Global Childhoods in International Perspective: Universality, Diversity and Inequalities

SAGE STUDIES IN INTERNATIONAL SOCIOLOGY

Series Editor Chaime Marcuello Servós (2016–ongoing)
Editor, Department of Psychology and Sociology,
Zaragoza University, Spain

Recent books in series

Key Texts for Latin American Sociology
Edited by Fernanda Beigel

Global Sociology and the Struggles for a Better World: Towards the Futures We Want
Edited by Markus S. Schulz

Sociology and Social Justice
Edited by Margaret Abraham

Global Childhoods in International Perspective: Universality, Diversity and Inequalities

Edited by **Claudio Baraldi** and **Lucia Rabello De Castro**

SSIS SERIES SAGE STUDIES IN INTERNATIONAL SOCIOLOGY: 68

Los Angeles | London | New Delhi
Singapore | Washington DC | Melbourne

Los Angeles | London | New Delhi
Singapore | Washington DC | Melbourne

SAGE Publications Ltd
1 Oliver's Yard
55 City Road
London EC1Y 1SP

SAGE Publications Inc.
2455 Teller Road
Thousand Oaks, California 91320

SAGE Publications India Pvt Ltd
B 1/I 1 Mohan Cooperative Industrial Area
Mathura Road
New Delhi 110 044

SAGE Publications Asia-Pacific Pte Ltd
3 Church Street
#10-04 Samsung Hub
Singapore 049483

Introduction © Claudio Baraldi and Lucia Rabello de
   Castro 2020
Chapter 1 © Claudio Baraldi 2020
Chapter 2 © Lucia Rabello de Castro 2020
Chapter 3 © Régine Sirota 2020
Chapter 4 © Isabelle Danic 2020
Chapter 5 © Sharmla Rama 2020
Chapter 6 © Tobia Fattore 2020
Chapter 7 © Doris Bühler-Niederberger 2020
Chapter 8 © Vinod Chandra 2020
Chapter 9 © Loretta E. Bass 2020
Chapter 10 © Asuncion Fresnoza-Flot and Itaru
   Nagasaka 2020

First published 2020

Library of Congress Control Number: 2019949072

British Library Cataloguing in Publication data

A catalogue record for this book is available from
the British Library

Editor: Natalie Aguilera
Assistant editor: Eve Williams
Production editor: Katherine Haw
Copyeditor: Jane Fricker
Proofreader: Bryan Campbell
Indexer: Silvia Benvenuto
Marketing manager: George Kimble
Cover design: Wendy Scott
Typeset by: C&M Digitals (P) Ltd, Chennai, India
Printed in the UK

ISBN 978-1-5297-1148-6
ISBN 978-1-5297-1147-9 (pbk)

At SAGE we take sustainability seriously. Most of our products are printed in the UK using responsibly sourced
papers and boards. When we print overseas we ensure sustainable papers are used as measured by the
PREPS grading system. We undertake an annual audit to monitor our sustainability.

Contents

About the Editors

Claudio Baraldi is Professor of Sociology of Cultural and Communicative Processes at the University of Modena and Reggio Emilia (Italy). His research includes works on interaction in educational systems, intercultural communication and mediation, and the development of dialogue. He has published widely in international journals and collections, he is co-author of a book (*Niklas Luhmann. Education as a Social System*, Springer, 2017), and he has edited and co-edited four other books (*Dialogue in Intercultural Communities. From an Educational Point of View*, John Benjamins, 2009; *Coordinating Participation in Dialogue Interpreting*, John Benjamins, 2012; *Participation, Facilitation, and Mediation. Children, Young People in their Social Contexts*, Routledge, 2012; *Theorizing Childhood. Citizenship, Rights and Participation*, Palgrave, 2018).

Lucia Rabello de Castro is Professor of Childhood and Youth, Institute of Psychology, Universidade Federal do Rio de Janeiro, Brazil. She was Founder and Chair from 1998 to 2011, and present Scientific Director of the Centre for Interdisciplinary Research and Exchange on Contemporary Childhood and Youth (NIPIAC/UFRJ/BRAZIL), Senior Researcher of the Brazilian Council of Science and Technological Development (CNPQ), and President of RC53 Sociology of Childhood (2018–2022). She is also Editor in Chief of *DESidades*, an international electronic peer-reviewed scientific journal in the area of childhood and youth (www.desidades. ufrj.br), published in Spanish and Portuguese, and President Elect of the National Association of Youth Researchers in Brazil (REDEJUBRA) 2017–2021. Professor Rabello de Castro has published widely on children and childhood in Portuguese, Spanish, French and English, covering issues of children's political and social participation, theory and methodology in childhood research and contemporary culture and children's subjectivities. A recent contribution, 'The study of childhood and youth in Brazil: dilemmas and choices of a "Southern" scholar', appeared in S. Koller (ed.) *Psychology in Brazil: Scientists Making a Difference* (Springer, 2019).

About the Contributors

Loretta Bass is Professor of Sociology and holds the Edith Kinney Gaylord Presidential Professorship at the University of Oklahoma in the United States. Loretta is a demographer who focuses her research on childhood and stratification issues in the United States, Africa and Europe. Her book *African Immigrant Families in Another France* (Palgrave Macmillan, 2014) examines the integration experiences of international migrants from Sub-Saharan Africa to France. Her earlier book, *Child Labor in Sub-Saharan Africa* (Lynne Rienner Publishers, 2004), offers a window on the lives of child workers in 43 African countries. She is currently the Series Editor for the *Sociological Studies of Children and Youth* (SSCY), and serves on the Editorial Board for the journals *Social Problems, Sociological Inquiry, Population Research and Policy Review* and *Current Sociology*. Also, she has served as President of Research Committee 53, Sociology of Childhood, within the International Sociological Association (ISA) and as a past Chair of the American Sociological Association's (ASA) Children and Youth Section.

Doris Bühler-Niederberger is a Professor of Sociology at the University of Wuppertal, Germany. In her research she focuses on institutions and professions dealing with childhood and on age as a dimension of social structure and social order in different societies. Publications include 'Marginality and voice: childhood in sociology and society', *Current Sociology*, Monograph Issue (2010), Vol. 58, No. 2; and *Victim, Perpetrator, or What Else: Generational and Gender Perspectives on Children, Youth, and Violence,* Sociological Studies of Children and Youth, Vol. 25 (with Lars Alberth) (Emerald, 2019).

Vinod Chandra is Head and Associate Professor of Sociology in J N Post Graduate College of Lucknow University, India. Dr Chandra is an established childhood researcher with a long-standing specialization in the study of child labour, child abuse and neglect. He has a strong interest in the study of youth and children's experience of education, work, labour and leisure. Dr Chandra obtained his doctoral degree from Warwick University, UK as Commonwealth Scholar and served as Secretary on the Research Committee of Sociology of Childhood, International Sociology Association during 2010–2014. Currently, he holds the posts of Vice-President (Asia Region) for the period of 2018–2022 in the Research Committee on Sociology of Youth (RC: 34) and Secretary in the Research Committee of Sociology of Population (RC: 41) in the International Sociology Association. He is also President of the Indian Association of Life Skills Education (IALSE). His field experience in the study of child abuse, neglect and child labour, children's wellbeing and mental health has been a continuous source for addressing the issues related to children who are in need of care and protection at Child Welfare Committees. He is currently involved in a multinational qualitative study of 'Children's Understanding of Well-being: Global and Local Contexts'. He has published six books on children and youth, the latest titled *Childhood Realities: Working and Abused Children* (Kalpaz Publications, 2016).

Isabelle Danic is Senior Lecturer at the University of Rennes 2, France and researcher in the CNRS Laboratory 'Espaces and Societies'. She has contributed to European and national research projects on childhood and youth, on education and socialization from a life course perspective (Danic, I. and Loncle, P. (eds), *Les Labyrinthes de verre. Les trajectoires éducatives en France dans un contexte européen*, Rennes: PUR, 2017; Danic, I. 'Access to higher education at the end of lower secondary for "disadvantaged" students: the interplay of structural, institutional frameworks and student agency', *European Education* (2015), Vol. 47, No. 1), and on the spatial dimension of these phenomena (Danic, I., Fontar, B., Grimault-Leprince, A., Le Mentec, M. and David, O. (eds), *Les Espaces de construction des inégalités éducatives,* PUR, 2019).

Tobia Fattore (PhD, USyd) is a Senior Lecturer in the Department of Sociology, Macquarie University, Australia. He is currently a coordinating lead researcher on the multinational study 'Children's Understandings of Well-being – Global and Local Contexts', which involves a qualitative investigation of how children experience wellbeing from a comparative and global perspective, to explore the relative importance of local, regional and national contexts for children's wellbeing (see www.cuwb.org/).

Asuncion Fresnoza-Flot is tenured Associate Researcher of the Belgian National Fund for Scientific Research (FRS-FNRS) and Senior Lecturer (*maîtresse d'enseignement*) at the Laboratory of Anthropology of Contemporary Worlds (LAMC) at the Université libre de Bruxelles (ULB) in Belgium. Her previous research focused on Filipino migration to France, specifically on its gender and family dimensions. Her important works include the monograph in French *Migrant Mothers without Borders: The Invisible Dimension of Filipino Migration to France* (L'Harmattan, 2013) and the two volumes in English, *Mobile Childhoods in Filipino Transnational Families: Migrant Children with Similar Roots in Different Routes* (co-edited with Itaru Nagasaka, Palgrave, 2015) and *International Marriages and Marital Citizenship: Southeast Asian Women on the Move* (co-edited with Gwenola Ricordeau, Routledge, 2017). Her ongoing research focuses on the contextual mobility of Belgian–Asian couples within their cross-border social spaces.

Itaru Nagasaka is an Associate Professor at the Graduate School of Integrated Arts and Sciences, Hiroshima University, Japan. He has been con- ducting anthropological fieldwork both in the rural areas of the Philippines and in Rome, Italy, on Filipino transnational migration since the 1990s. From 2009 to 2016, he headed a joint research project on the migratory experiences of Filipino children and youth living in different countries, the results of which form the core of the edited volume, *Mobile Childhoods in Filipino Transnational Families* (Nagasaka, I. and Fresnoza-Flot, A. (eds), Palgrave Macmillan, 2015). His recent research topics include men's identities in international division of reproductive labour, return migration and reintegration of migrants to the homeland society, poverty alleviation projects in the rural Philippines, patterns of marriage migration from the Philippines to Japan, and forms of identification of youth with Filipino background in Italy and Japan.

Sharmla Rama holds a PhD in sociology and is Senior Lecturer at the School of Social Sciences, University of KwaZulu-Natal's (UKZN) Pietermaritzburg campus. Her broad research interests include gender, and child and youth studies with a focus on, amongst others, mobility (transport and travel), place and space, and more recently the scholarship of teaching and learning sociology.

Régine Sirota is a Sociologist and Professor of Educational Sciences at Paris Descartes University. She is a member of Cerlis (Center for Research on Social Links, CNRS) and is responsible for the research committee 'Sociology of childhood' of AISLF (International Association of French-speaking Sociologists) and was a member of the ISA Sociology of Childhood Research Committee. She is mainly interested in the sociology of education and the sociology of childhood and Childhood Studies. She conducts research on socialization and more specifically on the rituals of childhood and especially the birthday. Her publications can be found on the CERLIS website http://www.cerlis.eu/.

Introduction

Claudio Baraldi and Lucia Rabello de Castro

Global Childhoods in International Perspective

Globalization processes, encompassing dynamic international capitalist markets, dissemination of knowledge, e.g. through media, education and medicine, and a wide gamut of national and international relationships, have affected present conditions of living worldwide. While European colonialism started to produce important influences in the world since the nineteenth century, in recent years, in a steadfast and devastating way, regions of the globe that had so far preserved their indigenous ways of living have been colonized by new forms of knowledge, communication and social and object relationships. Such significant and overarching processes that traverse national boundaries and connect nations and cultures in ways and on a scale not before witnessed (Kellner, 2009) pose the challenge of understanding their short- and long-term impact on human lives and social conviviality. Childhood studies have responded to contemporary demands of interrogating and analysing the relevance and the effects of globalization processes on childhood and children. One first issue that emerges concerns the terms in which the debate on globalization is going to be set and how problems are going to be defined and identified. Globalization processes reinforce the enduring hegemonic position of Northern countries over the South, economically and culturally, foregrounding the difficulties of establishing more symmetrical relationships in the international division of scientific labour. The idea of a global childhood that has become a major topic of discussion in this area of studies from early in the twenty-first century (Aitken, 2001; Hengst, 2005; Katz, 2004) calls for problematization insofar as it allows for the fixing of an apparent ideal of a good childhood embedded in the global design of European and American local histories (Mignolo, 2000). Here, global childhood refracts the construction of the generational position of children characteristic of the highly industrialized societies whose economic and social structuration circumscribes the production of childhood connected to the worlds of schooling and consumption. Besides, this ideal vision purports a moral agenda disseminated worldwide through international legislation and international aid intervention programmes setting forth norms and values to be pursued by different nations, North and South. As Nieuwenhuys (2007) comments on the issue of child labour, the new agenda concerning the abolition of children's labour on the wave of the ratification of the 1989 UN Convention on the Rights of the Child demands that Southern nations reinvent their national policies in the direction of securing the ideal order of a 'global childhood', a labour-free childhood, irrespective of the situated meanings and values of children's lifeworlds. Thus, to address a 'global childhood' constitutes itself an issue, one that must be able to clearly interrogate how its theoretical and scientific agenda remains aligned with, or poses questions to, the economic, cultural and political conditions of the globalized international scenario. In this vein, when Alanen (2000: 504) evaluates the advances made by recent sociological studies towards *an international* sociology of childhood, one cannot help wondering whether such an internationalization does not correspond to further consolidating an international division of scientific labour in global capitalism (Dirlik, 1998) whereby childhood scholarship is but transnationalized from Europe and the US to be circulated, reiterated and consumed in countries of the South. As Alanen herself acknowledges, given the enormous limitation of such Western scholarship, reflecting a Western minority standpoint, it would be surprising its capacity to circulate and establish scientific hegemony were it not for political and economic underpinnings that seem themselves unattended in the present debate in the area of childhood studies.

This brings us to a second and related issue, which consists of the impact of a 'global knowledge' about children and childhood in localities where social, cultural and political practices show very little resonance with Western values and ways of living. Although in many ways interconnected by the flux of capital investments, economic transactions and technologically mediated communication networks, regions of the world differ with regard to social and cultural practices surrounding children. Nieuwenhuys (2010: 294) comments, on this purpose, that 'we still have to better document and understand how the very definition of the child as a person below the age of 18 transforms the majority of citizens of entire countries into "children" – about 70% of Tanzania for example'. So, she asks, have children become a new trope to be imposed globally at the expense of other ideals? As far as global knowledge on children and childhood seems to serve and contract international policies and interventions 'in the best interests of children' worldwide, it seems important to evaluate the vicissitudes of such interventions with an eye to interrogate cherished assumptions and good intentions towards children. In the end, what may seem a failure from the point of view of rescuing children from abnormal, illicit and unhealthy living conditions, can forward a fully-fledged examination of veiled interests of globalized capitalist economic forces whose imperatives consist of appropriating the local for the global, admitting different cultures into the realm of capital, and homogenizing subjectivities in accordance with the requirements of production and consumption. Moreover, other aspects of a globalized Western culture influence the narrative of 'the best interest of children' and the intervention programmes, i.e. liberal politics, pedagogical theories, juridical values and scientific views, leading to define unquestionable truths. What happens at the local level of intervention programmes with children – including here the possibility of actually listening to children and sharing their experiences – can be instructive to defy the tenets of an encompassing global perspective against the backdrop of a situated, localized and incarnated perspective. Following Dirlik (1998: 84), the local can, in this sense, be the site – the only site (?) – of resistance to capital, and the location for imagining alternative future possibilities for the status quo. While this position is certainly intriguing, the relations and connections between the local and the global are an open and complex issue, which has raised divergent theoretical perspectives (e.g. O'Byrne and Hensby, 2011) and empirical observations (e.g. Twum-Danso Imoh and Ame, 2012). This debate cannot be faced here, as it is beyond the objective of this Introduction and this book.

The relevance of childhood with respect to globalization processes points further at issues of intergenerational solidarity, social justice and responsibility. The scope of choices that will allow for a better or worse reproduction of social life in the future is being conditioned by adults' actions, decisions and preferences in the present. Envisaging that the choice of certain courses of action can be severely harmed, or even completely barred, by today's greediness and vanity, 'children's best interests' stand not only as a rhetoric that must be invoked for setting up policies and programmes that involve them directly in their present conditions of life, but also as a political trope that expands the vision of our present demands, whatever they are, to one that encompasses the needs and the demands of future generations. In this vein, the topic of intergenerational solidarity directly articulates how social justice and responsibility between children, such as the methods and techniques of intervention with them (Nieuwenhuys, 2007). Therefore, lots of questions remain about how adequate the latter are for children's education, protection and participation. In short, in different societies across the globe the value and significance of relationships where children are involved vary enormously.

Against this background, the analysis of a plurality of childhoods across the world can highlight the diversity in the ways in which children express themselves and are socially relevant, and it can highlight inequalities and discriminations in the ways in which children are treated in different social contexts. This type of analysis raises the delicate problem of conceptualizing diversity. Diversity is frequently analysed in cultural terms by stressing that the conditions of children depend on specific cultural presuppositions. This approach has been labelled as 'essentialist', i.e. when it considers individual human beings as part of cultural groups which determine, or at least strongly condition, their ways of thinking and behaving (e.g. Holliday, 2011). Accordingly, one's belonging to the social and cultural group of children accounts for the ways individuals act and think *qua* children, taking into consideration that across societies not only are different criteria used for ascription in the group of children, but also different repertoires of action are thought to characterize childish-ness. An alternative approach to diversity problematizes the ascription of individuals, e.g. individual children, as members of permanent cultural groups, emphasizing how social differentiation is produced within societies and structures different social orders, one of them being the generational. Therefore, the generational order – and the social groups it encompasses – becomes itself an issue in terms of how it comes to be produced, both at the macro and micro levels. Furthermore, how individuals are ascribed to a certain social group, for instance, that of children, depends on negotiations at the level of social interactions whereby children's (lack of) opportunities of action are permanently actualized and transformed in the context of child–adult relationships (Alanen, 2009; Mayall, 2002). Thus, a sociological approach focusing on forms of child–adult relations and social structures seems to allow for an understanding of childhood as resulting from the interplay between structural and relational constraints of children's action, on the one hand, and children's initiatives, on the other.

The present impetus to particularize childhood and contrast its univocal and dominant constructions risks exerting a 'negativizing' function in theorizing and public policy, once certain particular social and cultural contexts can be disclosed as problematic as far as children's lives are concerned. This constitutes an important topic for sociological studies to ascertain in what ways conditions of marginality and abuse that frequently characterize children's lives throughout the globe, especially in countries of the Southern hemisphere, differentially impact their lives. In recent years, the economic crisis and the intense migration fluxes have expanded the problem of children's marginality to rich countries, such as the European nations. Children's problematic conditions are thus linked to two major types of social, political and cultural circumstances: to live in the Southern countries and to live as migrants and refugees in Europe and the United States.

The critical conditions of children, both in Southern countries and in situations of migration taking place in the global North, are historically, economically and politically grounded. The differentiation and interdependence of a global economy and a global politics, and their historical conditions are therefore important objects for the sociological analysis of childhood. Three important problems of analysis arise in this situation.

First of all is the issue of the historical conditions of social contexts of children's lives. The critical conditions of children's lives may be easily linked to the historical hegemony of Western societies in modernity, and in particular to the forms of colonialism and neo-colonialism that these societies have produced (and continue to produce). The historical impact of Western societies is strong and differentiated and determines the life and death of children (and their parents), both in countries in which the importance of children as individuals and childhood as a category has been greatly developed, and in countries in which it is substantially ignored.

The second is the issue of the present interplay of economic and political conditions of childhood. As Kupchan (2012) states, the present world is a no one's world. The political dominion of the West has diminished, despite the continuous attempts of neo-colonialism. The present situation highlights the impotence of states as political organizations, which are not able to prevent upsurges of nationalism and economic chaos. It also becomes doubtful whether a 'Western culture' stands as the emblematic cultural resource to which migrants feel most willing to adhere. Against this background of political impotence, the illusion of free markets leads to crises and failures, not only in poor countries and not only for reasons of corruption and inefficiency. Simplified analyses, for instance concerning the 'neoliberal state', the necessity of 'development' or the importance of 'cultural diversity', do not explain this situation with sufficient depth. The establishment of new trends in education and negotiation of intergenerational relations may be conceived as a way of managing local social conditions of children's lives, in which Western and non-Western values and ways of living are mixed. The problem therefore is not to imagine a positive 'development' towards the Western conception of children and childhood, but to interrogate ways and strategies of enhancing children's rights and wellbeing, i.e. ways and strategies of adult–children relations in all social contexts, from family and school education to economy and political institutions. Children's needs and problems can be associated with different definitions of children, adults and child–adult relations. In particular, institutional definitions of children's needs and problems become increasingly part of globalized expert markets, though it remains an important issue how local contexts can be empowered to change and/or shape them. The differentiation of ways and strategies of enhancing children's rights and wellbeing results in many different ways to conceptualize social intervention for and with children, from traditional educational methods, based on hierarchical relations between adult experts and incompetent children, to actions in which the adult expertise is used to enhance children's active participation. The interplay of political orientations and decisions, on the one hand, and social intervention, on the other, are therefore crucial to understand the plurality of childhoods.

Finally, the issue of analysing diversity in childhood challenges present epistemological, ethical and political tenets by which childhood is made visible, showing the ways in which global trends impact on children's life and wellbeing. This analysis can serve as a prompt to make positive 'other' theorizing and practice about children and childhood. For this purpose, a more complex type of analysis is needed, concerning the interplay between children's opportunity of action and structural constraints in different social contexts, through the investigation of their history, their educational, political and economic situation, and the forms of adult–children relations. This complexity requires a programme of macro- and microanalyses and a plurality of methods. This programme cannot be accomplished by a single researcher or team of researchers, it requires a collective effort, based on confrontation and exchange, i.e. transforming the present fragmentation of analyses in a sociological mosaic.

The Structure of the Present Contribution

This book does not aim at providing an exhaustive representation of sociological approaches to childhood, but, rather, at highlighting a variety of theoretical and empirical issues posed to social scientists concerning childhood in a globalized world. In this way, the book also proposes an original condensation of issues that have not been systematically analysed in the existing literature. Its main thrust invites readers into the complexities of childhood theorizing in face of the challenges posed by the widely differentiated childhood realities throughout the world. Empirical differentiation is discussed and analysed not only in relation to the problems it raises as far as theory construction of childhood is concerned, but also as challenges to intervention policies by national states.

This book explores the many ways in which the relationship between universality and particularities of childhood plays an important role in describing global childhoods. It gathers a wide spectrum of contributors coming from Europe, the USA, South Asia, South Africa and Latin America, who, attuned with present dilemmas in the area of childhood studies, discuss some key theoretical and empirical aspects of child scholarship, such as identity, child wellbeing, child mobility and migration, intergenerational relationships and child abuse.

The book fits in the ISA book series, as it concerns a debate of significant relevance for sociology, not deeply explored yet. It highlights childhood as a cross-cutting issue in sociological studies primarily aimed at researchers, practitioners and students interested in both childhood studies and the other areas including Community Research, Sociology of Education, Family Research, Social Transformations and Sociology of Development, Poverty, Social Welfare and Social Policy, Comparative Sociology, Regional and Urban Development, Social Stratification and Sociology of Migration.

References

Aitken, S. (2001) 'Global crises of childhood: rights, justice and the unchildlike child', *Area*, 33(2): 119–127.

Alanen, L. (2000) 'Review essay visions of a social theory of childhood', *Childhood*, 7(4): 493–505.

Alanen, L. (2009) 'Generational order', in J. Qvortrup, W. Corsaro and M.S. Honig (eds), *The Palgrave Handbook of Childhood Studies*. Basingstoke: Palgrave. pp. 159–174.

Ariès, P. (1960) *L'Enfant et la vie familiale sous l'ancien régime*. Paris: Seuil.

Dirlik, A. (1998) *The Postcolonial Aura: Third World Criticism in the Age of Global Capitalism*. Oxford: Westview Press.

Hengst, H. (2005) 'Complex interconnections: the global and the local in children's minds and everyday worlds', in J. Qvortrup (ed.), *Studies in Modern Childhood*. New York: Palgrave Macmillan. pp. 21–38.

Holliday, A. (2011) *Intercultural Communication and Ideology*. London: Sage.

James, A. and James, A. (2004) *Constructing Childhood: Theory, Policy and Social Practice*. Basingstoke: Palgrave.

James, A. and Prout, A. (eds) (1997) *Constructing and Reconstructing Childhood*. London: Falmer Press.

James, A., Jenks, C. and Prout, A. (1998) *Theorizing Childhood*. Oxford: Polity Press.

Katz, C. (2004) *Growing Up Global: Economic Restructuring and Children's Everyday Lives*. Minneapolis: University of Minnesota Press.

Kellner, D. (2009) 'Dialectics of globalization: from theory to practice', in S. Dasgupta and J.N. Pieterse (eds), *Politics of Globalization*. London: Sage. pp. 179–196.

Kupchan, C.A. (2012) *No One's World: The West, the Rising Rest and the Coming Global Turn*. New York: Oxford University Press.

Luhmann, N. (2002) *Das Erzhieungssystem der Gesellschaft*. Frankfurt am Main: Suhrkamp.

Mayall, B. (2002) *Towards a Sociology for Childhood: Thinking from Children's Lives*. Buckingham: Open University Press.

Mignolo, W. (2000) *Local Histories/Global Designs: Coloniality, Subaltern Knowledges and Border Thinking*. Princeton, NJ: Princeton University Press.

Nieuwenhuys, O. (2007) 'Embedding the global womb: global child labour and the new policy agenda', *Children's Geographies*, 5(1–2): 149–163.

Nieuwenhuys, O. (2010) 'Keep asking: Why childhood? Why children? Why global?', *Childhood*, 17(3): 291–296.

O'Byrne, D.J. and Hensby, A. (2011) *Theorizing Global Studies*. Basingstoke: Palgrave.

Twum-Danso Imoh, A. (2012) 'The Convention on the Rights of the Child: a product and facilitator of a global childhood', in A. Twum-Danso Imoh and R. Ame (eds), *Childhoods at the Intersection of the Local and Global*. Basingstoke: Palgrave. pp. 17–33.

Twum-Danso Imoh, A. and Ame, R. (eds) (2012) *Childhoods at the Intersection of the Local and Global*. Basingstoke: Palgrave.

Wells, K. (2015) *Childhood in a Global Perspective*. Cambridge: Polity.

Section One

Problematizing Universality, Diversity and Inequalities in Global Childhoods

Introduction

In this section, the three chapters deal with issues of universality, diversity and inequalities in narratives about children and childhood. Child scholarship faces the difficult task of producing theories with some degree of generality, whilst it has to take into account the vast empirical diversity in the conditions of living one's childhood and being a child worldwide. Despite the fact that in our contemporary age, especially the period from the second half of the twentieth century onwards, great social, cultural and political transformations have impacted childhoods all over the world, at stake lies the issue of what models are flexible and complex enough to account for the myriad of ways whereby children are produced as subjects, as well as a social category, in the scope of generational structures of different societies.

Universality has been a major aspect in theories about childhood as these strive to highlight commonalities in recurrent constructions of childhood through different social and empirical contexts, and/or as conceptual elements in the making up of theories. To postulate agency for the child in our current theories consists of an example of how conceptual models about childhood have evolved from regarding the child as a developing creature, a construction of internal maturational forces and environmental stimuli, to thinking about the child as contributing to make the social world as it is. However, what remains to be sorted out is to what purposes and when is agency mobilized, and how is it acted out in the various circumstances in which children live?

Diversity in child scholarship is frequently associated with how crucial factors such as race, ethnicity, gender and social class pluralize the conditions whereby children are produced, amplifying, and sometimes questioning, the canonical and current frameworks to study children. It is a fact that all these factors cannot be divorced from their cultural underpinnings, and this sums up to make analyses of diversity even more complex. Lately, it has been argued that the place and territory which children inhabit constitute a relevant variable that makes up the diversity of childhood and children. In this sense what can constitute an agenda for the study of diversity in childhood remains an open programme to be continuously searched for and investigated by child scholars.

The topic of inequalities has been a long-standing object of enquiry in child studies, as one of the foremost differentials in the conditions of becoming children has been accounted for by social class. However, the historical making up of social classes is embedded in the specific cultural and political context of different countries, so that this intersection of social class with other relevant factors has a significant impact on the ways that generational structures are produced.

The first chapter of this section, 'Roots and Problems of Universalism: The Concept of Children's Agency', by Claudio Baraldi, analyses a new form of universalism in the sociological study of the child introduced by the concept of agency. Starting with a radical critique of adult control, this theoretical standpoint analyses the meanings of social relations involving children, and forwards the view that children are competent actors of social relations and active agents of change. However, the universalized twist that the concept of agency proposes demands that one envisages the social structure which conditions children's agency as a hierarchical, although dynamic, generational order of relations. In this sense, agency is not a given in adult–child relationships but the result of structuring conditions of action. The analysis and enhancement of agency require the recognition of five presuppositions. First, the actions of adults differ in meaning according to different social structures. Second, although the significance of adult actions depends on the structure of the social system in which they are produced, only local conditions can promote more or less effective adult–child relations. Third, the actions of adults can enable various forms of children's action, coordination with and among children, and management of decisions. Fourth, the paradoxical dependence of children's actions on adults' actions may take two forms: either guided adaptation and socialization, or empowered choices and decision-making.

Fifth, empowering children's choices means enhancing unpredictability, which needs the additional enhancement of children's management of their own actions.

The second chapter of this section, 'Age Epistemology and the Politics of Age', by Lucia Rabello de Castro, addresses the universalism of the concept of age in child scholarship, whose pervasive capillarity in social and educational practices, legal texts and common sense may lead to the belief of a seemingly unequivocal narrative about childhood. It is argued that this category has played an important role in defining a politics of age by providing legitimacy to asymmetries in the distribution of human capabilities and social power. On this account human differentiation along the life-course has been reduced to a certain postulation of humanness as the unidimensional development and attainment of rational capacities and autonomy. The fact that legal systems throughout the world operate comfortably with the age episteme despite its diverse pitfalls points out that to this day the notion of age has served to sustain a universalized view of human differentiation as becoming rational and is used to reinforce a vision of social cohesion as based on the internalization of norms, and a rational and volitional capacity of individuals.

The third chapter of this section, 'Inequalities in French Speaking and Anglo-Saxon Childhood Sociologies', by Régine Sirota, takes up the issue of inequalities in distinct sociological traditions, the French and the Anglo-Saxon. In the French context, the 'republican universalism' has been the main reference for the sociological debate, therefore childhood inequalities have been mainly studied in terms of social stratification. On the other side, in the Anglo-Saxon context, diversity has been the main reference for this debate, therefore priority has been given to aspects such as gender or ethnicity. The thrust of the argument is to analyse how differences in the way that childhood inequalities have been studied affect theoretical categorizations and make it possible to address their intersectionality. Above all, this category, namely 'social class', is used to think about childhood inequalities, both in the sense of thinking about childhood in terms of social class, as well as thinking about social class through childhood so that, ultimately, the relevance of the concept of diversity can emerge. There are problems, however, of moving from one language to the other, a task which is neither simple nor the exchange between the Anglophone and the French traditions obvious.

1

Roots and Problems of Universalism

The Concept of Children's Agency

Claudio Baraldi

The Western Narratives of Children and Childhood

The social meaning of children and childhood may be analysed through narrative theory. According to Fisher (1987), narratives are social constructions, in which the observed reality is interpreted and storied in different ways, historically and culturally grounded. Somers (1994) differentiates among narratives of the self, public narratives, conceptual narratives, including scientific concepts, and metanarratives, concerning the basic features of society in a specific historical period. This chapter is interested in conceptual narratives, in particular sociological narratives, public narratives and metanarratives regarding children and childhood, and in the links among these types of narratives. Moreover, this chapter points out that the importance of narratives depends on the structural conditions which are created in society, in this particular case, the structural conditions of children's actions and relations.

The conceptual narratives of children and childhood have been enhanced in Western society since the beginning of modernity, and later expanded to the global society. In particular, I am interested in a recent conceptual narrative which has been proposed by the Sociology of Childhood and which aims to enhance new metanarratives and public narratives in the global society. Sociology of Childhood criticizes the traditional narratives of childhood and children in Western society, thus proposing a new form of universalism.

In Western society, the metanarrative of childhood is traditionally made up of the combination between the importance of children's self-realization and the need to exercise control on children (Prout, 2000). The importance of self-realization is associated with a more general historic tendency to observe that individuals choose their identities rather than finding them already prescribed by society and groups; this conception

The constraints of children's agency are prevalently explained in relational terms (Bjerke, 2011; Moosa-Mitha, 2005; Oswell, 2013; Valentine, 2011), in the context of a hierarchical, although dynamic, generational order of relations (Alanen, 2009; Mayall, 2002). The range of children's actions is predefined through a set of relational constraints, based on hierarchical relationships which can offer opportunities, but above all limitations for children's agency. This means that socially constructed structures of expectations predefine adult–children relations (Wells, 2015). These structures concern value orientations (e.g. the education and upbringing of children), the definition of social roles (e.g. teacher and pupil), and the definition of opportunities for personal expression. For instance, relationships in school are based on the value of the child's education and learning, the roles of teacher and pupil, the assessment of the results of learning and penalties in the event of non-success, but also on an increasing attention for children's personal expression (e.g. Mercer and Littleton, 2007).

The structural limitation of agency seems unavoidable, and particularly relevant for children. However, social structures cannot determine children's agency (Leonard, 2016). Agency means showing the availability of choices of action, so that a specific course of action is one among various possibilities (Van Langhenove and Harré, 1999). It means that children 'contribute to the reproduction of childhood and society' through negotiations with adults and peers (Corsaro, 1997: 43). Children's agency can be observed if children's action shows the availability of choices, which can enhance alternative actions and therefore change in social relations. In a nutshell, the concept of agency emphasizes that children can condition adults' actions. In the case of relations in which children participate as social agents, the actions of children and adults are correlated, and each action of children and adults influences another one. On the one hand, children's agency means that children's actions influence the actions of adults. On the other hand, children's agency must be accepted and enhanced by adults' actions (Baraldi, 2014; Wyness, 2013a). Therefore, adult–child relations take a form of reciprocity. Even educational control ultimately depends on the agency of children, as the idea of children requiring control is correlated with a concern for their ability in making choices. However, to evaluate the opportunities for children's agency, it is vital to consider that children may or may not be treated by adults as competent participants, and may be considered for their competence in different social situations.

The West and the Rest: Marginalization and Agency

An important question is if the conceptual narrative of agency can explain children's participation in problematic social conditions. In Western society, the public and conceptual narratives of children's problematic conditions are certainly not irrelevant. Considerable emphasis is placed on socialization pathologies such as self-damaging behaviour (e.g. anorexia), self-exclusion and diagnosed depression, violence suffered (e.g. sexual abuse) and inflicted on others (e.g. bullying). Conditions of significant psychosocial discomfort and deviancy arouse feelings of concern, disapproval, indignation and, in extreme cases, even repugnance, because they are in evident contrast with both self-realization and educational control. The main fear is that children reject or are unable to accept the orientations regarded as positive by society, and therefore grow up with mistaken values or 'without values'. The narrative of children's agency is also difficult to apply in situations where children are marginalized, including poverty, deviancy, psychosocial discomfort, social marginality. In such cases, children are often in a position of inferiority, weakness and inequality.

A broader view of the global dimension of society, including many countries which are not observed as Western-like, reveals other and more relevant problems of inferiority, weakness and inequality for children. First of all, it can be noted that although the most important metanarrative of children's rights and wellbeing, i.e. the United Nations Convention on the Rights of the Child (UNCRC), has been ratified by almost all the world's nations, there are serious violations of it concerning the rights of children. Forced migration, child labour, the abandoning of children in the street, illiteracy, genital mutilation, enforced enrolment in armed bands are just some of the most significant violations, in situations where children's rights are subordinate to the logic of social groups that do not consider them to be important (Boyden, 1997), or in the large urban conglomerates that have developed in many non-Western countries, where children face high exposure to poverty, decay and life-threatening conditions.

A number of studies have been dealing with the conditions of children in the global society (e.g. Honwana and de Boeck, 2005; Hunner-Kreisel and Bohne, 2016; Percy-Smith and Thomas, 2010; Twum-Danso Imoh and Ame, 2012; Wells, 2015), although the interest in marginalized children is still insufficient in Sociology of Childhood (Sarmento et al., 2018). One frequently analysed phenomenon is that of 'street children' (e.g. Cerqueira Filho and Neder, 2001; Davies, 2008; Glauser, 1997;

Invernizzi, 2003; Sarmento et al., 2018), because life on the streets is considered to be a sign of abandonment and a situation of risk. Another is that of child labour (e.g. Balagopalan, 2002; Bass, 2003; Bourdillon, 2005; Droz, 2006; Huijsmans, 2008; Sarmento et al., 2018): in conditions of extreme poverty, children may be 'sold' on the job market by their families, sometimes in order to avoid even more serious risks to their lives. Therefore, for child workers in majority world countries, protection can be deployed in an arbitrary way (Baraldi and Cockburn, 2018). Associated with these phenomena is another extensively studied problem: the lack of opportunities for formal education. A further situation of difficulty arises from intense migration flows, and the consequent presence of children belonging to cultural minorities in societies, which leads to children's marginalization stemming both from insufficient attention, or even rejection, on the part of the dominant narrative and the tendency of minority communities to shut themselves off. The development of these tendencies is favoured by local communities and national policies rejecting the Western model and insisting on alternative constructions of childhood (Twum-Danso Imoh and Ame, 2012).

In these situations, children's agency seems to be overshadowed by other, more pressing problems determined by inequalities and social constraints established at both local and global levels. Against this background, the question is if agency can be considered as a universal feature of childhood, or at least a universal opportunity to increase children's rights and wellbeing. The extent to which universalist narratives may be associated to childhood is a complex issue. For instance, Wells (2015) recognizes deep differences in the global society, stating that a global concept of childhood does not exist, but she also supports the universalist narrative of children's immaturity and children's needs for physical care, emotional attachment and adult teaching. Although denying the existence of global childhood, sociological studies can accept some characteristics of the Western narrative of childhood as universal, in particular the relevance of emotional bonds and adult caregiving for children's wellbeing. Although from a critical perspective, these studies tend to interpret the global society as conditioned by the Western narrative, and to express favour for the application of the 'best' parts of this narrative, regarding children's rights and wellbeing, in the global society (e.g. Fass, 2007).

Against this background, whenever their rights are violated, children may be viewed as 'minorities' who, at least potentially, might claim their rights if put in a condition to do so (James et al., 1998). Alternatively, children's action may be observed as the expression of a 'tactical' form of agency (Honwana, 2005), which copes with the concrete, immediate conditions of life, e.g. in military and violent contexts (see also Shepler, 2012; Wyness, 2016). Children can actively react to disintegration of families and communities, and show generational resentment when left behind by older generations (Wells, 2015). Tactical agency is associated with weakness, rather than with empowerment. Tactical agency is a form of 'interstitial agency', it is linked to a hybrid identity of child and adult, victim and perpetrator, and it allows children to exploit any given opportunity in their social context (Honwana, 2005).

This concept of tactical/interstitial agency may be applied to different situations and conditions. It may be applied to the case of street children, working on the streets to support their families financially or cooperating with peers (Mandel Butler, 2009; Mizen and Ofosu-Kusi, 2010; Wells, 2015). It may explain why the ideas of exploitation and slavery do not represent the full complexity and ambivalence of the reality of child labour (Abebe and Kjorholt, 2009; Morrow, 2010), which may also be conceived as an alternative to scholastic failure, violence, hunger and worse forms of exploitation, and may even represent a quest for economic and social mobility. It may explain why the introduction of formal education into the lives of illiterate children may require significant compromises with an informal education that appears more respectful of their rights. It may explain female mutilations as the result of children's choices to mark cultural identity and react to colonial and post-colonial domination (Wells, 2015). It may highlight the non-arbitrary trajectories of independent forms of children's migration (Wells, 2015), as well as the migrant children's different opportunities of action in marginalizing social conditions (Hunner-Kreisel and Bohne, 2016), i.e. their attempt to assimilate the models of the host society, their valorization of personal specificity, the reinforcing of their belonging to ethnic groups, their oscillation between different orientations and their refusal to belong to any one cultural group.

The concept of tactical/interstitial agency highlights that children are capable of tackling their problems actively, rather than merely being on the receiving end of changes imposed from outside. Thus, the analysis of children's agency may be extended to the global society. Children's tactical/interstitial agency is subordinated to adults' power. It allows children to cooperate in the social reproduction of social order, in particular in 'collectivistic' cultural contexts in which hierarchical arrangements and strong obligations towards the collective prevail (e.g. André and Godin,

2014; Bühler-Niederberger and Schwittek, 2014; Clemensen, 2016; Khalifa, 2012; Muftee, 2015). In these cases, children's agency means accepting the existing social and cultural orientations. This observation of different forms of agency in the global society has raised questions about the Western 'voice-based global standard' of children's participation (Wyness, 2013b). Moreover, this observation may raise some doubts on the meanings of children's rights: if they are universally based either on the golden standard of agency as autonomous choice, or on a plurality of forms of agency.

It is clear that marginalization is associated with the Western narrative of children's agency in a very ambiguous way. At a basic level, all children's actions change social relations, as each action influences the production of other actions. At this level, children's actions showing acceptance of adults' authority also influence social relations showing tactical agency. However, acceptance does not show either the availability of choices of action, nor change of children's social conditions. Therefore, the question concerns the difference among children's forms of agency, associated with subordination to or cooperation with adults representing the existing social and cultural order, on the one hand, and with autonomous choice of actions and social change, on the other. This question is particularly important in children's marginalized conditions, as in these cases children's opportunities to choose actions and change their social context may be low. The question is if children's tactical/interstitial agency can ensure respect of children's rights. In fact, according to the Western narrative, the tactical/interstitial agency of marginalized children is inadequate, the voice of these children is out of tune, and children cannot really become protagonists of the social relations they take part in, due to the power adults can wield over their lives. It is believed that only by changing the existing socio-cultural conditions will it be possible to ensure the establishment of full agency on the part of children, who are not able to achieve it 'on their own'.

While it seems clear that agency must be observed in the specific social and cultural contexts of children's lives (Lansdown, 2010), this observation raises the issues of both the contrast and the mix between Western narratives and local values (Twum-Danso Imoh and Ame, 2012) for what concerns power relations, (under-)representation of children, support of children's choices of action and participation in decision-making. In conditions of marginalization, children's actions cannot simply reproduce the Western narrative of agency, they necessarily reshape and hybridize this narrative, 'in various, often self-invented, spaces and practices of resistance, negotiation and opposition, but also of collaboration, negotiation and invention' (De Boeck and Honwana, 2005: 9).

Globalization of Children's Agency?

The Western narrative of agency requires that children are guaranteed the possibility to act in significant public situations. Publicly visible participation is considered a fundamental indicator of children's agency. This requirement is coherently enhanced by the UNCRC metanarrative: the UNCRC formalizes a long series of children's rights in public situations. However, this metanarrative is not sufficient to enhance children's agency, which cannot be guaranteed by a charter, however authoritative. The promotion of agency requires a societal shift from a narrative of children as being primarily subject to external orientation to one that considers them as competent individuals endowed with agency.

According to the Western narrative, this shift is associated to actual participation in decision-making, on the one hand, and interventions initiated by children themselves, on the other (Clark and Percy-Smith, 2006; Holland and O'Neill, 2006). Agency requires effective institutional intervention not only *for* children, but also, indeed above all, *with and by* children, who are legitimated to contribute to decision-making processes. Various methods for evaluating the promotion of this participation have been proposed, including categories such as active listening, the encouragement of personal expression, dialogue, power sharing and empowerment (e.g. Baraldi, 2012; Matthews, 2003; Shier, 2001). However, the public narrative of children's participation is criticized as incomplete, instrumental, or not applied by Sociology of Childhood (Percy-Smith, 2010; Thomas, 2007). Critical views mainly focus on two aspects. Firstly, not all children are involved in participatory initiatives: disadvantaged groups of children are neither consulted, nor involved in decision-making. Secondly, and more radically, the promotion of children's participation is subordinated to forms of adult control (Hill et al., 2004; James and James, 2004). Adult control determines a complex disciplinary apparatus which includes relations with teachers, home care assistants, doctors, psychologists and social workers, who act for the good of the child (Jenks, 1996). This apparatus builds the idea of a dependent, vulnerable child. The result is 'the normalization and institutionalization of the social settings and practices within which children in "modern" societies are taken care of, raised, looked after, instructed, supervised and controlled' (Alanen, 2005: 39). Children's participation is often viewed as an opportunity for education and political use. By participating children can develop an adequate understanding of their own competences, of the significance of shared responsibilities and of skills in planning, monitoring and managing social contexts, political awareness and democratic attitudes. The promotion of participation appears to be a strategy for integrating children into society.

Contrasting exclusion of disadvantaged children and adults' control is an important feature of the Western narrative of agency. However, an additional form of intervention is often proposed in situations of extreme marginalization, which are frequently observed in the global society. In these situations, most interventions, inspired by the Western metanarrative of children's rights and wellbeing, aim to offer children protection (e.g. Canavera et al., 2016; Wyness, 2016). According to Wells (2015), this global child-saving narrative is guided by a liberal conception of the child (and the human being in general). Wells rejects both this liberal narrative, aiming to universalism, and its critique, which encourages the acceptance of cultural diversity, thus legitimizing the reproduction of inequalities in global society.

The problem of accepting cultural diversity arises when the marginalization affects minority cultural groups, for instance in conditions of migration in Western society. In this society, the idea that cultural diversity can be a positive resource in society is frequently associated with the function of education, which is considered fundamental for promoting and valorizing respect and participation. The challenge for the intervention is to promote intercultural education, which, however, may have two different objectives. On the one hand, it may aim to preserve and enhance the value of children's cultural identity (e.g. Mahon and Cushner, 2012). On the other hand, it may set out to develop in children the capacity for enhancing effective relationships and to adopt cultural decentring (e.g. Byrd Clark and Dervin, 2014). This second objective underlines the increasing importance assigned to children's agency.

In the narrative of international organizations, the increasing importance assigned to children's agency has led to a partial change in the focus of child-saving: the new idea is to create the conditions for children to recover a 'normal' level of agency, to listen actively to their agency in community interventions, and to support their self-protective actions, as for example in the case of child worker associations. Taking account of agency is not, however, simple when it is observed to be inadequate: in these cases, children's agency can be considered a secondary or even counter-productive factor. The degree to which child-saving can be effectively combined with the promotion of agency is thus an open issue. What seems clear is that it is difficult to assign a unitary significance to the typology of interventions designed to promote children's agency because there is no unitary significance of agency. For this reason, the promotion of children's agency in conditions of extreme marginalization is problematic.

Significant dilemmas arise regarding the goals of the intervention, for instance between better working conditions for children and the abolition of child labour. Children's organizations do not aspire to abolishing their work but claim the right to work in reasonable conditions, seeking to generate an awareness about their work and to combat exploitation, leaving open the possibility for education, play and access to social and cultural services. The mixture of protection and the promotion of agency is a characteristic of this type of intervention, which attempts to generalize the concept of children's agency, but at the same time to negotiate on the values that guide it, such as the ban on child labour or the aversion to children living on the streets. This mixed approach characterizes, for example, programmes aimed at children who live on the streets within protected communities in Brazil (Cerqueira Filho and Neder, 2001), promoting interventions based on a methodology that considers the educator as co-producer of knowledge and children as active learners. This type of intervention is designed to encourage the participation of marginalized children by providing protection and by supporting their cognitive development. Other examples of this mix in conditions of marginalization are presented in research into the application, in various parts of the world, of the UNCRC (Lansdown, 2001).

This conception of social intervention is paradoxical to say the least: it must maintain the children's diversity and agency, but also protect and educate children. This paradox is determined by the wish to assign a positive value both to personal and cultural diversity, and to equality of social conditions and possibility of action. The paradox emerges, then, in the attempt to accept and at the same time to overcome diversity. Against this background, the insufficient reflection on the social and cultural presuppositions of the intervention makes the promotion of children's agency problematic. Therefore, despite the growing emphasis on the importance of children's agency, promoting it is fraught with difficulties stemming from the prevalence of hierarchical structures in adult–child relations. It is a question of understanding whether conditions exist that enable the actions of adults and of children to be considered equally important in social relations.

If adults and children are regarded as equally important and competent participants, the coordination between their actions in creating an 'effective relationship' comes to be of central importance. In Western society, a form of coordination between the actions of adults and children, which has been enhanced with the aim to promote children's participation, is that of *facilitation of dialogue* (Baraldi, 2012, 2014). Facilitation of dialogue may be understood as a specific form of communication based on three assumptions. First, the fair distribution of participation, in which no hierarchical disparity emerges in communication, nor a prevalence of the actions of one participant over those of another. Second, the manifestation of sensitivity towards children, allowing them to express their needs, interests and desires. Third, the treatment of disagreement and alternative perspectives as enrichment, in other words the primary importance of the empowerment of the participant children.

Facilitation of dialogue requires that adults support and acknowledge children's personal expressions, check children's perceptions, actively listen to children's utterances, introduce personal points of view, and appreciate children's contributions. Adults' actions can function as a catalyst for children's actions. Facilitation of dialogue is not, however, the product of an adult's action, but rather of the coordination between facilitative actions by the adult and instances of personal expression by the child: therefore, the success of facilitation depends on the manifestation of agency by the child. If the adult's action effectively promotes the child's agency, the hierarchical form of the interaction is subverted and the conditions for dialogue created. Thus, facilitation also enhances reflection on the meanings of the communicative process and the children's management of decisions.

In global society, facilitation of dialogue with and among children is enhanced by some important international organizations, which are based in Western society (e.g. Amnesty International, 2011; CISV, 2002/2003). It is impossible to say if facilitation of dialogue can become a widespread practice in the future. An important presupposition is combining the Western sensitivity for children's agency with the local conditions of facilitation of dialogue, in order to enhance hybrid forms of children's agency, rather than liberal narratives of childhood. The enhancement of liberal narratives of childhood would not only prolong the domination of the Western narrative, but also arouse suspicions and negative reactions in many parts of the global society. The challenge for a new metanarrative of children's rights and wellbeing is not enhancing the best (Western) form of agency, but a facilitative process through which some form of children's agency is constructed and accepted at the local level. The challenge is the promotion of the metanarrative of children's rights and wellbeing through local forms of dialogue, rather than the definition of what the child is or should be.

For this purpose, two structural features of facilitation of dialogue must be taken into account. First, facilitation of dialogue is no less paradoxical than education. The relevance of children's agency depends on the relevance of adults' action in promoting children's agency, i.e. children's availability of choices of action depends on adults' enhancement. This paradox originates from the positioning of children, who have no access to the most important decision-making processes in society. Second, facilitation of dialogue paves the way for unpredictability, which stems from the expression of diversity between points of view. The increasing attention towards dialogue and agency also involves a growth in social unpredictability and therefore requires a growth in skills for managing it. This means that facilitation of dialogue must create the conditions for children's active participation in decision-making processes to manage unpredictability. An open issue is if, and to what extent, paradoxical facilitation of dialogue can be achieved and unpredictability can be effectively managed outside specific and protected contexts.

Conclusions

The quest for effective adult–child relations, which promote children's agency, is evident where there is a strong interest in the social and cultural presuppositions of children's participation. Sociology of Childhood often argues that there should be a more decisive shift away from adult control and towards the recognition of children as competent social agents. This conceptual narrative has come in for criticism on the grounds that it subordinates research to moral and political narratives (King, 1997). But interest in the concept of children's agency primarily regards research, not politics or morality. Defining policy and intervention goals on the basis of research results is an important way of including research in society and of applying its outcomes to it.

The interest in children's participation may enhance efforts to find forms of relations that also function in conditions of marginalization, creating the conditions for the empowerment of marginalized children, taking into account the global dimension of society. Marginalized children can be empowered if actions which are available make facilitation of adult–children dialogue effective. Facilitation of dialogue can be pursued if five social and cultural presuppositions are recognized. First, the actions of adults differ in meaning according to different social structures. In particular, value and expectations of children's personal expression contrast with value and expectations enhanced by hierarchical structures. Second, although the significance of adult actions depends on the structure of the social system in which they are produced, only local conditions can promote more or less effective adult–child relations. Third, the actions of adults can enable various forms of children's action, coordination with and among children, management of decisions. Fourth, following these presuppositions, the paradoxical dependence of children's actions on adults' actions may take two forms: either guided adaptation and socialization, or empowered choices and decision-making. Fifth, empowering children's choices means enhancing unpredictability, which needs the additional enhancement of children's management of their own actions.

The challenge is globalizing dialogue rather than universal narratives of childhood and children, as dialogue is a hybrid social structure that can promote effective local and differentiated narratives of children's agency (e.g. Shier, 2010). However, globalizing dialogue is particularly challenging since, following the dominant narratives, the recognition of the above cited five presuppositions is very difficult.

The identification of the structure of dialogue is a result of research that cannot predict the future and in particular cannot imply that dialogue and agency are the best possible future for which to hope in the global society. The future of children and their relations with society is not the result of a conceptual narrative, of a moral commitment or of a political programme, but the consequence of the evolutive success of the structures of relations in which children are involved. It is an unpredictable future, above all because the more important dialogue is in society, the more necessary it is to allow for the unpredictability of its outcomes.

References

Abebe, T. and Kjorholt, A.T. (2009) 'Social actors and victims of exploitation: working children in the cash economy of Ethiopia's South', *Childhood*, 16(2): 175–194.

Alanen, L. (2005) 'Women's studies/childhood studies: parallels, links and perspectives', in J. Mason and T. Fattore (eds), *Children Taken Seriously: In Theory, Policy and Practice*. London: Jessica Kingsley. pp. 31–45.

Alanen, L. (2009) 'Generational order', in J. Qvortrup, G. Valentine, W. Corsaro and M.S. Honig (eds), *The Palgrave Handbook of Childhood Studies*. Basingstoke: Palgrave. pp. 159–174.

Amnesty International (2011) *Facilitation Manual: A Guide to Using Participatory Methodologies for Human Rights Education*. London: Amnesty International.

André, G. and Godin, M. (2014) 'Child labour, agency and family dynamics: the case of mining in Katanga (DRC)', *Childhood*, 21(2): 161–174.

Balagopalan, S. (2002) 'Constructing indigenous childhoods: colonialism, vocational education and the working child', *Childhood*, 9(1): 19–34.

Baraldi, C. (2008) 'Promoting self-expression in classrooms interactions', *Childhood*, 15(2): 239–257.

Baraldi, C. (2012) 'Participation, facilitation and mediation in educational interactions', in C. Baraldi and V. Iervese (eds), *Participation, Facilitation, and Mediation: Children and Young People in their Social Contexts*. Abingdon and New York: Routledge. pp. 66–86.

Baraldi, C. (2014) 'Children's participation in communication systems: a theoretical perspective to shape research', in M.N. Warehime (ed.), *Soul of Society: A Focus on the Leaves of Children and Youth*. Bingley: Emerald. pp. 63–92.

Baraldi, C. and Cockburn, T. (2018) 'Introduction', in C. Baraldi and T. Cockburn (eds), *Theorising Childhood: Citizenship, Rights, and Participation*. Basingstoke: Palgrave. pp. 1–27.

Bass, L. (2003) 'Child labor and household survival strategies in West Africa', *Sociological Studies of Children and Youth*, 9: 127–148.

Bjerke, H. (2011) 'It's the way to do it: expressions of agency in child–adult relations at home and school', *Children & Society*, 25(2): 93–103.

Bourdillon, M.F.G. (2005) 'Working children in Zimbabwe', *Sociological Studies of Children and Youth*, 10: 7–21.

Boyden, J. (1997) 'Childhood and the Policy Makers: A Comparative Perspective on the Globalization of Childhood', in A. James and A. Prout (eds), *Constructing and Reconstructing Childhood: Contemporary Issues in the Sociological Study of Childhood*. London and New York: Routledge. pp. 190–229

Bühler-Niederberger, D. and Schwittek, J. (2014) 'Young children in Kyrgyzstan: agency in tight hierarchical structures', *Childhood*, 21(4): 502–516.

Byrd Clark, J.S. and Dervin, F. (2014) 'Introduction', in J.S. Byrd Clark and F. Dervin (eds), *Reflexivity in Language and Intercultural Education*. Abingdon and New York: Routledge. pp. 1– 42.

Canavera, M., Lanning, K., Polin, K. and Stark, L. (2016) '"And then they left": challenges to child protection systems strengthening in South Sudan', *Children & Society*, 30(5): 356–368.

Cerqueira Filho, G. and Neder, G. (2001) 'Social and historical approaches regarding street children in Rio de Janeiro (Brazil) in the context of the transition to democracy', *Childhood*, 8(1): 11–29.

CISV (Children's International Summer Villages) (2002/2003) 'Effective cross-cultural facilitation', *Interspectives. A Journal of Transcultural Education*, 19: 1–50.

Clark, A. and Percy-Smith, B. (2006) 'Beyond consultation: participatory practices in everyday space', *Children, Youth and Environment*, 16(2): 1–9.

Clemensen, N. (2016) 'Exploring ambiguous realms: access, exposure and agency in the interactions of rural Zambian children', *Childhood*, 23(3): 317–332.

Cockburn, T. (2013) *Rethinking Children's Citizenship*. Basingstoke: Palgrave.

Corsaro, W. (1997) *The Sociology of Childhood*. Thousand Oaks, CA: Pine Forge Press.

Davies, M. (2008) 'A childish culture? Shared understandings, agency and intervention: an anthropological study of street children in northwest Kenya', *Childhood*, 15(3): 309–330.

De Boeck, F. and Honwana, A. (2005) 'Introduction: children and youth in Africa', in A. Honwana and F. de Boeck (eds), *Makers and Breakers: Children and Youth in Postcolonial Africa*. Oxford: James Currey. pp. 1–18.

Droz, Y. (2006) 'Street children and the work ethic: new policy for an old moral, Nairobi (Kenya)', *Childhood*, 13(3): 349–363.

Fass, P. (2007) *Children of a New World: Society, Culture, and Globalization*. New York: New York University Press.

Fisher, W. (1987) *Human Communication as Narration: Toward a Philosophy of Reason, Value, and Action*. Columbia: University of South Carolina Press.

Giddens, A. (1984) *The Constitution of Society*. Cambridge: Polity Press.

Glauser, B. (1997) 'Street children: deconstructing a construct', in A. James and A. Prout (eds), *Constructing and Reconstructing Childhood*. London: Falmer Press. pp. 145–164.

Hill, M., Davis, J., Prout, A. and Tisdall, K. (2004) 'Moving the participation agenda forward', *Children & Society*, 18(2): 77–96.

Holland, S. and O'Neill, S. (2006) '"We had to be there to make sure it was what we wanted". Enabling children's participation in family decision-making through the family group conference', *Childhood*, 13(1): 91–111.

Honwana, A. (2005) 'Innocent and guilty: child-soldiers as interstitial and tactical agents', in A. Honwana and F. de Boeck (eds), *Makers and Breakers: Children and Youth in Postcolonial Africa*. Oxford: James Currey. pp. 31–52.

Honwana, A. and de Boeck F. (eds) (2005) *Makers and Breakers: Children and Youth in Postcolonial Africa*. Oxford: James Currey.

Huijsmans, R. (2008) 'Children working beyond their localities: Lao children working in Thailand', *Childhood*, 15(3): 331–353.

Hunner-Kreisel, C. and Bohne, S. (2016) *Childhood, Youth and Migration: Connecting Global and Local Perspectives*. Dordrecht: Springer.

Invernizzi, A. (2003) 'Street-working children and adolescents in Lima: work as an agent of socialization', *Childhood*, 10(3): 319–341.

James, A. (2013) *Socialising Children*. Basingstoke: Palgrave.

James, A. and James, A. (2004) *Constructing Childhood: Theory, Policy and Social Practice*. Basingstoke: Palgrave.

James, A. and James, A. (2008) *Key Concepts in Childhood Studies*. London: Sage.

James, A. and Prout, A. (eds) (1997) *Constructing and Reconstructing Childhood*. London: Falmer Press.

James, A., Jenks, C. and Prout, A. (1998) *Theorizing Childhood*. Oxford: Polity Press.

Jenks, C. (1996) *Childhood*. London: Routledge.

Khalifa, H. (2012) 'Caught up in between change and continuity: challenging contemporary childhood in Saudi Arabia', in A. Twum-Danso Imoh and R. Ame (eds), *Childhoods at the Intersection of the Local and Global*. Basingstoke: Palgrave. pp. 160–173.

King, M. (1997) *A Better World for Children?* London: Routledge.

Lansdown, G. (2001) *Promoting Children's Participation in Democratic Decision-making*. Florence: UNICEF.

Lansdown, G. (2010) 'The realisation of children's participation rights: critical reflections', in B. Percy-Smith and N. Thomas (eds), *A Handbook of Children and Young People's Participation: Perspectives from Theory and Practice*. Abingdon: Routledge. pp. 11–23.

Leonard, M. (2016) *The Sociology of Children, Childhood and Generation*. London: Sage.

Luhmann, N. (1995) *Social Systems*. Stanford, CA: Stanford University Press.

Luhmann, N. (2002) *Das Erzhieungssystem der Gesellschaft*. Frankfurt am Main: Suhrkamp.

Mahon, J. and Cushner, K. (2012) 'The multicultural classroom', in J. Jackson (ed.), *The Routledge Handbook of Language and Intercultural Communication*. Abingdon: Routledge. pp. 434–448.

Mandel Butler, U. (2009) 'Freedom, revolt and "citizenship": three pillars of identity for youngsters living on the streets of Rio de Janeiro', *Childhood*, 16(1): 11–29.

Matthews, H. (2003) 'Children and regeneration: setting an agenda for community participation and integration', *Children & Society*, 17(4): 264–276.

Mayall, B. (2002) *Towards a Sociology for Childhood: Thinking from Children's Lives*. Buckingham: Open University Press.

Mercer, N. and Littleton, K. (2007) *Dialogue and Development of Children's Thinking*. Abingdon: Routledge.

Mizen, P. and Ofosu-Kusi, Y. (2010) 'Asking, giving, receiving: friendship as survival strategy among Accra's street children', *Childhood*, 17(4): 441–454.

Moosa-Mitha, M. (2005) 'A difference-centred alternative to theorization of children's citizenship rights', *Citizenship Studies*, 9(4): 369–388.

Morrow, V. (2010) 'Should the world be free of "child labour"? Some reflections', *Childhood*, 17(4): 435–440.

Muftee, M. (2015) 'Children's agency in resettlement: a study of Swedish cultural orientation programs in Kenya and Sudan', *Children's Geographies*, 13(2): 131–148.

Oswell, D. (2013) *The Agency of Children: From Family to Global Human Rights*. London: Routledge.

Percy-Smith, B. (2010) 'Councils, consultations and community: rethinking the spaces for children and young people's participation', *Children's Geographies*, 8(2): 107–122.

Percy-Smith, B. and Thomas, N. (eds) (2010) *A Handbook of Children's and Young People's Participation: Perspectives from Theory and Practice*. Abingdon and New York: Routledge.

Prout, A. (2000) 'Children's participation: control and self-realisation in British late modernity', *Children & Society*, 14(4): 304–315.

Sarmento, J.S., Marchi, R. and Trevisan, G. (2018) 'Beyond the modern "norm" of childhood: children at the margins as a challenge for the Sociology of Childhood', in C. Baraldi and T. Cockburn (eds), *Theorising Childhood: Citizenship, Rights, and Participation*. Basingstoke: Palgrave. pp. 135–157.

Shepler, S. (2012) 'The rites of the child: global discourses of youth and reintegrating child soldiers in Sierra Leone', in A. Twum-Danso Imoh and R. Ame (eds), *Childhoods at the Intersection of the Local and Global*. Basingstoke: Palgrave. pp. 174–189.

Shier, H. (2001) 'Pathways to participation: openings, opportunities and obligations', *Children & Society*, 15(2): 107–117.

Shier, H. (2010) '"Pathways to participation" revisited: learning from Nicaragua's child coffee workers', in B. Percy-Smith and N. Thomas (eds), *A Handbook of Children's and Young People's Participation: Perspectives from Theory and Practice*. Abingdon and New York: Routledge. pp. 215–229.

Somers, M. (1994) 'The narrative constitution of identity: a relational and network approach', *Theory and Society*, 23(5): 605–649.

Thomas, N. (2007) 'Towards a theory of children's participation', *International Journal of Children's Rights*, 15(2): 199–218.

Twum-Danso Imoh, A. and Ame, R. (eds) (2012) *Childhoods at the Intersection of the Local and the Global*. Basingstoke: Palgrave.

Valentine, K. (2011) 'Accounting for agency', *Children & Society*, 25(5): 347–358.

Van Langenhove, L. and Harré, R. (1999) 'Introducing positioning theory', in R. Harré and L. van Langenhove (eds), *Positioning Theory*. Oxford: Blackwell. pp. 14–31.

Wells, K. (2015) *Childhood in a Global Perspective*. Cambridge: Polity.

Wyness, M. (2013a) 'Children's participation and intergenerational dialogue: bringing adults back into the analysis', *Childhood*, 20(4): 429–442.

Wyness, M. (2013b) 'Global standards and deficit childhoods: the contested meaning of children's participation', *Children's Geographies*, 11(3): 340–353.

Wyness, M. (2016) 'Childhood human rights and adversity: the case of children and military conflict', *Children & Society*, 30(5): 345–355.

2

Age Epistemology and the Politics of Age

Lucia Rabello de Castro

Children are a type of critic in all kinds of ways: because of their incessant questioning; because they are parasitically dependent on a language they nonetheless find baffling and alien; because, being outsiders, they can see both more and less than insiders; because they are isolated 'intellectuals' not fully conversant with common practices of feeling yet also more emotionally sensitive than most; because their social marginality is the source at once of their blindness and insight.

(Terry Eagleton, 'The critic as clown', 1988: 620)

Children's peculiarities have intrigued adults' minds and have been a source of scientific interest and otherwise. In the above epigraph Eagleton provokes us, pointing at children's unremitting capability of 'standing outside' and, *ipso facto*, questioning our own sense of reality and being. Within child studies the foundational question about what is a child (Honig, 2011) has brought about many different attempts to account for the specificity and the particularity of beings we call children.

One main notion that has surrounded the child question across different disciplines and throughout a century-long period of scientific interest in children is that of age with its regime of divisions, scales and characterizations. Although the concept of age has benefited from different statuses in child studies, it has been of paramount importance to define the child in scholarship (Thorne, 2004, 2008), professional practice (Kelle, 2010; Mantle et al., 2006) and ordinary child–adult relationships. It would not be an overstatement to say that the minutiae of children's lives in modern societies are deeply affected by age indicators, used by adults as a rule of thumb to understand and decide about what children should and should not do, to forbid and authorize them, and to reproach or celebrate their actions and behaviours. Most importantly, in modern societies age has become a quantifiable and universal index of children's level of understanding and overall capacity. The label of childish attached to a child's behaviour is often pejoratively invoked whenever children deceptively show attitudes and behaviours below what is perceived to be their chronological age. The legal system of modern societies reverberates conventional wisdom deferring to age to define individuals' autonomy, rights and duties. Parameters of moral agency and legal responsibility are couched in age cutting points. For instance, age comes to define thresholds of criminal responsibility, of civic participation in elections and of individual autonomy and choice to wander about without anyone's consent. The criterion of age has become what authorizes the entrance of adolescents into the brave new world of paid work, licensed drugs and unaccountable sex.

The universality of the concept of age – across legal texts, ordinary use or scientific explanation – calls for an examination of its widespread diffusion as well as its resiliency in face of criticisms of essentializing what the child is. The relevant fact to this day that what children are and what capacities they have are still associated with their age inspires an analytical treatment of the episteme articulated by this concept. This consists of a complex and diversified knowledge whose variety of principles and rationales derives from different disciplines comprehending multilayered trajectories of scientific enquiry. Here, we use the term age epistemology to account for the array of issues and discussions that the age concept has encompassed, such as the conceptualization of human life as the acquisition of rational competences according to a progressive temporality, the perspective of the future as indeterminate and demanding early preparation, the view of human abilities and competences as individualized assets and others. In this chapter some of these issues are tackled as we pursue the debates about the child question engendered by the concept of age. At stake lie key issues about human differentiation along the life cycle where distances, reciprocity and affiliations among generations forward frontiers of disputes and struggles between generational groups whose positions and access to symbolic and material resources depend on ongoing definitions of what it is to be a child, a youth, an adult or an elderly. It is argued that the category of age has played an important role in defining such a politics – often providing legitimacy to asymmetries in the distribution of human capabilities and social power – on account of its irremediable connections to a certain postulation of humanness as the unidimensional development and attainment of rational capacities and autonomy.

The Evolving Child: Human Differentiation as Sequential and Progressive

The view of the child as a developing organism emerges in the context of Western modernity when human differentiation was foregrounded in the scope of debates about human evolution. At play was the concept of human ontogeny, derived from nineteenth-century biology, which consisted of a general model of change related to the individual organism. At the cornerstone of such a model lay a linear and cumulative conception of temporality which organized the transformative process of individuals, species and societies along biographical and historical dimensions. On the one side, the concept of chronological age, constructed as an individual scale starting at point zero, organized the timing of human changes; on the other, the great epochal historical stages depicted the progressive development of Western civilization. Change along the continuum only permitted a forward and univocal movement, so that entities positioned at the initial point of the temporal continuum were supposed to evolve into something else eventually, whereas it was logically impossible to go the other way round. The focus on ontogenetic changes led inevitably to an interest in the child – as the baseline of human ontogenetic development; although the child, as such, was not the question, but, most importantly, how human attributes would evolve from the very start and be superseded by more complex and adaptable characteristics.

Early psychologists, like Arnold Gesell (1928) and Charlotte Bühler (1951 [1935]), who investigated children's thoughts, motives and other psychological attributes, considered them internal organismic entities, which, like other biological entitlements such as stature, developed from intrinsic causation. Ontogeny underscored the progressive nature of human development, the 'evolution-development-progress complex' (Morss, 1992: 241), a sort of 'image ladder … in which the trunk represents the main line of progress, with the most developed point at the very top' (Morss, 1992: 249). Oyama points out that in this transformational model of development, change is conceived to be generated from within, and 'maturation, as it is traditionally conceived, is the quintessential internally driven process' (1992: 215). The inexorable passage of calendar time in days and years served well to systematize the unfolding human changes whose process associated internality (of causation), fixity (regular normative pattern) and 'innatism' (a reductionism of the biological to the innate). However, as Oyama (1992) cautions, the association made of biology with internality and fixidity leading to inopportune dichotomies, such as biology vs culture, nature vs nurture, has made it more difficult to envisage alternative ways to conceive human changes other than caused by internal factors. Thus, 'in developmental theory the transformational model dominates' (Oyama, 1992: 215), although it does not constitute the sole model of accounting for change in biology. Noteworthy is the assumption often made that the only way that biology constructs development is based on this transformational model, accounting thus for reducing biology to a non-constructivist and naturalized perspective on human change.

Not only early psychologists, but also quite a number of scholars dedicated to human development, were captivated by the neatness of this model to explain human change along biographical time. In the first place, age provided a simple objective scale along which regular patterns of maturation could be mapped and pinpointed. Statistical methods became a helpful device to ascertain the incidence of behaviour patterns in the population so that regularity was at once assimilated as a normalizing and normative aspect of evolving capacities to be expected as desired outcomes. In this sense, development was conceived as *naturally* unfolding as time went by, and despite the acknowledgement of the plasticity of human psychological universals (Buller, 2006), development was teleologically conceptualized as not going wherever, but fulfilling a stage by stage sequence towards completion at an expected apex. Peters summarizes: 'I take it as axiomatic that, in talking about development, there must be *a prior conception of the end-product* and that the processes which contribute to it must be sequential' (1980: 113, my italics). Following Jean Piaget, he sees the acquisition of rationality and autonomy as a natural process – inherited as human specific – to be adequately accomplished, it is admitted, with correct environmental stimuli.

The tenets of development – its regularity and sequential staging, the presupposed outcomes it entails and its basically inner driving force – remain effective to this day to figure out what best provisions should lead to these expected results. Children, as those beings whose capacities are not still what they are likely (and ought) to be, become depicted as subjects of *evolving capacities* whilst adults are those with evolved capacities who can devise adequate treatment for the former's 'optimum development' (Lansdown, 2005). The conception of the evolving capacities of the child, also embodied in Article 5 of the UN Convention on the Rights of the Child, entails a process to be duly continued and completed, an *evolving* child condition, for which, at the same time, a certain optimum outcome is envisaged and fostered by adults' intervention. Lansdown notes that children do not acquire competencies merely as a consequence of age, although he acknowledges that 'age is widely assumed as a proxy for competence' (p. 55), and that 'it is impossible to discount the concept of phases altogether ... there is clear evidence of biologically based universality in children's physical development' (p. 23).

As a proxy for competencies that are acquired as time goes by, age stood as the foremost index of human differentiation, be they changes of physical appearance and body shape, be they relevant intellectual and social abilities. It seems that age differentiation theories have served the purpose of foregrounding, or even producing children's peculiarities – the most obvious case being when they serve commercial purposes. As for children, their provoking peculiarities (to the adult's mind and not probably to themselves) have been attributed the status of evolving capacities that should change to ulterior end states, defined as such by what adults foresee as socially and culturally relevant, a process that naturalizes the effects of differential power relations between age groups. Thus, in effect, children's peculiarities – understood as their evolving capacities – have become of interest to the extent that they should be superseded in the direction of other capacities (say, peculiarities). A case in point can be illustrated by bodily changes and differentiation. Children's bodies and appearance take part in the process of construction of children's identities as an outcome of their naturalized body difference from adults. Adultcentric norms as regards body shape, functions, capacities give way to the assignment of characteristics to children on account of their differential appearance, for instance, being vulnerable and immature. The issue, therefore, is that whenever criteria of performance, perfection and end states are at stake, as in the case of evaluations of children's bodies, the production of knowledge on children starts off mediated by the differential power relations between adults and children and what adults conveniently stipulate as the best parameters. However, as the epigraph of this article suggests, children's capabilities as compared to adults' can be seen as more advantageous depending on what social, cultural and political purposes they serve. Turning to other human age differentials, Labouvie-Vief (1981) has cautioned in relation to old age, that human capabilities and competencies are multifaceted, diverse, transitory and often contingent making it impossible to elect a few of them as having an absolute value over the others. Age differentiation in Western modernity has underscored adults' peculiarities as completeness – evolved socialization and humanness – and, on the other hand, children's imperfect and transient competencies as part of a theory of progress whereby an adult ideology came to be enforced (Nandy, 2010).

The age scale, based on calendar time, begins at point zero and goes on continuously along standard and homogeneous intervals of years. It informs a psychometric apprehension of human existence conceiving its beginning as a liminal state. Accordingly, humanness is not yet fully recognizable in the infant. If everything goes well, children are then slowly integrated into the social world. The view that the beginning of human life is emptied and devoid of any substantive or relevant disposition has raised opposite appraisals from both philosophical and empirical sides. Henri Bergson has noted that it is in childhood that there lies a whole range of human possibilities that are acted out as if one could play different personalities at the same time. However, as one grows old choices have to be made that constrict human life: one is gradually reduced to being one sole subject, owner of one sole life (Bergson, 1959). In the same vein, following Henri Michaux, Charbonnier (2012) notes that children disclose an enormous privilege vis-a-vis other life phases: being strangers in the world nothing is given or evident for them, which constitutes in itself a most potent ethical horizon for human action. Similarly, arguing from the perspective of empirical studies with babies, Stern (2000, 2010) has shown the intense, rich and complex forms of vitality that make up the lives of infants from the very start – a picture quite at odds with the view that describes it as asocial and emptied. Some of these initial capabilities, many of them untapped by scientific enquiry, show that infants and small children dispose of different and complex ways of subject–object relationship and that this primary intersubjectivity is impregnated by a dense body-affect-sensory experience (Ogden, 1989).

These points draw attention to the pitfalls of age scales based on psychometric assumptions that bar whatever insights on the human capabilities of the child that do not corroborate the notion of a univocal progressive movement of human differentiation in the direction of rationality and autonomy. As linear time can only march onwards, childhood's destiny is sealed towards adulthood. Children's peculiarities must be then superseded and regressive movements deemed as inadequate and labelled as childish consist of a reminder that once one is 'of age', to act, feel and be as a child can only invoke social disapproval. Age scales conform a rigid separation of beings in time, so that if one is a child one cannot be an adult. Intermingling states and ambiguity of beings become a logical aberration, thus the difficulty to think of the adult as not the child yet

(Charbonnier, 2012), or that children and adults are not opposite states or beings (Alderson, 2013) and that children and adults have more in common than they differ.

'Social Age': The Limits of Undoing the Fixed Linearity of Age Scales

The pervasiveness of age as a proxy for children's competences of reason, autonomy and independence cannot be underestimated. Western modernization and rationalization processes brought about the structuring of the human life-course as a sequenced order of phases characterized by evolving human dispositions accorded with different social prerogatives and legal entitlements. An increasing state regulation of the phases of the life-course – childhood, youth, adulthood and old age – contributed to the institutionalization of age-related processes and transitions, such as schooling, age of majority and marriage, entry to paid work, retirement (Kohli, 1986; Meyer, 1986; Narvanen and Nasman, 2004). In this context important societal changes such as the emergence of retirement and of a post-employment stage of life (Blaikie, 1997) took place enhancing the relevance of age as a structuring feature of society and, at the same time, of the individual life-course process (Riley, 1987). As Heinz and Kruger have remarked, 'age-related social expectations still provide measuring sticks or markers for plans and aspirations that people expect to engage at various time points in their lives' (2001: 42).

The social construction of age relates then to the process of age categorizations immersed in the social demands for rights and prerogatives of different social groups allowing for the differential access to social and material resources. Societal values about longevity and productive labour, child-rearing and reproduction practices, and gender roles, among others, play an increasingly important role in social age categorizations. A case in point concerns the contemporary definition of Western youth which in modern industrialized societies has gradually evolved to encompass a longer chronological lifespan – from 15 to 29 years of age – indicative of a social condition characterized in different degrees by a long economic dependence, a longer permanence in the educational system and a delayed parenthood. The social construction of age takes place in the wider process of social distinction interacting conjointly with gender, race and social class constructions. It consists of a process of intertwining both fixation and deconstruction of meanings and values around age following the changing social dynamics of modern societies where entitlements and norms concerning age roles become increasingly a matter of dispute. In this vein, Thorne (2008) draws attention to the situationally specific ways whereby children and youth themselves name and negotiate their age positions within the scope of objective age terminologies which tend to obfuscate these contextually and culturally constructed meanings of age differentiation. Adults often use age indicators as a rule of thumb orientation to understand and decide about what children should and should not do; however, as Solberg (1990) cautions, 12-year-olds living in the same city in Norway are differently regarded as to their capabilities, responsibilities and accountabilities in relation to what they do by their parents as the latter hold different conceptions of what social roles can be expected from their 12-year-olds. Notwithstanding its relevance in Western societies, for many non-Western societies, as noted by Morrow (2013), such a temporalization of human life according to age is of no relevance, making this notion dispensable. Children's entitlements and responsibilities are not decided by the criterion of age, but by their social positions in the intergenerational order defined by what they are expected to do in their home and environment as young people.

As part and parcel of modernization and rationalization processes, as well as the increasing focus on the individual as a rational actor, age indicators continue to play a preponderant part in positioning actors with respect to their social and intergenerational roles, embedding the biographical point of their life-course in the wider interpretive framework of historical and cultural dimensions of societies. In this sense social age remains an attempt to substantially disengage age markers from the chronological and evolutionary linearity and its maturational determinacy, making more salient historical, cultural and spatial (Hopkins and Pain, 2010) aspects that structure the differential subject positions along the life-course.

What seems of relevance in the theorizing about age that brackets uniform chronological linearity in order to foreground spatial and cultural dimensions of age categorizations is that the *relational construction* of children's position becomes prominent. As argued by Danic et al. (2006), social age becomes the social production of an age group whereby a naturalistic conception of children is refuted in view of childhood as a social construction produced by social relations and children's own construction (p. 30). Accordingly, they claim a missing term which could be deployed in contraposition to age, as in the pair of gender and sex. The term age would then characterize the epitomized naturalistic state of being a child, whereas social age – for lack of another term – would refer to the social acting, performing, negotiating and constructing of a child position. However, it can be argued that the keeping of the term age, as in 'social age', speaks of the theoretical impasse concerning giving up the life-course frame of analysis – the biographical temporality constructed as a social and cultural structure – to order different social positions. Social age remains captive of a 'naturalized' vision of human differentiation whose cornerstone consists of the attainment of higher rational and moral competences. Even if generational groups can negotiate their positions with respect to each other, it seems that the conditions of possibility for being a child *or* an adult are not questioned, based on the assumption of the higher competences attributed to the role model of the adult – rationality, autonomy. In this sense, what is left un-problematized is the vision of the subject that reduces their humanness to becoming rational. Age groups and age classes (Criado, 1998) can be the sites of social dispute resulting in situationally constructed age categorizations although the rationale that produces them is left un-problematized.

Bracketing the Structure of the Life-course: Differentiation as Intrinsically Relational

As noted, it has been an issue how to include the dimension of the human biographical temporality in theorizing about children and childhood. Anthropologists have reiterated the relevance of age and aged cultures to anthropological theory (Berman, 2016; Duarte, 2001), rescuing age as an important category to understand differential entitlements and roles along the life cycle. In a different vein, answers to the child question have focused on the processes that create relations of difference based on *internally* connected relationships rather than deploying age as an external index of differentiation defined by one's belonging to a certain stage along the life-course. Accordingly, differences between adults and children take place, as 'people become (are constructed as) "children" while other people become (are constructed as) "adults" ' (Alanen, 2001a: 21). Relationality of positions makes them necessarily reciprocal so that children's becoming is part and parcel of the same process that makes adults' becoming. Alanen (2001b) highlights the importance of generation as a structural condition of difference that bridges a system of relationships among social positions. She says: 'A generational order is a structured network of relations between generational categories that are positioned in and act within necessary interrelations with each other' (2011: 161).

Such a definition of generational order leaves open the question about what makes a category to be generational (other than something else), and how we should approach social relationships in view of mapping out and pinpointing generational structures as specific social structures different from those of class, gender and ethnicity. Alanen proposes that empirical studies should find out what actually is the constitutive principle in the social ordering of child–adult relationships (2011: 167). Talking about children, as experts do and the author of this chapter is doing right now, is part of the process of generationing, or generational ordering, to which Alanen would agree (2011: 170). As social actors bring about notions such as those of the child and/or the adult in whatever social interaction, they are indeed reinforcing and producing generative positions. However, if generative positions are relevant to social ordering it becomes a relevant task to extricate what principle of differentiation they serve and what logic of exclusion they legitimate. Thus, if age derives from conceptualizing the structure of the human lifespan and its unfolding trajectory towards rationality and autonomy as the cornerstone of human differentiation, the principle of social ordering in generational analysis seems lacking. In the same way that, for instance, gendering responds to the principle of sexual differentiation in social ordering, generation calls for an explanation of what systematizes the social relationships it entails. The contribution offered by Alanen underscores the relational and the interactional aspects of social ordering that create the child and the adult positions avoiding to be captured by the external framework of age markers that differentiates people along the lifespan. It seems questionable, however, whether human temporality can be left out altogether when tackling the child question. The notion of generativity proposed by Honig (2011) seems promising in this respect, if it is understood as the capability of generating, an asset which differentially qualifies all moments of biographical time. In this vein, generativity opens a ground of disputes among different social groups as they face the intertwined and contradictory demands of human growth and decline, birth and death, which directly address the conditions of possibility of species and human life (re)production and social conviviality.

The Ages of Life: The Diversity of Humanness Along the Life-course

The subject of 'the ages of life' ('des âges de la vie') has been for long intriguing poets, painters and philosophers. The fact that human life

evolves, taking different forms from birth to death, demands to understand how such disparate moments of existence interrelate as a meaningful trajectory and what meanings they can disclose about what it is to be
born man/woman. Ariès, in his *Centuries of Childhood* (1962), begins his
social history of childhood by presenting an initial discussion on 'the ages
of life' tracing back to the Middle Ages the popularization of interest in
ages. Other child historians (Cunningham, 2005; Heywood, 2009) have
shown how conceptions and values of children accompany the transformations of ampler meanings about the life cycle. More recently, the subject of the ages of life has been renewed on account of the issues posed by
the emergence of a 'novel' childhood (Deschavanne and Tavoillot, 2007;
Gauchet, 2004; Renaut, 2002). Modern childhood has inflected the meanings of what it is to be human in the direction of a massive investment of
adults on children through education. Renaut points to the paradoxical
condition of children in modernity, considered equal albeit different from
adults. It is, according to him, under the aegis of education that adults
conceive their relationships with children who provoke the recognition of
otherness or 'the dissimilarity of the same' even in societies invested with
the recognitions of the other under a juridical regime of equal rights for
all. For Renaut, children pose the paradox of their difference as 'they are
incapable of being what they are legally invested to be under a democratic
dynamics that leads to establish that they already are' (p. 18). Thus, the
'ages of life' in our present time condense the tensions of conceptions of
hominization that include the value of difference, but also, the search for
one's autonomy and identity and the responsibility for oneself and one's
acts. At the same time that education sets in motion a process of recognizing
the difference posed by children's dissimilarity, these efforts should, paradoxically, be imbued with the respect for the difference – the alterity – of
children, rendering education itself highly problematic in that it reduces
children's alterity by imposing (adults') norms and codes. This, for
Renaut, contains core issues for democracies today as the apprehension of
human universality, deeply differentiated throughout the life cycle, instan-
tiates the appreciation of dissimilarities in their articulation to the value of
a common human identity shared by all humans. Present legal conditions
of equal human dignity and humanness pose impasses for democratic
societies, especially concerning the normative basis of authority of adults
vis-a-vis children in education, as well as in the stipulation of minimum
ages for civic autonomy, penal responsibility and formal political agency.
Modern societies struggle to find solutions to the impasses posed by such

a political economy of alterity, the crisis of education being one and an important one. This has destabilized the seemingly unmovable frontiers of the biological immaturity of children – physiological and intellectual – which, as argued by Renaut, placed them in a position of incapacity and submission to the other concerning their survival.

The topic of the ages of life gains momentum in the face of the radical changes that have affected the human life cycle in the past century. An important one concerns human longevity, which has been extended by more than 30 years along the twentieth century, affirms Marcel Gauchet. In his 'The redefinition of the ages of life' (2004), Gauchet notes that societies are faced with issues posed by an extension of human life which has changed the meaning of all the life phases. Childhood, for instance, together with youth, constitutes the moment for the accumulation of resources for a long life whose content and outcome are not liable to be previously defined. Thus, it is in view of a future 'as distant as unknown' (p. 34) that individuals must prepare themselves, children being thus identified as 'the holders of a future that is known to be different and hoped for as better' (p. 31). Preparation lies mainly on the premises that human existence is now understood as personal history constructed in the individual exercise of rational capacities, autonomy, personal choice and freedom. Accordingly, self-construction *is* education: the process that caters for the discovery of a singular self. For Gauchet childhood acquires the connotation of a mythical time, pregnant with pure potentiality and indeterminacy in the adventure of self-construction. By the same token, a redefinition of maturity is called for, as now nobody is constrained to become mature in the sense of having to assume public constraints and obligations of collective reproduction, once procreation and family life are regarded as private affairs. Therefore, 'there is no model of adult existence, conditioned by the foothold of the foundation of a household' (p. 41); contrarily, it is youth that acquires a model value for the whole of human existence whose gains attached to ageing become increasingly eroded. To grow old is to become the least adult possible able to deploy the advantages of such a position and avoid as far as possible its inconveniences. For the individuals unconstrained by the obligation of maturity, it is their own development that constitutes the only legitimate horizon of their existences.

Both Renaut and Gauchet agree on the understanding that our contemporary time demands a reconfiguration of collective representations about the ages of life and, consequently, of childhood. For both authors, there seems to be an irrevocable fact about the form of life in childhood which continues to provoke adults' minds in terms of its immaturity, be it regarded in the positive sense of indeterminacy, but also, in its less advantageous singularity, *as not being able yet*, and therefore dependent on others. Therefore, the biological stands for both authors as a foundational and irreducible fact about childhood (its immaturity) concurring to pinpoint the social dependency of children as *the* relevant aspect of their life. In this sense, the discussion about the ages of life leads to a politics of human becoming, as what is at stake is the differential qualification of forms of life: adults' form of existence remaining the norm and being held superior with regard to children's. The former's privileged position is justified in relation to three sources of normativity (Monjo, 2012): experience, in the Hegelian sense of reconciliation with the world; responsibility, whose model remains parenthood in the exercise of solicitude; and authenticity, in the sense of coincidence with oneself.

It seems noteworthy that the discussion of the redefinition of the ages of life has actualized the issues about human differentiation along the life cycle in the context of present-day challenges as well as enhanced the understanding of the life phases in their articulation about what it is to be human. However, the child's contribution to humanness has been spelt out from the exclusive viewpoint of the pedagogization of the adult–child relationship, in a legal position of equal dignity with regard to adults. Children's peculiarities seem to remain inchoate capabilities phantomized by notions of immaturity and dependence. The normativity of the human life cycle, though curbed by present ideals of universal equality and dignity of all humans whatever their appearance and modes of existence, continues to reflect the privileged point of enunciation of adults whose peculiarities of reason, maturity and autonomy corroborate their own partial vantage point and power position.

By Way of Conclusion: The Age of Criminal Responsibility in Brazil

Age and age characterizations have had a paramount importance in the legal system of modern societies where a liberal idea of the human agent – individualized, free, rational and autonomous – is at stake. In Brazil, a most important debate that has been going on for some time concerns proposals to amend the 1988 Brazilian Constitution so as to lower the age of penal responsibility from 18 to 16 years of age (and even 14 years). The relevance of this debate for the lives of Brazilian children is enormous and raises questions concerning what issues are involved in a seemingly trivial lowering of two or more years in the age of criminal responsibility.

Brazilian children up to 18 years of age have a specific legal statute – the Children's and Adolescents' Statute (ECA)/Federal Law 8069 of 1990 – which considers children up to 18 not accountable to be criminally condemned. Although from 12 years of age children can be legally held responsible for committing acts in disaccord with the law, they are subject to a special regime of socio-educational measures which can include from deprivation of freedom and internship in youth centres to other measures such as official reprimand, duty to repair the damage and carrying out community service. Under this statute, offences committed by minors are not conducive to penal responsibility as in the case of adults. The ECA considers that minors cannot be imputable of penal responsibility on account of 'their peculiar condition of development'. Here, the peculiarity of children is regarded as granting them a certain guarantee that eventual offences against the law should not constitute a matter of punishment but rather corrective socio-educational measures.

The moral panic against youth violence and delinquency finds an echo in the proposals for constitutional amendments forwarded to lower the age of criminal responsibility, the main argument claiming that many youth offenders know perfectly well what they are doing when they are trans-gressing the law thus able to cognitively discern what is illicit. This should justify treating them with no safeguard to their peculiarities. Finally, it is also claimed that Brazilian law has lowered both the age of voting and of driving to 16 years of age which concurs with regarding youth as capable and owners of exercising rights and duties.

The fact that modern states have taken over the task of legislating over and regulating the lives of children and youth, apart from the control of parents, has positioned them as the most governed group in our societies. The nature of the relationship between children as a social category and the state is shown in this dual arrangement: on the one hand, children are destitute of full civic and political rights; on the other hand, tutelage and protection of children are heralded as foremost duties of the state and parents. Both aspects condition the dependence and subordination of chil-dren, quite often their oppression, exploitation and abandonment. Political regimes that uphold children's lack of political rights should commit themselves to obligations of tutelage, but, most importantly, obligations of educational and cultural transmission to the young as a key feature of the social pact between generations.

Nevertheless, 'when things go wrong' as Hanson (2016) puts it, if outcomes of the tutelage imposed by parents and the state do not correspond to what is socially expected, as in the case of children's acting in disaccord with the law, this seems to justify proposals to raise the duly protective safeguards granted to children and to give up the embarrassing commitment of a failing educational relationship. Children's *maladroit* peculiarities become then not the object of intriguing enquiry on the part of the older generation, but assume a menacing effect which calls for a vehement demand to control and punish children levelling off the responsibility of adults.

It seems that age markers – be it 16 or 18 years – constitute a frail criterion to objectify key subjective elements of social transition in complex modern societies (McDiarmid, 2013). In the first place, this depends on what educational processes have contributed to a child's becoming, and in Brazil an enormous contingent of children suffer from serious disadvantages in this respect. For many, there has been no effective opportunity to enjoy and appreciate the ever dilemmatic adhesion to the social pact (Castro, 2013). They have been outsiders to all social endeavours – educational, cultural, emotional – and in this sense they have been wilfully excluded from participating in the social creation of citizenship in our society. Secondly, the implicit model of the subject in the legal system based on the individual's rationality to know about his or her acts and autonomy to choose and to act reinforces a vision of human completeness based on a fiction of adulthood that seems both derogative of the differential humanness of children and out of date with respect to present-day adults' capabilities. In this sense, it is no wonder that till now the legal system operates by deploying age criteria to determine penal responsibility. Humanness is reduced to rational autonomy to be achieved as a developmental task. Besides, it is expected that societal cohesion can be based solely on the internalization of norms, as a rational and volitional aspect of individuals that 'should know what is morally desirable'. Finally, adults' tutelage and protection of children seems to presuppose a univocally incapable child, one who cannot act agentically in any circumstances. Therefore, there is either the protective rule of adults over acquiescent children, *or* the granting them rights and entitlements which means that they are made similar to adults and penalized accordingly. As argued before, children have been regarded as distinctively contributing to humanness on account of holding untapped human potentials to be discovered and fulfilled. Therefore, adults' commitments to their others, and to this imaginary (re)production of human life, are carried out through the process of education, which today should include reciprocity between generations, a modern value that demands far different arrangements between protection and participation than those of present-day societies. The arguments forwarded to lower criminal responsibility in Brazil point to the malaise between generations emergent nowadays over disputes on the nature of the obligations and commitments of adults towards children and the value of children in a country where black adolescents in the peripheries are literally exterminated by the police force. Age markers and the episteme they presuppose have for long been used to constrict the view about humanness to a progressive scale towards rational and autonomous 'completion' resulting in differential social power attached to social positions. It is not surprising that legal systems have operated so comfortably with age markers so as to reinforce and reproduce social positions of power and prestige to the detriment of children. A politics of age seems needed to face present demands for better answers concerning what is the child and their contribution to expanding our knowledge about what it is to be human.

References

Alanen, L. (2001a) 'Explorations in generational analysis', in L. Alanen and B. Mayall (eds), *Conceptualizing Child–Adult Relations*. London: Routledge Falmer. pp. 11–22.

Alanen, L. (2001b) 'Childhood as a generational condition: children's daily lives in a central Finland town', in L. Alanen and B. Mayall (eds), *Conceptualizing Child–Adult Relations*. London: Routledge Falmer. pp. 129–143.

Alanen, L. (2011) 'Generational order', in J. Qvortrup, W. Corsaro and M.-S. Honig (eds), *The Palgrave Handbook of Childhood Studies*. Basingstoke: Palgrave Macmillan. pp. 159–174.

Alderson, P. (2013) *Childhoods Real and Imagined*. Vol. 1. Abingdon: Routledge.

Ariès, P. (1962) *Centuries of Childhood*. London: Penguin.

Bergson, H. (1959) *Oeuvres*. Paris: PUF.

Berman, E. (2016) 'Aged culture'. Available at: http://acyig.americananthropo.org/2016/02/08/aged-culture/

Blaikie, A. (1997) 'Age consciousness and modernity: the social construction of retirement', *Self, Agency and Society*, 1(1): 9–26.

Bühler, C. (1951 [1935]) *From Birth to Maturity*. London: Routledge and Kegan Paul.

Buller, D. (2006) 'Evolutionary psychology: a critique', in E. Sober (ed.), *Conceptual Issues in Evolutionary Biology*. Cambridge, MA: MIT Press. pp. 197–216.

Castro, L.R. de (2013) 'A infância e seus direitos: são eles a única via de emancipação das crianças?', in *O Futuro da Infância*. Rio de Janeiro: 7 Letras. pp. 175–194.

Charbonnier, S. (2012) 'La conquête de l'enfance: uchronie de l'émancipation', in A. Kerlan and L. Loeffel (eds), *Repenser l'enfance?* Paris: Hermann. pp. 219–230.

Criado, E.M. (1998) *Crítica de la sociologia de la juventud.* Madrid: Istmo.

Cunningham, H. (2005) *Children and Childhood in Western Society since 1500.* Harlow: Pearson.

Danic, I., Delalande, J. and Rayou, P. (2006) *Enquêter auprès d'enfants et de jeunes: objets, méthodes et terrains de recherche en sciences sociales.* Rennes: Presses Universitaires de Rennes.

Deschavanne, E. and Tavoillot, P.-H. (2007) *Philosophie des âges de la vie.* Paris: Grasset et Fasquelle.

Duarte, L.F. (2001) 'Prefácio', in L.R. de Castro (ed.), *Crianças e jovens na construção da cultura.* Rio de Janeiro: Nau/Faperj. pp. 11–15.

Eagleton, T. (1988) 'The critic as clown', in C. Nelson and L. Grossberg (eds), *Marxism and the Interpretation of Culture.* Urbana: University of Illinois Press. pp. 619–632.

Gauchet, M. (2004) 'La redefinition des âges de la vie', *Le Débat*, 132: 27–44.

Gesell, A. (1928) *Infancy and Human Growth.* New York: Macmillan.

Hanson, K. (2016) 'Children's participation and agency when they don't "do the right thing"', *Childhood*, 23(4): 471–475.

Heinz, W. and Kruger, H. (2001) 'Life course: innovations and challenges for social research', *Current Sociology,* 49(2): 29–45.

Heywood, C. (2009) *A History of Childhood: Children and Childhood in the West from Medieval to Modern Times.* Malden, MA: Polity.

Honig, M.-S. (2011) 'How is the child constituted in childhood studies?', in J. Qvortrup, W. Corsaro and M.-S. Honig (eds), *The Palgrave Handbook of Childhood Studies.* Basingstoke: Palgrave Macmillan. pp. 62–77.

Hopkins, P. and Pain, R. (2010) 'Geographies of age: thinking relationally', *Area*, 39(3): 287–294.

Kelle, H. (2010) 'Age-appropriate development as measure and norm: an ethnographic study of the practical anthropology of routine paediatric checkups', *Childhood*, 17(1): 9–25.

Kohli, M. (1986) 'Social organization and subjective construction of the life course', in A. Sorensen, F. Weinert and L. Sherrod (eds), *Human Development and the Life Course: Multidisciplinary Perspectives.* Hillsdale, NJ: Lawrence Erlbaum. pp. 271–292.

Labouvie-Vief, G. (1981) 'Proactive and reactive aspects of constructivism: growth and aging in life span perspective', in R. Lerner and N. Busch-Rossnagel (eds), *The Individuals as Producers of their own Development.* New York: Academic Press. pp. 197–227.

Lansdown, G. (2005) *The Evolving Capacities of the Child.* Florence: UNICEF/Save the Children.

Mantle, G., Leslie, J., Parsons, S., Plenty, J. and Shaffer, R. (2006) 'Establishing children's wishes and feelings for family court reports: the significance attached to the age of the child', *Childhood*, 13(4): 499–518.

McDiarmid, C. (2013) 'An age of complexity: children and criminal responsibility in law', *Youth Justice*, 13(2): 145–160.

Meyer, J. (1986) 'The self and the life course: institutionalization and its effects', in A. Sorensen, F. Weinert and L. Sherrod (eds), *Human Development and the Life Course: Multidisciplinary Perspectives*. Hillsdale, NJ: Lawrence Erlbaum. pp. 199–216.

Monjo, R. (2012) 'Philosophie et politique des âges de la vie. Enfance et justice', in A. Kerlan and L. Loeffel (eds), *Repenser l'enfance?* Paris: Hermann. pp. 67–84.

Morrow, V. (2013) 'What's in a number? Unsetting the boundaries of age', *Childhood*, 20(2): 151–155.

Morss, J. (1992) 'Against ontogeny', in P. Griffiths (ed.), *Trees of Life: Essays in Philosophy of Biology*. Dordrecht, The Netherlands: Kluwer. pp. 241–270.

Nandy, A. (2010) 'Reconstructing childhood: a critique of the ideology of adulthood', in A. Singh and S. Mohapatra (eds), *Indian Political Thought*. New York: Routledge. pp. 203–214.

Narvanen, A.-L. and Nasman, E. (2004) 'Childhood as generation of life phase?', *Young*, 12(1): 71–91.

Ogden, T. (1989) *The Primitive Edge of Experience*. Northvale, NJ: Jason Aronson.

Oyama, S. (1992) 'Ontogeny and phylogeny: a case of metarecapitulation?', in P. Griffiths (ed.), *Trees of Life: Essays in Philosophy of Biology*. Dordrecht: Kluwer. pp. 211–240.

Peters, R. (1980) 'The development of reason', in S. Modgil and C. Modgil (eds), *Toward a Theory of Psychological Development*. Windsor: NFER.

Renaut, A. (2002) *La Libération des enfants*. Paris: Hachette.

Riley, M. (1987) 'On the significance of age in sociology', *American Sociological Review*, 52(1): 1–14.

Solberg, A. (1990) 'Negotiating childhood: changing constructions of age for Norwegian children', in A. James and A. Prout (eds), *Constructing and Reconstructing Childhood*. London: Falmer Press. pp. 118–137.

Stern, D. (2000) *The Interpersonal World of the Infant*. New York: Basic Books.

Stern, D. (2010) *Forms of Vitality*. Oxford: Oxford University Press.

Thorne, B. (2004) 'Theorizing age and other differences', *Childhood*, 11(4): 403–408.

Thorne, B. (2008) 'What's in an age name?', *Childhood*, 15(4): 435–439.

3

Inequalities in French Speaking and Anglo-Saxon Childhood Sociologies

Régine Sirota

Introduction

Academic traditions and socio-political contexts have addressed the issue of inequalities in childhood in different ways. In particular, the French speaking sociological analyses are quite different from the Anglo-Saxon ones. This difference will be presented and discussed in this chapter. Paradoxically, it is in putting aside the question of democratization and inequalities of opportunities that the child emerged as an actor in French speaking sociology. On the one side, in the French context, the 'republican universalism' has been the main reference for the sociological debate, therefore childhood inequalities have been mainly studied in terms of social stratification. On the other side, in the Anglo-Saxon context, diversity has been the main reference for this debate, therefore priority has been given to aspects such as gender or ethnicity. I aim to examine how these differences influence the way in which childhood inequalities have been studied and how the different categorizations have been transformed and their intersectionality has been addressed.

Thinking of Childhood, Inequality and Diversity: Two Sociological Traditions

The first question is how the issue of inequalities has been addressed in the Sociology of Childhood. Conceptualizations have evolved considerably and differently according to the socio-political contexts and academic traditions. First of all, let us focus on the vocabulary which has been used to address the issue of childhood. The most important terms used in French and English speaking contexts are inequality and diversity. While the term 'inequality', or the expression 'inequality of opportunities', is frequently used in Francophone sociology, the term 'diversity' is widespread in the

Anglo-American sociology and has only recently emerged on the French sociological scene – in particular as a common theme in the social and media spheres. The term 'diversity' has been used to talk about urban segregation, youth unemployment and social movements, in consequence of the ongoing crisis in suburban housing estates and the curtailment of social mobility. It has become a 'politically correct' slogan to refer to anything sensitive or incorrect, particularly in public policies.

Against this background, several questions arise. The first question is whether the term 'diversity' can replace the term 'inequality'. The second question is whether the notion of 'diversity' can make differences as equivalent, laying the cards on the table as they are, next to each other. The third question is whether this mean that there are no longer relations of hierarchization, stratification, or even discrimination or domination, and, if this is the case, what is the regime of equality or inequality that is implicitly involved in this position? The fourth question is whether different diversities in childhood are conceptually equivalent, and if the different relations – regarding social class, gender, generation, ethnicity – in which childhood can be included are equivalent. The fifth question is whether it is possible to talk either about relations of power, solidarity, competition, stratification, domination or about reconfiguration of the different elements which compose the individual identity. The sixth questions is whether these questions are specific to the French context, and if this conceptualization depends on the French linguistic and/or national framework. The final question is whether this conceptualization is still relevant in the face of migrations between South and North and North and South, and what is the significance of this conceptualization in a globalized perspective. I will address these questions in what follows.

Two cultural traditions have enhanced two very different ways of addressing the issue of inequality: the French (and Francophone) context and the American (and Anglophone) one. In the French context (Sirota, 2010a), the universalism of 'republican egalitarianism' was originally based on the denial of differences, as all individuals were considered equal before the Republic. For a long time, the model of French assimilation, transcending all individual affiliations (whether cultural, religious, social or economic) has blocked the formulation of inequality in terms of race, ethnicity or origins. The weight of Marxist sociology emphasized the question of inequalities of opportunities and social discrimination in relation to social class (Doyetcheva, 2010; Masclet, 2012). This was particularly evident in the educational sphere, where inequality of opportunities was

stressed almost exclusively in terms of social mobility and democratization (Sirota, 1994, 2005). This type of sociology reached its apex in France
in the 1970s and 1980s when 'social class worked as a total concept, as
that which must be explained and as that which explains what needs to
be explained' (Dubet, 2012: 260). Later on, the rise of symbolic interactionism and social constructivism, on one side, and individualism, on the
other, contributed to articulate the issue of inequalities in a different way,
considering individuals as 'plural' (Lahire, 1998) and facing the challenge
of developing individuality. This approach allowed for the slow emergence of other social relations, such as gender, on the sociological scene.

Ethnicity was not focused on, particularly because after the Second
World War it was seen as a taboo or 'a forbidden variable' in the French
debate (Fassin and Fassin, 2006). However, the current social situation
and the crisis in the suburbs have forced politicians to address the question of discrimination based on race or origins, whether ethnic, national,
migratory or, more recently, religious (Keppel, 2012). The French sociologists hesitate to choose a vocabulary to qualify and to name these
'visible minorities' – in other words, to classify diversity – as they know
that words create objects. Even the collection of statistics about ethnicity
opens a heated debate in both the scientific and political spheres; therefore, it is conducted under the careful watch of public bodies such as CNIL
(Commission de l'Informatique et des Libertés), HALDE (Haute authorité
de lutte contre les discriminations et pour l'égalité) and more recently the
Ombudsman (le Défenseur des droits).

The question of inequality and discrimination was historically raised
in a very different way in the United States. Against the background of
the heritage of slavery, racial differences and affirmative action policies,
and in order to respond to criticism about the implementation of affirmative action policies (via the quota policy), the notion of diversity was
developed as it was seen as fitting into the American tradition. The path
towards equality therefore starts with the principle of equality rights, that
is to say 'civil rights', and the recognition that discrimination needs to
be corrected, which was soon reformulated in a discourse of diversity
(Laufer, 2009). The aim was to allow the people, whose words had long
been stifled, whether on account of race, gender, class or other forms of
hierarchization such as disability, to speak up (Paperman, 2013), and to
allow the people, who are in asymmetrical, unequal or unjust relations, to
express themselves in order to reconstruct the matrices of domination. One
effect of this approach was the segmentation of different relationships of

domination: white and coloured people, women and men, youth or elder, dependent or independent people, disabled or abled people, dominant or dominated people. This led to the emergence of what have been called 'subaltern theories'.

The Issue of Inequalities in the Sociology of Childhood

In the first stage of the Sociology of Childhood, whether Anglophone or Francophone, the main concern was to allow an invisible actor, the child, who had largely been marginalized or ignored by general sociology, to step onto the sociological stage (Ambert, 1986; James and Prout, 1990; Sirota, 1994). This aim was repeatedly stated, loud and clear: it was necessary to let certain aspects of differentiation be overshadowed, at least momentarily, in order to focus on the emergence of the hidden figure of the child, by granting it 'full rights' and 'full status'. The critical revision of the socialization process allowed not only the child to access the sociological scene as a subject and as an actor, but also children to emerge as a social group and childhood as a social category (James and James, 2004; Sirota, 1998, 2019). This was proposed in various contexts, historically and interculturally, thus also taking into account the structural constraints on childhood.

This stage primarily developed a general vision of childhood, in order to focus primarily on the difference of childhood as opposed to adulthood. This structural position interpreted difference and inequality as intergenerational differences or what can be considered a 'generational order' (Alanen, 2016). This approach sees the intergenerational difference as the main one, which absorbs all other differences, such as gender or class differences. In this perspective, childhood is seen as a social category which depends on other social categories, and which has a minority status involving a relationship of protection and domination. This minority condition is described in the French context by political philosophers such as Gauchet (2004) as a 'paradoxical ego'. In this stage, the aim of Sociology of Childhood was to allow a 'normal' childhood, in the sense of ordinary childhood, to come out of the shadows (Corsaro, 1997; James and Prout, 1990; Qvortrup et al., 2009). How should we understand this concern?

An important question is whether the growth and weight of the middle classes, during the 30 years of the postwar boom (known as the *Trente glorieuses* in France), and the corresponding dilution of differentiation due to the rise of consumption (Morin, 1963), might have made it possible to think of childhood in this way, and/or if it is a result of class ethnocentrism. This aspect has not been studied enough, therefore we know very little about its conditions of socialization, which should be deconstructed. In any case, this approach breaks away from the perspective of the *dispositifs* and measures invented by developmental psychology, which mainly focuses on deviance and pathology, for example through IQtests. This psychological focus was linked to the concerns of philanthropists (Fass, 2007) and paediatricians at the time of industrial development (Rollet, 2007; Segalen, 2010), who wanted to eradicate misery and poverty by formulating the norms and criteria of appropriate care. The idea was to focus primarily on childhood issues that were (and still are) a problem for the improvement of industrialized societies, which need to preserve, anticipate and maintain the human capital.

Each identified problem of childhood enhanced a specific field of sociology, linked to how different institutions dealt with the problem, and adapted to it, while anthropology focused mainly on the countries of the global South and on the conditions of neo-colonialism. Childhood thus only appeared indirectly on the sociological scene, through the analysis of public policies in schools, the health administration and the legal system. It appeared in terms of differentiation rather than inequalities, with the consequent production of diversity of institutions, professionals, social concerns and sociological territories. The diffraction of the object and the concealment of the subject were produced together, as childhood had become the object of multiple public policies and the child did not exist per se but only as a social problem, through various and differentiated official bodies, dealing with marginal or 'irregular' childhood.

How Categorizations Affect Childhood and How Childhood Affects Categories

The question then is how one can think about childhood, i.e. what interpretative framework can be used about childhood, in particular what categorizations of inequality or diversity should be used and what frame of analysis can be applied? In other words, the question is how different categorizations can affect the way of thinking about childhood and whether it is necessary either to review the history of these categorizations one by one or to understand their intersectionality. An integrated approach is necessary in order to go beyond juxtaposing, partitioning and hierarchizing the most important orientations to social differentiation, namely gender, class, race, ethnicity, disability and sexual orientation (Bilge, 2009). I choose here a specific angle, which is still controversial on the French linguistic scene. I will try to look at how the issue of inequalities or the categories of diversity affect childhood and, conversely, how childhood affects these categories. I will focus more specifically on the use of one category, namely 'social class', to think about childhood inequalities. I will look at how thinking about childhood in terms of social class allows different thinking, and how thinking about social class through childhood leads to thinking about childhood differently, and to introduce or put aside diversity.

The question here is if social class can be interpreted as a 'forgotten variable' as Goffman (1988 [1964]) might have put it, or a 'useful category', as Scott would have argued about 'gender' (Scott and Varikas, 1988). It is possible to identify a succession of stages in the use of the concept of 'social class' in the field of Sociology of Childhood. Against this background, Bourdieu's claim that 'Youth is just a word' (1981) might be applied to childhood, seen as an age category which conceals the inequalities and class relations that affect it, and that should be articulated in terms of social stratification and class relations. To what extent does such an approach, which emphasizes class hierarchies, conceal other issues, such as generational, gender, racial and ethnic factors? On the other hand, did the 'sacralization' of the child – the 'priceless child' (Zelizer, 1985) – which resulted from the focus on the changes in the social value of children, discourage any analysis based on social disparities? Indeed this sacralization was originally a case of intentional avoidance of assimilation of children to their families, in order to set children apart from the household, to allow them to escape from the 'patriarchal reasoning', assimilating all family members to the socio-professional category of the father, considered as both the breadwinner and the head of the family. The goal was to keep outside the issue of inequality of opportunities, which confined the analysis to the entities symbolized by the expression 'son or daughter of executives or workers' (*fils ou fille de cadres supérieurs ou d'ouvriers*), with little or no questioning of what these categories might consist of. Childhood was thus only considered as either a potential social prospect, or an updated past. The present and the tangible conditions of children's socialization were not questioned.

This pervasive issue in the sociology of education relegated the child behind the pupil and only considered children's social life through success or failure at school. A perspective of social mobility was made possible, partly by prosperity during the 30-year postwar boom, and partly by the mythology of school meritocracy. The aim was to reintroduce the child as a fully-fledged social actor, with a dual definition of the condition of childhood, socially defined as variable in time and space and therefore multiple. This aim also included the introduction of the child as a social actor who has some agency, either to update or to negotiate the modalities of their social conditions. The child was therefore interpreted as partly, but not exclusively, dependent on these structural conditions. This theoretical position considers both structure and agency. Both aspects must be taken into account, but the place of the child must be balanced against the structural factors. As the British sociologists James and Prout (1990) have argued, childhood, as a variable of socio-analysis, can never be entirely separated from other variables such as class, gender or ethnicity. This raises significant methodological issues. Two main types of approaches have been used, raising several methodological problems with regard to the use and analysis of social categories, i.e. ethnographic approaches and statistical methods.

Ethnographic approaches, researching children as social actors, have generated some carefulness in the understanding of variations in social contexts. This perspective relies on an 'anthropology at home', which restricts access to the field. While in-depth analysis allows researchers to draw general conclusions, initially the ethnographic approach allowed little or no comparative work about different social contexts (Diasio, 2010). Despite this, in her book *Unequal Childhood: Class, Race and Family* (2003), the American sociologist Annette Lareau discusses the role of race and social class in the daily education of children. Through a sociological analysis inspired by French sociologist Bourdieu, she concludes at the end of her ethnographic study that social class plays a part in the construction of inequality, through two theoretical models that she outlines as 'concerted cultivation' and 'accomplishment of natural growth'. The title of Lareau's article, published in 2002, is very clear in its identification of the variables that are at play: 'Invisible inequality: social class and childrearing in Black families and White families'.

While the child had long remained totally invisible from a statistical point of view, it has now become a potential 'homo statisticus', by considering her or him as an actor, but in a perspective that is dynamic. The concurrent emergence of a statistical understanding of the child and Sociology of Childhood (Octobre, 2004; 2010; Qvortrup, 1993) implies taking these children into account differently, especially as theories of social constructivism and individualism lead us to consider the complexity of the cultural strategies of the child as plural individual. The statistical analysis, which uses the most classical sociological variables, makes apparent the multiplicity of childhood situations and their inequalities. In the French context, for instance, there has been an emergence of studies and surveys by the Ministry of Culture on the cultural practices of children (Octobre, 2004; Octobre et al., 2010; Octobre and Sirota, 2013; Sirota, 2010b). The analysis concerns cultural transmission and cultural practices (Cook, 2013; Pugh, 2011) when the child has become a consumer of culture. The analytical process requires taking into account children's voices and their growing autonomy. This however does not mean forgetting to see childhood as a social construction, caught in multiple structural determinants, such as social class or gender. These social factors need to emerge, not only for what concerns their respective weight, but through the evolution of cultural practices in the various stages of this period of life, from toddlerhood to childhood and from pre-adolescence to adolescence.

How Taking Childhood Into Account Affects Social Class as a Social Categorization

The point was raised from the beginning: the child is an actor. But an actor of what type of sociology (Sirota, 1998, 2006)? To answer this question, it is important to reflect on the type of conceptualization of social relations that is involved in this definition of social actor. This implies going back to classical debates, related to the evolution of general sociology, where it is possible to observe the evolution in the vocabulary used, in order to show how the multiplicity of childhood conditions may depend on the social context, how the theoretical turn 'towards the actor' can be taken into account, what the relevant categorizations and differentiations of childhood are as a stage of life, for example how age and social class differentiations work, and finally what the relevant differentiations in childhood are.

Let's see, in French sociology, how much social class categorization can depend on the evolution of general sociology, its certainties and ambiguities. The weight of Marxist sociology has led to strongly emphasize the question of inequality of opportunities and social discrimination in relation to social class, especially in the educational sphere, where the inequality of opportunities has been addressed in terms of social mobility and democratization, as mentioned above. An important transformation happened through the passage from an analysis mainly focused on labour and relations of production, in terms of objective social classes, to an analysis of complex and mobile social affiliations, as François Dubet indicated (Paradeise et al., 2016). This has given rise to the classical usage of the circumlocutions *enfants d'ouvriers* (children of workers) and *enfants des classes supérieures* (children of the upper class). But we can observe a further evolution of this categorization: *enfants pauvres* (poor children) has given way to *enfants d'ouvriers* (children of workers), and then *enfants des classes populaires* (working-class children), before shifting to *enfants de catégories défavorisées* (children of underprivileged categories) or to *jeunes de banlieues* (youth from the suburbs) and *jeunes des cités* (young from housing estates), or *jeunes des quartiers* (children from urban ghettos). More recently, this evolution has led to *enfants de migrants* (children of migrants), *enfants de réfugiés* (children of refugees) and *mineurs non accompagnés* (unaccompanied minors). In parallel, expressions such as *enfance en danger* (threatened children), *enfance vulnérable* (vulnerable children), *enfant victime* (child victim) have been used. Recently, the categories of 'poor children', 'street children' and even *enfances précaires* (precarious childhood) have been retrieved in the debate (Hirsch and Villeneuve, 2006; Stettinger, 2014; Zaouche Gaudron, 2017). The reference for this terminology has thus shifted from the patrons of nineteenth-century philanthropy to the UN Convention on the Rights of the Child, via the following representation of the fractures and tensions in French society.

Alain Chenu's analysis has described this evolution very well, in an article in the journal *Socio-économie* (2012) about the evolution of the general use of socio-professional categories and of the French National Institute of Statistics (INSEE) nomenclature: 'The new descriptions of the social world increasingly give way to spatial categories; community categorizations that refer to ethno-racial social origins are emphasized in a context increasingly described as "postcolonial" ' (2012: 239). Diversity in childhood, which was taken into account from the beginning in the Anglophone context, is slowly penetrating the French sociology, making its analyses more complex.

This leads to a new series of questions. Firstly, to what extent is the notion of social class the most relevant categorization to identify social inequalities concerning childhood and how is it connected with other categorizations? Secondly, which other types of discrimination are relevant? Thirdly, how might family and personal migratory trajectories redistribute this diversity and these inequalities, either in the Northern or the Southern part of the world? Finally, are the social disqualification and precariousness, depending on poverty, no more significant than socio-economic and socio-cultural inequalities? The question of social inequalities was raised from the very beginning in the Anglophone sociological studies on childhood, for example by Corsaro, who stated that 'of all the factors that contribute to the social problem of children, poverty is the most pervasive and the most insidious' (1997: 297), and by some British sociologists. In France, this question is rarely confronted directly, even though almost two million children are estimated to live below the poverty line by the few organizations that tackle the issue (Stettinger, 2014), either private foundations or public or international bodies (UNICEF, 2012, CERC). The French sociologist Serge Paugham (2016), for example, in a study commissioned by UNICEF, stresses that growing up in an underprivileged area is in itself a source of inequality. He uses a study conducted with children between six and 18 years old, to analyse how the areas they live in are a social marker that has a notable impact on the risk of experiencing difficulties in integration into wider society, in terms of ethnic and religious discrimination. The analysis is formulated directly in terms of spatial segregations and social disqualification, rather than social class.

The debate around colour-blindness and the construction of identities that animates the Anglophone sociology is also spreading in the French sociology. In the first instance, this controversy was mainly present in the media and in political debates. For some, the republican model of integration into the nation-state relies on two identity criteria: legal nationality and socio-professional category (Noiriel, 2006); while for others this model is 'colour-blind' (Ndiaye, 2006). Universalism and communitarianism clash. It becomes important to shift from the social to the racial and ethnic question, to reflect the evolution and the tensions in French society, to quote Fassin and Fassin (2006), whose book published in 2006 marks this turning point. Academic perspectives and political speech feed the debate on the public policies about immigrants and the classification of the social inequalities and discriminations affecting young immigrants. The representation of society and of its tensions purely in terms of social class is thus questioned. These debates, while not directly concerned with that age group, have ended up influencing the scientific agenda of childhood studies, as what is at stake, in the media and politics, are young second and third generations of immigrant descent who are challenging the French model of integration. These issues become part of the sociological debate. 'Crossing borders, crossing eras: migratory policies and childhood agency' was the title of a conference held in 2016. The political and academic debates on the reasons behind religious radicalization (Keppel, 2012) have increased the pressure to take into account the cultural conditions (Lagrange, 2010) and not only the economic ones of childhood, and to pay more attention to the variable of religion. The question of the connection between these different variables, on the one hand, and social class and various types of discrimination, on the other, has become acute and has prompted heated debates. But the topics related to immigration or religion are often studied from specialized fields within sociology, depending on the specialization of researchers, and 'ideological preconceptions are crucial in the way everything that has to do with immigration is addressed' in France, to quote the opening of a book entitled *Les Yeux grands fermés* ['Eyes Wide Shut'] by a specialist on the matter (Tribalat, 2010: 2).

Last but not least, the question is what the 'child actor' makes of social differences and differentiations. Taking the child as the unit of measurement or central point of analysis leads to consideration of several obvious points regarding the use of categorizations; however it is not clear in what ways the child is a carrier of these categorizations. Taking the perspective of reproductive sociology, this question may be reformulated in terms of how the 'habitus' is constructed and evolves and of 'cultural capital' as a productive hierarchy in an era of eclecticism and omnivorousness. Again, this problem involves family and personal migratory trajectories redistributing diversity and inequalities, and the ways in which gender identity is connected with these inequalities and can redistribute them. Asking these questions implies taking a theoretical standpoint, and this is where the researcher's theoretical and ideological choices clearly come into play.

Although the question of childhood inequalities is considered in the Francophone sociology as the only valid question, it is still only formulated in terms of social class or gender, considered as the main front, if not the only legitimate one, for sociologists, and leaving aside other differentiations or discriminations. This shows how much this sociology remains dependent on the issues tackled by general sociology, and on the way in which the researchers position themselves as academics or activists (Galland and Muxel, 2017). However, the situation is not so simple when thinking and rethinking inequality. Though social class is certainly making a comeback in general sociology, with the advent of individualism and the development of consumption, the object of investigation is now a complex and pluralistic individual, caught in the multiplicity of identities and their evolution. This brings us back to the question of interconnections among these variables, intersectionality, weight and time frames. A small individual, but a big sociological subject.

A Child Lost in Translation

While asking the most relevant questions, it is not possible to ignore the problem of translation because the move from one language to another is far from simple (Pouly, 2017), and the exchanges between the Anglophone and the French traditions is far from obvious. The rules of the game can be quite different in the two traditions, implicitly or explicitly, as a French-American researcher, Rebecca Rogers, summarized it during an oral debate: 'When I write in English I use it, in French I avoid'. Firstly, Anglophones generally ignore Francophone studies, unless they are translated – which they seldom are – and Francophone academics do not read much in English. Secondly, the difficulties of translation between English and French, the weight of the different theoretical traditions, the complexity of transposing these debates in different academic and socio-political contexts lead to misunderstandings, which deepens ignorance (Sirota, 2012). This is notably the case for the debate around structure and agency: the child as an actor, the child as an agent, and *le métier d'enfant*.

From the beginning, in *Le Vocabulaire européen des philosophies* ['European Philosophical Vocabularies'] (Balibar and Laugier, 2004), the word 'agency' was deemed to be untranslatable in French; one can nonetheless note that it has appeared and is used in Childhood Studies, and especially in the Sociology of Childhood, but also, in the same period, in social sciences in general. It has been especially used to emphasize the reversal in the position of researchers, away from the classical Durkheimian position which considered the child as *un acteur faible* (a weak actor) (Payet, 2011), understanding children's agency by looking at what they do and not only at what is done to them. However, the notion of 'agent' is not at all similar in the Anglophone and Francophone contexts, and the word has a very different meaning depending on the theoretical positioning of the author. Symbolic interactionism, theories of individualism, social constructivism and sociology of reproduction give a different weight to the child's agency, above all to the child's capacity to negotiate or to be trapped in the weight of structural determinisms.

To these problems of translation, one must add the weight of disciplinary divides, which sometimes delineate research areas and perimeters differently (Sirota, 2012), depending on national contexts. If sociology and anthropology have mingled in the Anglophone childhood studies – which strongly challenge the relevance of all of these categorizations and their transpositions, if not the relevance of their globalization in a universalist vision (Delalande, 2014; Lancy, 2012) – in the Francophone academia, the perimeters of the different disciplines are quite distinct, and the researchers who come from anthropology and work in countries of the global South are those who question these categorizations and their transpositions, by focusing, for example, on the 'child of development' (*l'enfant du développement*) (De Suremain and Bonnet, 2014). This leads back to the norms of politics and international law, and to the questions about the relevance of the figures of childhood that are implicitly or explicitly used. This new perspective on children and the attention paid to their voice, in very different socio-cultural contexts, demand an articulation of local tensions and global norms, to question these categorizations and to generate new outlooks on institutional realities, capable of altering the analysis, among others, of the ways in which the *corps politique* (political body) of the child is treated (Diasio, 2010; Jaffré and Sirota, 2013). From the analysis of daily situations in hospital, for example, including the pain of the child (Kane, 2019), to that of street children, reinterpreting them through local familial or professional figures of childhood, these studies raise questions about the formation of new imaginary figures, whether compassionate or strictly activist (Schlemmer, 2006; Stoecklin, 2000), in the imagination of researchers and political actors.

'Observing sociological views is always an act of authority. It defines what is and what is not, it distinguishes between fields, specialties, subfields and sub-specialties, it divides things in two, public and private, feelings and rationality, facts and values, and it fixes hierarchies. Mapping sociology and its architectural principles is like touring one's land and pushing to the edges of the discipline the questions and theorizations coming from subaltern points of views (Paperman, 2013:61)'. Asking the question of inequalities from the perspective of childhood is like holding a mirror that reflects not only the evolution of society or of the societies used as a point of reference, but also the relevance or irreverence of sociological categories, shining a light on their rigidities, as well as on their transformations and ambiguities.

References

Alanen, L. (2016) 'Intersectionality and other challenges to theorizing childhood', *Childhood*, 3(2): 157–161.

Ambert, A.-M. (1986) 'Sociology of sociology: the place of children in North American sociology', *Sociological Studies of Child Development*, 1: 11–31.

Balibar, E. and Laugier, S. (2004) 'Agency', in B. Cassin (ed.), *Vocabulaire européen des philosophies*. Paris: Le Robert/Seuil. pp. 26 –32.

Bilge, S. (2009) 'Théorisations féministes de l'intersectionnalité', *Diogène*, 1(225): 70–88.

Bourdieu, P. (1981) 'La jeunesse n'est qu'un mot', in *Questions de sociologie*. Paris: Editions de Minuit. pp. 143–158.

Chenu, A. (2012) 'Les catégories socioprofessionnelles: sous la nomenclature, quelles institutions', *Revue Française de Socio-économie*, 10(2): 235–240.

Cook, D. (2013) 'La notion de "culture" dans la culture de la consommation des enfants', in S. Octobre and R. Sirota (eds), *L'Enfant et ses cultures, perspectives internationals*. Paris: Ministère de la Culture et de la Communication. pp. 91–122.

Corsaro, W. (1997) *The Sociology of Childhood*. Thousand Oaks, CA: Pine Forge Press.

De Suremain, C.-E. and Bonnet, D. (2014) 'L'enfant dans l'aide internationale. Tensions entre normes universelles et figures locales, L'enfant du développement', *Autrepart, Revue de Sciences Sociales au Sud*, 4(72): 3–21.

Delalande, J. (2014) 'Le concept d'enfant acteur est-il périmé? Réflexions sur des ouvertures possibles pour un concept toujours à questionner', *AnthropoChildren*, 4. Available at: http://popups.ulg.ac.be/2034-8517/index.php?id=1927

Diasio, N. (2010) *Le gouvernement de l'incertitude: corps, culture matérielle et maillage des temps à l'enfance*. HDR: Université Paris Descartes.

Doyetcheva, M. (2010) 'Usages français de la notion de diversité', *Sociologie*, 1(4): 423–438.

Dubet, F. (2012) 'Classes sociales et description de la société', *Revue Française de Socio-économie*, 2(10): 259–264.

Fass, P.S. (2007) *Children for a New World*. New York: New York University Press.

Fassin, D. and Fassin, E. (eds) (2006) *De la question sociale à la question raciale*. Paris: La Découverte.

Galland, O. and Muxel, A. (2017) 'Face au terrorisme, la recherche en action, une vaste enquête sur la radicalisation des lycéens' (Interview), *Journal du CNRS*, May.

Gauchet, M. (2004) 'L'enfant du désir', *Le Débat*, 132: 98–131.

Goffman, E. (1988 [1964]) 'La situation négligée', in Y. Winkin (ed.), *Les Moments et leurs homes*. Paris: Seuil/Minuit. pp. 143–149.

Hirsch, M. and Villeneuve, S. (2006) *La Pauvreté en héritage, deux millions d'enfants pauvres en France*. Paris: Robert Laffont.

Jaffré, Y. and Sirota, R. (2013) 'Les corps sociaux de l'enfance', *Corps*, 1(11): 197–202.

James, A. and James, A. (2004) *Constructing Childhood: Theory, Policy and Social Practice*. London: Palgrave Macmillan

James, A. and Prout, A. (1990) *Constructing and Reconstructing Childhood: Contemporary Issues in the Sociological Study of Childhood*. London: Falmer Press.

Kane, H. (2019) 'Parcours d'enfant malades entre douleurs, non-dits et lacunes des prises en charge (Nouakchott, Mauritanie)', in Y. Jaffré (ed.), *Enfants et soins en pédiatrie en Afrique de l'ouest*. Paris: Enspedia/Karthala.

Keppel, G. (2012) *Banlieue de la République. Société, politique et religion à Clichy-sous-Bois et Montfermeil*. Paris: Gallimard.

Lagrange, H. (2010) *Le Déni des cultures*. Paris: Editions du Seuil.

Lahire, B. (1998) *L'Homme pluriel*. Paris: Fayard.

Lancy, D. (2012) 'Unmasking children's agency', *AnthropoChildren*, 2. Available at: http://popups.ulg.ac.be/2034-8517/index.php?id=1253

Lareau, A. (2002) 'Invisible inequality: social class and childrearing in Black families and White families', *American Sociological Review*, 67(5): 747–776.

Lareau, A. (2003) *Unequal Childhood: Class, Race and Family Life*. Berkeley: University of California Press.

Laufer, J. (2009) 'L'égalité professionnelle entre les hommes et les femmes est-elle soluble dans la diversité ?', *Travail, Genre et Sociétés*, 21: 29–54.

Masclet, O. (2012) *Sociologie de la diversité et des discriminations*. Paris: Armand Colin.

Morin, E. (1963) 'Une nouvelle classe d'âge', *Le Monde*, 6 July.

Ndiaye, P. (2006) 'Questions de couleur, histoire idéologie et pratique du colorisme', in D. Fassin and E. Fassin (eds), *De la question sociale à la question raciale*. Paris: La Découverte. pp. 37–54.

Noiriel, G. (2006) '"Color blindness" et construction des identités dans l'espace public français', in D. Fassin and E. Fassin (eds), *De la question sociale à la question raciale*. Paris: La Découverte. pp. 158–174.

Octobre, S. (2004) *Les loisirs culturels des 6–14 ans*. Paris: Ministère de la Culture et de la Communication.

Octobre, S. (2010) 'L'enfant en culture, sortir de l'invisibilité statistique', in A. Arléo and J. Delalande (eds), *Cultures enfantines*. Rennes: Presses Universitaires de Rennes. pp. 85–96.

Octobre, S. and Sirota, R. (2013) *Enfance et culture, perspectives internationales*. Paris: Ministère de la Culture et de la Communication.

Octobre, S., Detrez, C., Mercklé, P. and Berthomier, N. (2010) *L'Enfance des loisirs*. Paris: Ministère de la culture et de la communication.

Paperman, P. (2013) *Care et sentiments*. Paris: PUF.

Paradeise, C., Lorrain, D. and Demazière, D. (2016) *Les Sociologies françaises*. Paris: PUF.

Paugham, S. (2016) 'Consultation nationale des 6/18ans. Écoutons ce que les enfants ont à nous dire. Grandir en France, le lieu de vie comme marqueur social'. Available at: www.unicef.fr/consultation

Payet, J.P. (2011) 'L'enquête sociologique et les acteurs faibles', *Sociologies. Experience de reserche. Champs de recherche et enjeux de terrain*. Available at: http://sociologies.revues.org/3629

Pouly, M.P. (2017) 'Formations of class and gender /Des femmes respectables. Remarques sur la traduction en sciences sociales', *Biens Symboliques/Symbolic Goods*, 1. Available at: http://revue.biens-symboliques.net/19

Pugh, A.J. (2011) 'Distinction, boundaries or bridges? Children, inequality and the uses of consumer culture', *Poetics*, 39(1): 1–18.

Qvortrup, J. (ed.) (1993) *Childhood as Social Phenomenon: Lessons from an International Project*. Vienna: European Centre for Social Welfare Policy and Research.

Qvortrup, J., Corsaro, W. and Honig, M.-H. (2009) *The Palgrave Handbook of Childhood Studies*. London: Palgrave Macmillan.

Rollet, C. (2007) *Les Carnets de santé des enfants*. Paris: La Dispute.

Schlemmer, B. (2006) 'Le travail des enfants, étapes et avatars dans la construction d'un objet', in R. Sirota (ed.), *Eléments pour une sociologie de l'enfance*. Rennes: Presses Universitaires de Rennes. pp. 173–183

Scott, J. and Varikas, E. (1988) 'Genre: une catégorie utile d'analyse historique', *Les Cahiers du GRIF*, 37–38: 125–153.

Segalen, M. (2010) *A qui appartiennent les enfants?* Paris: Taillandier.

Sirota, R. (1994) 'L'enfant dans la sociologie de l'éducation, un fantôme ressuscité?', *Enfances et Sciences Sociales, Revue de l'Institut de Sociologie, Université Libre de Bruxelles*: 147–163.

Sirota, R. (1998) 'L'émergence d'une sociologie de l'enfance: évolution de l'objet, évolution du regard?', *Education et Sociétés*, 2: 9–33.

Sirota, R. (2005) 'L'enfant acteur ou sujet dans la sociologie de l'enfance. Evolutions des positions théoriques au travers du prisme de la socialisation', in G. Bergonnier-Dupuy (ed.), *L'Enfant acteur ou sujet dans la sociologie de l'enfance*. Paris: ERES. pp. 33–41.

Sirota, R. (ed.) (2006) *Éléments pour une sociologie de l'enfance*. Rennes: Presses Universitaires de Rennes.

Sirota, R. (2010a) 'French childhood sociology: an unusual, minor topic or well defined field?', *Current Sociology*, 58(2): 250–271.

Sirota, R. (2010b) 'De l'indifférence sociologique à la difficile reconnaissance de l'effervescence culturelle d'une classe d'âge', in S. Octobre (ed.), *Enfance et culture, transmission, appropriation et representation*. Paris: Ministère de la Culture et de la Communication. pp. 17–36.

Sirota, R. (2012) 'L'enfance au regard des sciences sociales', *AnthropoChildren*, 1. Available at: https://popups.uliege.be/2034-8517/index.php?id=921

Sirota, R. (2019) 'Positions et dispositions de la sociologie de l'enfance, retour et discussions sur le processus de socialisation', in S. Depoilly and S. Kakpo (eds), *La Construction des dispositions durant l'enfance*. Paris: Presses de l'Université de Vincennes.

Stettinger, V. (2014) 'Pour une approche sociologique renouvelée des enfants pauvres', *Sociologie*, 4(5): 441–453.

Stoecklin, D. (2000) *Enfants des rues en Chine*. Paris: Karthala.

Tribalat, M. (2010) *Les Yeux grands fermés, l'émigration en France*. Paris: Denoël.

UNICEF (2012) *Mesurer la pauvreté des enfants*. Florence: Centre de Recherche Innocenti.

Zaouche Gaudron, C. (2017) *Enfants de la précarité*. Toulouse: Eres.

Zelizer, V. (1985) *Pricing the Priceless Child*. Princeton, NJ: Princeton University Press.

Section Two

Issues of Children's Agency in Global Childhoods

Introduction

In Section 1 we have seen the problematic universalization of the concept of agency. This second section includes three chapters regarding the application of this concept to different social functions (education, mobility and health), and in different socio-cultural contexts (Burkina Faso, South Africa and Australia). The intersection between different functions and different socio-cultural contexts leads to three types of social conditions of agency.

The first chapter, 'Globalization, School and Redefinition of Childhood in Burkina Faso', written by Isabelle Danic, argues that the extension of schooling and transformation of childhood in Burkina Faso are linked to the process of globalization. According to the author, the globalization process has changed childhood representation and the attention paid to it in Sub-Saharan Africa in general. What is interesting here is the link between globalization and colonialism, as an ambivalent trigger of change. The education system introduced by the colonialist dominion has been affected by new educational issues arising from four intersecting factors: (1) migration processes, (2) international media exposure, (3) international lender agencies' requirements to increase the school enrolment rate and (4) the building of schools thanks to international donors. The author stresses that these factors have combined with the local conditions, leading to two relevant consequences. First, the crisis of farming, which is the country's main economic activity, has led farmers to hope that their children will access other types of jobs. Second, parents and children feel increasingly responsible for their own life and act to define its course, thus showing increasing agency. The final consequence is that childhood is redefined as a specific age that requires education, and children are redefined as individuals who should be involved in the decisions regarding their life.

The author also outlines the children's different opportunities of showing agency in Burkina Faso, which depend on different external resources and attitudes towards their lives. This highlights the generational order in Burkina Faso, as Alanen defines it. In particular, children's agency can be reduced by their families' economic conditions, religious beliefs, fatalistic and passive attitudes, and by children's past experiences, e.g. illnesses or loss of parents. Thus, children's opportunities of action are highly differentiated. In particular, they are enhanced by the expectation of the need to educate children so that they have access to better conditions of life.

This chapter highlights the paradoxical outcome of the intersection between societal and family conditions, on the one hand, and individual opportunities of action, on the other. This paradox is that children's agency is limited both when it is impeded by societal and cultural factors, and when it is enhanced through the redefinition of children as beings to educate, i.e. as not-yet-agents.

The second chapter in this section, 'Examining Child Mobility and Transport in South Africa: Challenges for Theory and Practice' by Sharmla Rama, examines children's social representation and inclusion in South Africa's transport policy and interventions. In particular, the chapter focuses on the extent to which these policies and interventions understand children's everyday activities, in terms of transport and mobility. The author highlights the potential relevance of the Sociology of Childhood in orienting transport experts and decision-makers to understand the complexity of children's mobility and transport. The current mobility and transport discourses highlight that mobility and transport experiences as well as needs are important conditions of equality of lives and voices. Against this background, however, studying child mobility only in terms of its impact on adults' mobility is insufficient. It is also necessary to analyse children's daily lives and schedules, considering their experiences and needs, i.e. their agency. The author's conclusion is that the marginality of children's experiences and needs, on the one hand, causes a gap of knowledge, and insufficient policies and practices, and on the other hand, it generates a passive, univocal and constrained view of children in society.

In this chapter, children's agency is seen as a fundamental and universal concept not only theorized within the Sociology of Childhood, but also certified by the United Nations, through the recognition of children as active participants, citizens and social agents in society. Against this background, on the one hand, participation is considered as an important strategy for sustainable development and the realization of democratic principles; on the other, children are seen as absent and dismissed from the decision-making spaces, processes and structures.

The third chapter, 'The Limits of Healthism: Understanding Children's Conceptions of Health' by Tobia Fattore, deals with another, more Westernized context, thus completing the 'journey' from an African country hybridized by Western influence to a Western country. This chapter regards children's health in relation to the discourse of healthism. The author highlights that health is an area of children's life in which normative expectations regarding parenthood and childhood have always been fundamental. Against this background, an important change concerning dominant health discourses is healthism, which has important consequences for the conceptualization of health and the healthy individual. The chapter presents a qualitative research with children, showing the ways in which children understand and act health, in relation to the idea of wellbeing, their agency, the social context, and the idea of body. According to the author, healthism emphasizes the individual responsibility but presents a limited view of children's agency, as children are subjected to parents' decisions and actions concerning their health, Children themselves enact agency in health practices, but they also acknowledge that their agency is socially built above all through parent–child relations. In this chapter, agency is not interpreted as an asserting choice, but as embedded in daily practices that may be taken for granted by children. Moreover, although they engage in health practices that are different to those of their parents, children assume the existence of health rules set by their parents, recognizing their guidance, even if they may disagree with such rules.

These three chapters show how agency is the result of children's actions and choices, on the one hand, and social conditions of these choices, on the other. These three chapters also share a critical perspective about the social conditions of children's agency, including family and policies. Social conditions and limitations of agency are assumed as unavoidable, and this shows the generalized importance assigned to the generational order, although it is observed critically. This also shows the oscillation between a social dimension as a necessary presupposition of children's agency, on the one hand, and the social restrictions that prevent the exercise of children's agency, on the other.

Against this background, an interesting question is to what extent the concept of agency is conditioned by the implementation of the analysis in different social and cultural contexts, such has Burkina Faso, South Africa and Australia. While in Burkina Faso, the focus is on the basic conditions of children's agency through education, in the other two contexts the focus is on more sophisticated conditions, such as policies of mobility and healthism. This difference is reflected in the identification of different social conditions of children's agency and different critical assumptions about these conditions. The social conditioning of schooling on children's agency in Burkina Faso seems to be much more compelling than the social conditioning of mobility in South Africa and health discourse in Australia. In Burkina Faso, recognition of agency is a basic struggle for education, in South Africa mobility is considered a basic right, in Australia it is a practice concerning health behaviours, although not completely recognized in the discourse of healthism.

These differences may show the problem of universalizing the concept of agency, even if this concept is used in all these contexts. Against this background, these three chapters may also lead to reflect on what policy-makers need to take into account to enhance children's agency, in different societal contexts and for different social functions.

4

Globalization, School and Redefinition of Childhood in Burkina Faso

Isabelle Danic

Introduction

This chapter is intended to show the link between globalization, the extension of schooling and changes in childhood. The data and analysis are based on social science studies on education and socialization in Sub-Saharan Africa and in Burkina Faso in particular, and on my fieldwork in Burkina Faso. This research was carried out in 2008 in two areas of the Sanmatenga region, one of which is urban (a neighbourhood of Kaya, a city of 100,000 inhabitants, some 100 kilometres north of Ouagadougou) and the other rural (a village of 2,000 inhabitants). It consisted of observation in public spaces and in a public primary school in each area, of interviews with the two school principals, three teachers and the parents of 10 families, and of collective interviews with the children in the two schools concerned.[1]

Based on a direct analysis of my study and on the findings of other research, this chapter highlights the societal, economic, cultural and social determinants, as well as the micro-social ones and the agency of social actors that redefine children as beings to educate.

State of the Art

Several research fields, including education, childhood and social change, are involved in defining the relationship between globalization, societal transformation, schooling and conceptions of childhood.

The sociology of education in Sub-Saharan Africa has focused primarily on schooling, on the absence of schooling, and on the social determinants of access to school. In the 1960s and 1970s, the first published studies on teaching in Africa (Campion-Vincent, 1970; Lê Thanh Khoi, 1971; Martin, 1972) showed the culturally random nature of schooling imported into Africa. This new phenomenon introduced by the colonial authorities was intended primarily to train an elite and secondly to 'civilize' a broader segment of the population for the administrative machinery.

Theories from the North proved however to be unsuited to the analysis of countries of the South. As the notion of social class was not applicable, researchers turned to the effects of ethnic group and the colonial determinants of schooling. Then, in the 1990s, ethnic determinants were excluded and even challenged, as scholars focused on gender. Today, the sociology of education in Africa is still oriented primarily towards schooling and especially the globalization of teaching and its effects.

A number of studies nevertheless focused on the articulation of socialization at and through school, in relation to community and family socialization, and on the effects of schooling on other educational processes (Bonini, 1996; Erny, 1987; Gérard, 1997; Mercier-Tremblay and Santerre, 1982). In parallel, Jack Goody (1987) studied changes in the transmission of knowledge, with the switch from the oral to the written, and the social changes generated by ways of thinking related to writing.

Additionally, there have been many reports on schooling in Africa, commissioned by international organizations, which link economic development to the extension of schooling. These often statistical and economic approaches claim that the development of the 'schooling offer' will entail an increase in school attendance, and will thus boost the country's development. They have strongly influenced the educational policies imposed on countries by international institutions.

Africanist sociologists who attempt to link schooling practices to social phenomena and to national and international education policies have identified several factors such as the 'schooling offer', the 'demand for schooling', the 'educational strategies of families' in Sub-Saharan Africa, as well as families' ability to afford schooling (enrolment fees, supplies, clothes; the possibility of replacing the labour that children out of school provide, etc.), the family's social status and the child's gender (Baux, 2007; Bonini, 1996; Compaoré et al., 2007; Gérard, 1997; Lange and Martin, 1995; Pilon and Yaro, 2001). These studies show that schooling is not automatically determined by the 'schooling offer' nor by the family's economic capacity, but rather by a variety of political, economic and ideological factors.

Childhood itself has received scant attention from sociologists, especially in the global South. Since the 1990s a few studies have investigated child labour and street children. Child labour is a varied and complex phenomenon, ranging from unlimited exploitation to family help (agricultural, commercial, artisan), through independent work enabling the child to pay for his or her schooling and care. This research has highlighted the fact that the worst forms of exploitation, found for instance in Burkina Faso in child kidnapping to do forced labour in Côte d'Ivoire,[2] are a result of economic globalization that focuses on the financial costs of production and disregards the human cost (Schlemmer, 2000). There is very little real research on street children (Panter-Brick, 2002), although a recent book investigates the phenomenon in Burkina Faso (Maiga and Wangre, 2009). Street children are found essentially in societies undergoing transition, when family and community solidarity breaks down without being replaced by the state. These children form groups to protect themselves and survive.

Ultimately, research on children in Burkina Faso or, more broadly, in Sub-Saharan Africa, consists mainly of ethnological studies on traditional education. Unlike American cultural studies that examined childhood and socialization in the 1930s, French speaking ethnologists did not turn to the subject until the 1960s and 1970s (Erny, 1987; Moumouni, 1974; Salifou, 1974). They then studied traditional education, covering the treatment of children from the pre-colonial period until the present day, in the family and community spheres. It was as if colonialization and then globalization had had no effect on education, and anything not perceived as traditional was virtually excluded from these descriptions. From these ethnological studies we can, nevertheless, learn about the traditional conception of childhood embedded in the traditional representation of the world, in which life on earth and the beyond overlapped. At birth, a child is frightening because he or she comes from the invisible world of spirits and could be a reincarnated ancestor. When children are weaned and walk, they become full members of the human community here on earth. Traditional education functions by practical initiation: children observe, apply and integrate the know-how, knowledge, norms and values of their environment, through practices, words, proverbs and stories (Badini, 1992).

Societal changes in Sub-Saharan Africa, investigated by anthropology and sociology, have proved to be paradoxical. A process of modernization can be seen in the constitution of a state, the development of a market economy, the emergence of rival social classes, and a process of individualization. At the same time, the persistence of community logics is leading to 'political despotism' that ensures integration by way of distribution through clientelism and community solidarity. Globalization and structural adjustment plans have compounded economic difficulties, resulting in the state's withdrawal, inadequate basic public services, high unemployment rates, lack of job security, and poverty. This in turn has restored the importance of community solidarity (Marie, 1997). As regards schooling, the state played a determinant role until the end of the 1970s (Lange, 2003). At the end of the 1980s, the government engaged in structural adjustment plans that led to a 'globalized and decentralized school order' in which international technical and financial partners took precedence over the state, teachers, parents and students (Lange, 2003). In the context of globalization, African states have lost their sovereignty to other national and international players (Tidjani Alou, 2001).

Taking into account explanations for the massification of schooling through a greater offer, families' economic capacities, families' social integration and the child's gender, and drawing on my own fieldwork, I posit that child schooling is essentially the result of its redefinition, which itself is part of a process of societal change tied to globalization.

The Life Contexts of the Children Studied

Burkina Faso has 20 million inhabitants[3] living on 274,000 km² in Sub-Saharan Africa. The country was formed when the French colonial authorities grouped together several small autonomous territories under the name of Upper Volta, which gained independence in 1960. The population is often presented and presents itself by reference to an ethnic group: half of them are Mossis, and the rest primarily Peuls, Gourmantchés, Gourounsis and Lobi. In total, there are some 60 ethnic groups.[4] Several languages coexist but the official language is French. The population of the region under study here consists mainly of Mossi, speaking Moré. The main religion is Muslim, as in the country as a whole. On the United Nations Development Programme's Human Development Index, Burkina Faso is one of the poorest countries in terms of access to drinking water, electricity, healthcare and schooling.

Children under the age of 15 constitute half of the population and are present and visible everywhere. In the two study areas, the children share common spaces and activities with other age groups: farming, artisanal or commercial work and domestic tasks (fetching water, shopping, washing). When they have time, they play in the public spaces or in the yard with objects they have found (e.g. football with an empty tin can) or made (e.g. rag doll, wire car). We still find some of the aspects in the ethnologists' description of childhood. For instance, babies are still perceived as belonging to the invisible world: they are named only after one week, and arouse suspicion. The idea that a child could be a reincarnation of an ancestor is excluded by monotheistic religions but Muslim and Christian parents often remain ambivalent in this respect: 'I believe but I can't believe with religion. We lost a son who died because he was our father's reincarnation [this man is still alive], so this child couldn't stay alive. So we don't believe that, we can't believe that' (father, hardware dealer working in town, Muslim).

Yet the conceptions of children and their care are changing. Circumcision is becoming a family ritual and less and less a community affair. Initiation has disappeared and more and more children attend school.

With the exception of street children, who go to the cities, all children live in families, whether monogamous or polygamous, with their parents or entrusted to a family of relatives or friends. The latter case is very frequent and may be on the initiative of parents in economic difficulty, to ensure that the child is cared for, or so that the child can attend school when it is too far away or too expensive for the parents. It may be on the initiative of the host family: the child may be needed by several beneficiaries to help in their home, for instance a sick grandmother or a cousin shopkeeper. A Mossi proverb says that 'children belong to everyone'. The child him- or herself may be at the origin of the initiative, to avoid difficult relations with his or her parents or to be closer to a school. Multiple parenting is normal. In Mossi culture, for example, the category of fathers includes the biological father and all his brothers, and the category of mothers includes the biological mother, her husband's other wives, and her sisters.

Concessions, consisting of huts or small breeze-block houses around a common courtyard, group together people who may be relatives or not. Monogamous families often live in a two-room house: one room for meals and receiving guests, and the other for sleeping. Toilets, where one also 'showers', are common to all the inhabitants of the concession. In the homes visited in this study, the inhabitants of the town had access to water from a tap in the courtyard, while those in the village got water from a collective pump. Many homes use oil lamps for lighting at night, although some urban homes have electricity and some rural homes are connected to a generator. In towns and rural areas, meals are prepared on a wood fire in the yard, and consist mainly of rice or of millet porridge. Families are often able to have only one meal a day, including farmers whose crops are insufficient.

In this context, the children have responsibilities at a very early age. Some of them work for themselves or for a tradesperson, an artisan or a private individual (e.g. girls as domestic help). Despite Burkina Faso's economic problems, the gross rates of enrolment in primary school[5] rose from 38.4% in 1996 to 56.8% in 2005, and to 83% in 2014 (Source: Ministère de l'éducation nationale et de l'alphabétisation – MENA).

In the urban area studied in 2008, the population has a wider and more diverse choice of schools. In the Kaya 1 district, there were 23 state schools (8,120 pupils) and 12 private schools (1,931 pupils).[6] The private schools consisted of: two Catholic schools (308 pupils in total), one Protestant school (306 pupils), one Muslim school (95 pupils), seven madrasah Franco-Arabic schools (1,195 pupils) and one specialized school for the deaf (28 pupils).[7] In the rural area studied, there is one public primary school (212 pupils), one Catholic school (229 pupils) and one madrasah Franco-Arabic school (120 pupils). In the Sanmatenga district, the gross rate of schooling was 24% in 1996, 47.7% in 2005 and 69% in 2009 (Source: SDAU -Schéma Directeur de l'aménagement urbain- Kaya). Although imprecise and probably overestimated, this shows that, as in Burkina Faso as a whole, there has been a rapid increase in school attendance.

A Redefinition of Childhood

Children's schooling is of course related to national and international policies such as increasing the school offer and assisting families who enrol their children in school. But this accessibility in practical terms is not enough to explain the sudden rapid growth of schooling, without looking at the wishes of the parents and their children.

All the parents interviewed, whether they had been to school or not, were in favour of schooling as a pathway to employment: 'nowadays, if you haven't been to school and you don't have a qualification, getting a job is a nightmare' (mother, trader in town). Some of them also saw it as a way to acquire personal skills: 'someone who's gone to school expresses himself easily and to explain something he doesn't really have a problem' (father, farmer in the village). In a poor country where price increases in staple products are impoverishing the population even more, the parents interviewed (small farmers, low ranking civil servants, traders, artisans) expressed their hopes that an education would enable their children to lift themselves out of poverty. 'I don't want them to become farmers.

We enrolled them at school. God willing, they'll be able to succeed, have a job, earn their living and also help us' (mother, farmer in the village). 'We really try so that at least they don't end up like us' (father, hardware dealer in town).

The children interviewed also expressed this wish to go to school: 'a child who doesn't go to school has no chances' (8-year-old boy, urban area). Those who are in school say how pleased they are: 'we learn to read and write' (12-year-old girl, rural area); 'in June, July, August, September (during holidays), we're bored' (8-year-old girl, urban area). Those who are not or no longer in school express their regrets: 'I can't go to school anymore because my mother can't pay' (9-year-old girl, urban area).[8] In-class observation shows that the children are attentive and participate fully, and that they comply with school's functioning.

In this still largely agricultural and community-based society, the pro-school attitude stems from a new conception of children: they are no longer little beings learning from experience with their peers and with adults, but instead are becoming beings different from adults, who require particular treatment: 'We'd like all our children to go to school, to be able to come out of the darkness, to be able to understand' (father, farmer in the village). This wish of parents for their children to attend school is supported by a distancing from the conception of a child who learns in his or her daily life what he or she needs to know. Raising children, making them human by physically and mentally shaping them, teaching them through sharing in adult activities is no longer enough; they now require particular attention and treatment, education – through explanations and exercises – in reading, writing and abstract knowledge. Children are thus considered as different to and separate from adults, and therefore have to be treated specifically, especially through education:

> It's very important for a child to go to school, to learn to read and write. It develops a child's mind and intelligence, and opens him to others. You see the advantages of education: children can be useful to themselves and to society as a whole. I'd have liked all children to be able to go to school. Even if they don't all succeed, their minds will be more open than those who didn't have the opportunity to go. (Mother, nurse in town)

At the same time, parent–child relations are changing. Greater value is being attached to children; there is more closeness and affection, and a less hierarchical structure. 'In the past and now, it's not the same anymore. Children are less obedient. That's how life's become. We're not supposed to hit a child anymore, that's why they're not really obedient' (mother, street trader in town). All the parents interviewed nevertheless considered it normal to ask children for their help with family work (domestic, agricultural, commercial, artisanal). A father quoted a Moré proverb: 'If donkeys give birth, it's to rest'. But today children are less help and more of a financial burden: 'It's difficult for us to send our children to school, to take care of them, to feed them, it's not easy! In the past it wasn't easy either, but today it requires a lot of resources, really a lot, a lot. Oh yes' (father, farmer in the village).

While most parents still see life from the perspective of a large family ('we'll have as many children as God gives us', said a father who was a farmer in the village), in three of the 10 families interviewed the new conception of childhood was expressed by the limiting and spacing out of births: 'so that we can take care of them better because it's a responsibility of its own. We'll be accountable for our children's education … We're obliged to show them the right way. But when there are a lot of them it's difficult', commented a mother of three who is a nurse in town. These parents limit the number of children to be able to provide support for their children's development. According to the report 'Catalyzing Collaboration' produced by the Family Planning 2020, access and use of modern contraception increase in Burkina Faso.[9]

My fieldwork has revealed a redefinition of the child as a being who has to be educated, guided and emotionally cared for. This concerns the social elite (a small minority who has not been investigated in this fieldwork) and parents of modest means who themselves went to school for a few years and/or are part of the modern economic sector or urban environment.

Macro and micro processes of an economic, cultural and social nature, and agency of social actors explain the changes of conception and the pathways observed.

The Economic, Cultural and Social Determinants of this Redefinition

The societal determinants stemming from national and international policies, such as poor economic situation, the high rate of unstable employment and unemployment, and the fact that public healthcare and education are not free, are all impediments to school attendance. The environmental problems that are causing a critical lack of water for agriculture and are thus increasing poverty in this region constitute a meso-social determinant that compounds the economic constraints requiring child labour.

Other societal determinants are favourable to school attendance, such as the increase in the offer (many more public and private schools have been built), a limit on the costs of public schooling for families (free enrolment for girls, free supplies and free meals at lunch).

As noted above, research shows that schooling in Sub-Saharan Africa and in Burkina Faso depends on this offer being available to families and on their economic capacities, as well as on the child's gender. As the husband is socially defined as being economically responsible for the family, boys' school attendance is considered to be more important than that of girls (Lange, 1998).[10] Moreover, the family's social insertion (religious or socio-economic insertion; family structure; network of relatives and acquaintances) favours or impedes school attendance (Baux, 2007; Bonini, 1996; Gérard, 1997; Lange and Martin, 1995; Pilon and Yaro, 2001). On this last point, the economic theory of human capital (Becker and Lewis, 1973) contends that parents adjust the number of children in direct proportion to the educational investment they can offer (budget, time), as a quantity/quality calculation. In Europe (Hanushek, 1992) and in South Asia (Maralani, 2008), a lower number of children is linked with higher school enrolment. But in Sub-Saharan Africa, the link is not so clear (Kravdal et al., 2013) because of family solidarity networks. Bougma et al. (2014) show that family networks in Ouagadougou are able to offset the negative effect of large family size on school enrolment, but only for a part of the population that excludes the poorest (24% of the mothers in the survey).

Whether they had been to school themselves or not, the parents who were interviewed wanted to send their children to school in the hope that this would enhance their job opportunities. In some cases they also believed that it would enhance their personal skills. Exogenous and endogenous factors of Burkina Faso society explain this cultural change. Colonization and then globalization introduced and developed schooling, the modern definition of childhood, the value placed on scientific knowledge and on education and examinations, even on a distancing from local knowledge and traditional conceptions of the world and of childhood. More broadly, the cultural globalization that operates via the media, especially television and Internet, and through the growth of migration to neighbouring or European countries, conveys this new representation of the child to be educated.

Endogenous factors are also at play. Social relations combine community and individualist logics at this time (Marie, 1997). A modernization movement, with the development of a market economy and rational-legal domination, is underway. This process is attended by individualization, especially among the educated urban classes (Marie, 1997); it is visible among the young generations seeking to climb the social ladder, in the creation of a small nuclear family that is independent of the broader family and the community. This type of family leads to closer interactions between parents and children, and more distant relations with others. It implicitly redefines the child as a being to educate.

A Redefinition of Childhood in Progress

The societal change underlying the rapid increase of school attendance is still underway and is not so complete as to preclude children not attending school or dropping out of school. Despite a discourse in favour of schooling, three families interviewed had enrolled only some of their children in school, and of those, few completed the six years of primary schooling. The school offer is not the reason here for this non-attendance at school, for all the children whose parents took them to enrol were accepted, even if the classes were already crowded (Gérard, 1997). The decreasing numbers of pupils during the course of primary school years[11] show that children drop out or are expelled. To explain the non-attendance or drop-out rate, parents mention material difficulties such as distance from the school, cost of schooling, the need for help in the home, on the farm or for herding animals, or the child's illness. But in comparable situations, the definition of the child as a being to educate will be decisive. Parents who have not been to school, who have not migrated, who are part of a subsistence economy, living in the village community, envisage a child's physical and intellectual development as a natural process: children acquire necessary know-how and knowledge through practice. When parents do not have a specific conception of childhood and they see a child as a member of the family group who has to contribute to the collective survival, school-related practices are more conjunctural. School is perceived in a more instrumental way, as something that might be useful for getting a job, but not necessary for personal skills. We then find practices of 'reserved schooling' (Gérard, 1997): different choices from one son to another (school attendance of some, in different types of institution), or dropping out of school for reasons that are coherent and meaningful in the context of the family unit and with its representation of childhood.

Two ideal types of conception of the world become apparent, including two definitions of childhood and two attitudes towards schooling: a community conception that values the collective, with a non-specific representation of childhood; and a modern conception that values the individual, with a representation of childhood as a particular age that requires education. Both of these conceptions are witnessed in Burkina Faso. Older parents who never attended school, in rural areas, usually have the former conception. Others, who have been to school or are exposed to the individualist conception in their job (modern market economy) or in their neighbourhood (town), espouse the latter. The majority refers to one or the other, depending on the situation, without totally adhering to either one, and without being able to create a syncretic conception of these two antagonistic perspectives.

In these societal pre-structurings, childhoods are constructed by way of micro-social determinants and by the agency of social actors. Micro-social determinants create constraints and economic, social, cultural resources for the family. But families are not entirely bound by determinants; they co-create their child's living conditions and those of his or her schooling: enrolment and attendance of school; acceptance of decisions by the school authorities or negotiations to influence decisions (refusal of admission, redoing a year, expulsion, etc.). The children are also actors of their situation, by accepting, refusing or negotiating the school authorities' decisions, by appealing to their parents to let them stay in a particular home so that they can attend school, by working to pay for their school fees, or by refusing to start or to carry on attending school. Within their constraints, both children and parents encounter situations that afford opportunities, generate favourable or unfavourable situations, and participate by their agency in their schooling, exit from schooling, or absence of schooling. It nevertheless seems useful to point out that the actors do not all have the same ability to act, depending on their resources and their feeling of having a 'grip' on their lives. Children develop a capacity for action that reflects that of their family. A fatalistic attitude or passivity in their surroundings reduces their chances of building a feeling of having some control over their life. Past experiences can also cause a child to develop him- or herself as an actor or an agent (impacted by outside factors). Serious illness, loss of his or her parents, or being entrusted to an unkind family can cause some children to develop a motivation to 'make it in life'.

Ultimately, the economic, social and cultural situations of families differ significantly, and constitute as many constraints or resources in childhood. Situations that enable a child to attend school vary, from virtually 'locked-in' situations with very strong determinants, to situations that are more open to different possibilities. Action logics vary from positions of withdrawal, related to a feeling of abandonment, to the attitude of an actor seeking all opportunities for action. Passivity, related to social or religious fatalism, and situations of powerful constraints strongly limit the eventuality of a child attending school. By contrast, the conception of a child having to be educated to develop fully and to have access to a different situation makes it more likely.

Conclusion

Based on an earlier qualitative study and other research findings in Burkina Faso, this chapter argues that the extension of schooling and transformation of childhood are linked to globalization.

Over the last decades, representations of childhood and the attention paid to it in Sub-Saharan Africa have changed substantially. This change has taken place through the perpetuation of the schooling system introduced by colonization, through the diffusion of new educational concerns arising from migration and international media exposure, and also through international lender agencies' requirements to increase the school enrolment rate, and the consequent construction of schools by international donors. These elements have combined with endogenous ones. As the problem of the survival of farming (the country's main economic activity) has grown, farmers today hope that their children will access other jobs. Moreover, in a process of individualization, more and more parents and children feel responsible for their own lives and consequently act to define its course. Along with the massification of schooling, childhood is redefined as a specific age which requires education, and children are redefined as individuals who should be involved in the decisions regarding their lives. These massive transformations viewed positively in reference to the UN Convention on the Rights of the Child must not mask other negative effects of globalization on Burkinabe children: the dissymmetry of global economic relations, environmental degradation, and economic or sexual exploitation.

Notes

1 The majority of the population in this region are Mossi and Muslim. I met 10 families who were willing to be interviewed, and of those 10 families, eight were

Muslim and two Catholic. The 2006 national census showed that 60% of the population is Muslim, 23% Christian, 15% is animist, 1% other religion or without religion. The question was not included in the next census. In the village, all the parents interviewed were farmers; in the city, the interviewees were traders, artisans or civil servants.

2   This example was given to me by André Nyamba, Professor of Sociology at the University of Ouagadougou.

3   The population was estimated at 20,244,080 in 2018 (INSD – Institut National de la Statistique et de la Démographie).

4   Several researchers consider that the racist colonial ideology produced ethnic labelling, which was then appropriated by the population to support their identity and their political demands. Cf. in particular Gallisot et al. (2000).

5   Gross rates of school enrolment are the ratio of children attending school, over children of a school-going age. The gross rate of schooling was 24% in 1996, 47.7% in 2005 and 69% in 2009, in this region (Source: SDAU – Schéma Directeur de l'Aménagement Urbain – Kaya).

6   Since the 2008 survey, two private schools have been created.

7   What the population calls 'Koranic schools' offer teaching to children that it seems difficult to call schooling, due to the absence of a school programme and of a place and staff specifically devoted to teaching. The children learn the Koran and have to attend to their own needs under the authority of a marabout. The creation of madrasahs is intended to offer modern Muslim teaching, as opposed to these 'Koranic schools'. Cf. Pilon, 2004.

8   In Burkina Faso, relations between children and adults are strictly hierarchical and the former have a great deal of reserve and deference for the latter. This makes interviews or informal conversations with children more difficult, as they will say little to the researcher.

9   In 2018, 22.8% of women between 15 and 49 years old were using a modern contraception method in Burkina Faso. The report 'Catalyzing Collaboration' produced by Family Planning 2020 is available on line: https://www.familyplanning2020.org/resources/fp2020-catalyzing-collaboration-progress-report-webinar

10   The question of gender in school attendance has been studied extensively owing to researchers' interest in it, and to the fact that international research funding has been oriented towards it since the 1990s. I will therefore not expand on this aspect of the data, and instead consider mainly the redefinition of childhood that has largely been overlooked in the literature.

11   In the village, there were 100 pupils in the first year of primary school and 15 in the last year; and in the town, 95 pupils in the first year and 54 in the last year.

References

Badini, A. (1992) *Naître et grandir chez les Moosé traditionnels*. Paris and Ouagadougou: Ed. Sepia-ADDB.

Baux, S. (2007) *Les Familles lobi et l'école: entre rejets mutuels et lentes acceptations*, PhD dissertation. Paris: École des Hautes Etudes en Sciences Sociales.

Becker, G. and Lewis, H. (1973) 'On the interaction between the quantity and quality of children', *Journal of Political Economy*, 81(S2): S279– S288.

Bonini, N. (1996) *Education non scolaire et école primaire: les conséquences d'une rencontre. Une étude anthropologique de la transmission du savoir chez les Maasai de Tanzanie*, PhD dissertation. Paris: École des Hautes Etudes en Sciences Sociales.

Bougma, M., Pasquier-Doumer, L., Legrand, T.K. and Kobiané, J.-F. (2014) 'Fertility and schooling in Ouagadougou: the role of family networks', *Population*, 69(3): 391–418.

Campion-Vincent, V. (1970) 'Système d'enseignement et mobilité sociale au Sénégal', in G. Balandier (ed.), *Sociologie des mutations*. Paris: Anthropos.

Compaoré, F., Compaoré, M., Lange, M.-F. and Pilon, M. (eds) (2007) *La Question éducative au Burkina Faso. Regards pluriels*. Ouagadougou: Éditions du CNRST.

Erny, P. (1987) *L'Enfant et son milieu en Afrique noire: essai sur l'éducation traditionnelle*. Paris: L'Harmattan.

Gallisot, R., Kilani, M. and Rivera, A. (2000) *L'Imbroglio ethnique en quatorze mots clés*. Lausanne: Payot.

Gérard, E. (1997) *La Tentation du savoir en Afrique. Politiques, mythes et stratégies d'éducation au Mali*. Paris: Karthala/Orstom.

Goody, J. (1987) *The Interface of the Written and the Oral*. Cambridge: Cambridge University Press.

Hanushek, E.A. (1992) 'The trade-off between child quantity and quality', *Journal of Political Economy*, 100(1): 84–117.

Kravdal, Ø., Kodzi, I. and Sigle-Rushton, W. (2013) 'Effects of the number and age of siblings on educational transitions in Sub-Saharan Africa', *Studies in Family Planning*, 44(3): 275–297.

Lange, M.-F. (ed) (1998) *L'école et les filles en Afrique*. Paris : Karthala.

Lange, M.-F. (2003) 'École et mondialisation. Vers un nouvel ordre scolaire?', *Cahiers d'Études Africaines*, XLIII(1– 2):143–166.

Lange, M.-F. and Martin, J.-F. (eds) (1995) 'Les stratégies éducatives en Afrique subsaharienne', *Cahiers des Sciences Humaines*, 31(3).

Lê Thanh Khoi (ed.) (1971) 'L'enseignement en Afrique tropicale', *Revue Tiers Monde*, XXV(97).

Maiga, A. and Wangre, N.J. (2009) *Enfants de rue en Afrique. Le cas du Burkina Faso*. Paris: L'Harmattan.

Maralani, V. (2008) 'Family size and educational attainment with socioeconomic development', *Demography*, 45(3): 693–717.

Marie, A. (ed.) (1997) *L'Afrique des individus*. Paris: Karthala.

Martin, J.-Y. (1972) 'Sociologie de l'enseignement en Afrique noire', *Cahiers Internationaux de Sociologie*, 53: 337–362.

Mercier-Tremblay, C. and Santerre, R. (eds) (1982) *La Quête du savoir. Essais pour une anthropologie de l'éducation camerounaise*. Montréal: Presses de l'Université de Montréal.

Moumouni, A. (1974) *L'Éducation en Afrique*. Paris and Dakar: Présence Africaine.

Panter-Brick, C. (2002) 'Street children, human rights, and public health: a critique and future directions', *Annual Review of Anthropology*, 31: 147–171.

Pilon, M. (2004) 'L'évolution du champ scolaire au Burkina Faso: entre diversification et privatization', *Cahiers de la Recherche sur l'Éducation et les Savoirs*, 3: 147–169.

Pilon, M. and Yaro, Y. (eds) (2001) *La Demande d'éducation en Afrique. Etat des connaissances et perspectives de recherché*. Dakar: UEPA/UAPS.

Salifou, A. (1974) *L'Éducation traditionnelle africaine*. Paris and Dakar: Présence Africaine.

Schlemmer, B. (ed.) (2000) *The Exploited Child*. London: Zed Books.

Tidjani Alou, M. (2001) 'Globalisation: l'État africain en question', *Afrique Contemporaine*, special issue, *L'État en Afrique: entre le global et le local*.

5

Examining Child Mobility and Transport in South Africa

Challenges for Theory and Practice

Sharmla Rama

Introduction

'Defamiliarization of the familiar' is about understanding the distinction between common sense and sociological thinking (Bauman and May cited in Jacobsen and Poder, 2008). The notion encapsulates the need to question or debunk some of the everyday common-sensical ideas or beliefs we hold, and in particular those resulting in social actions and behaviours that disempower, marginalize or exclude some individuals, social groups, social classes or communities. In thinking about such aspects, we raise questions about why and how we come to hold, reproduce and legitimatize harmful beliefs, actions and behaviours. This idea is important to our (re)thinking about research on, about and with children, and in this context, child mobility and transport. Adult and institutional mobility and transport behaviour, patterns and challenges are generally considered an apt proxy of children's everyday transport and mobility needs, challenges and experiences (Rama, 2014). This formulation usually relates to children's subordinate social positioning, their familial dependency status, as well as assumptions that children form a homogeneous unit and childhood is universal. In the transport sector in South Africa, such generalizations are internalized (whether consciously or subconsciously) within research, decision-making and policy-making, and by the researchers, policy-makers and other related communities of practitioners.

The argument here is that the present assumptions and generalizations about child mobility and transport in the sector remain fragmentary, limiting and parochial. The current knowledge production and decision-making derive from traditional beliefs and conventional ways of researching, thinking, listening to, writing and talking about, or valuing, children and childhood. There is an idealization about children and childhood, and as a result, children's voices about their challenges, experiences and needs, including mobility and transport aspects, remain largely muted. The disjuncture between rhetoric and reality, and the subsequent challenges for theory and practice, therefore stem from underlying unreflected habits, truths and social actions in the sector. Whether self-imposed or the result of some form of intra-field closure (Murphy, 1983), this can lead to assumptions and generalizations that can exclude or negatively impact on children in general, and some age classes in particular.

Unreflected orientations, and the reproducing of norms, beliefs and values which disempower children and relegate them to being passive observers, have particular implications for children's inclusion, participation, movement, mobility, quality of life and wellbeing in society. They also shape the philosophical assumptions, or nested epistemologies, to social enquiry. Syprou (cited in Alanen, 2011: 147) argues that researchers' lack of reflexive practice stems from three issues: firstly, the lack of reflection on one's own role in knowledge production; secondly, how our own assumptions and the social forces acting on our lives constrain children's voices; and thirdly, lack of awareness about the power dimensions, epistemological hierarchies and hegemonies, and epistemic injustice. The conceptualization and problematization of child mobility and transport are therefore important for critical reflection.

At a local level (South Africa), the conceptualization, problematization and theorization of child mobility and transport needs, and associated experiences and challenges, are in conflict with contemporary and global shifts in childhood and mobility studies, including the adoption of rights-, participatory- and capabilities-based approaches. Any political, philosophical, empirical, ontological, ethical and epistemological marginality, injustices and hegemonies, subordinate children's social positioning and representation, thus rendering their voices muted. This undoubtedly drives the knowledge, policy and practice chasms. It has particular implications for policy prioritization, agenda-setting and policy and programme implementation on behalf of children, and for their future wellbeing and quality of life. It is important then to confront, contest, reframe or dismantle parochial assumptions when examining children and childhood, and how child mobility and transport are articulated.

Recent estimates indicate that, in South Africa, 30% of the population (total estimated at 58 million) is younger than 15 years of age (Statistics South Africa, 2018). Those in the age range 15–19 years comprise about

8% of the total population. The cohort aged 0–19 years (about 38% of the total population) represents a significant social, political and economic transport user and mobility group in South Africa, yet there is no or little policy and programme prioritization to suit their needs. It is important then to take cognizance of the multiplicity of diverse childhoods and everyday lived realities and experiences within this cohort, and the range of mobility and transport patterns, behaviours and challenges that emerge.

The chapter begins with a brief overview of contemporary mobility (mobilities) and transport debates and discourses. The subsequent section examines the complementarity of the tenets advocated in the Sociology of Childhood and in the child rights frameworks, with the emergent mobility rights discourse. Some of the examples of challenges for theory and practice in the sector in South Africa will be highlighted. The arguments presented here are of relevance to global contexts and draw attention to the wider implications for children's lives, realities, wellbeing and quality of life, despite their being particular and partial.

Thinking Through Mobility and Transport

Globally, children's daily journeys to attend school remain the central focus of child transport studies (Rama, 2014). Usually, the focus is on the impact of children's educational journeys on, amongst others, adult (particularly women's or mothers') travel times, patterns and constraints, the urban built environment, transport planning and networks, and more recently, childhood obesity and road traffic injuries and deaths. Such accounts include concerns about physical improvement of streets, particularly in the immediate vicinity of schools, traffic congestion during drop-off and pick-up times, traffic calming, speed zones, cycle lanes and safe crossings. They also include open, public or park spaces, providing bicycles to children living in rural or inaccessible places, and identifying risk-taking behaviours. These prioritizations are rooted in adultist, heteropatriarchal, filial, androcentric, institutional, state-orientated, technocentric and metrocentric agendas and actions. Focus remains on the expenses incurred on behalf of children or on children as mere consumers of adult time. Children's narratives and voices remain muted, undervalued and marginalized; they are seldom the primary 'unit' of analysis, observation or concern, signalling epistemic injustice.

The age and age group disaggregation of transport and related data does not necessarily demonstrate a child-centred approach. However, some disaggregated data, although not child-centred, do elevate international concerns about child health, wellbeing and quality of life. The global studies on traffic injury and death demonstrate the significance of quality and comparable age-disaggregated data contributing to the monitoring of the rights and wellbeing of children. On a global level, the adverse effect of traffic injuries and death is captured under Goal 3 ('Ensure healthy lives and promote wellbeing for all at all ages') of the Sustainable Development Goals (SDGs) (ICSU and ISSC, 2015), where one of the targets is to 'by 2020 halve the number of global deaths and injuries from road traffic accidents'. The *World Report on Child Injury Prevention* (Peden et al., 2008) estimates that, globally, road traffic injuries account for about 30% ($N = 262,000$) of child and youth deaths for the age group 0–19 years. The highest rates of road traffic deaths are in the African and Eastern Mediterranean regions. In Africa, the road traffic death rate among children is about 20 per 100,000 population. Child factors, vehicle and safety equipment, physical environment and socio-economic environment were investigated. The report shows, for example, that age, gender, type of road user and extent of independent mobility are important factors to take into account. Road traffic injuries were shown to be the leading cause of death globally in the age group 15–19 years. The World Health Organization (WHO, 2017) also released the *Save LIVES: A Road Safety Technical Package* report, which focuses on speed management, **L**eadership, **I**nfrastructure design and improvement, **V**ehicle safety standards, **E**nforcement of traffic laws and post-crash **S**urvival.

In South Africa, the 2009 Injury Mortality Survey (Matzopoulos et al., 2013) shows that transport-related injuries were the second highest cause of death (34%, $N = 17,077$) in the country. In the age range 0–19 years, more than 96% ($N = 2,883$) of transport fatalities ($N = 2,974$) were from road traffic injuries. These data, along with the anecdotal evidence, suggest that despite the South African government's efforts to police, regulate and monitor scholar transport, for instance, there continue to be tragedies with far-reaching consequences. In terms of scholar transport, the regulations for public transport operators and vehicles are easily flouted. There are perennial problems of overloading, recklessness and safety contraventions (MasterDrive SA, 2017). For example, in April 2017, an 18-seater taxi (minibus) carrying 27 school children in the age range 7–15 years collided with a truck (Pijoos et al., 2017). Eighteen children died. One family lost three children, and another lost two children and their father. In May 2017, a 16-seater taxi was found to be carrying 26 school children

(Joubert, 2017). The driver had no professional driving permit, and the vehicle had no licence disk and was also unroadworthy. In November 2018, 20 school children were injured when a taxi they were travelling in collided with another vehicle on their way home from school in Durban, KwaZulu-Natal Province (Mngadi, 2018).

Data from the 2013 South African National Household Travel Survey (SANHTS) show that for about 13% (about 1.6 million) of scholars, the taxi is the main mode of transport to and from school (Statistics South Africa, 2014). Globally, progress in the area of providing scholar transport seems stalled, or at best uneven. The automotive-orientated, technical and state-aimed actions provide a useful framework, but regardless of the overwhelming empirical evidence and localized interventions, there seems to be insignificant change in some quarters.

The reliance on non-motorized and corporeal transport (walking and head-loading) is characteristic of Sub-Saharan Africa, particularly in the rural areas (Porter, 2002). For some, walking is the most affordable choice, as the utilization of public transport depends on income levels, proximity and affordability, or even disability, status. In South Africa, pedestrians (32.8% – all ages) were the leading category of road traffic deaths (Matzopoulos et al., 2013). The WHO has also produced guidelines on pedestrian safety: *Make Walking Safe* (2013a) and *Pedestrian Safety: A Road Safety Manual for Decision-makers and Practitioners* (2013b). These focus on regulations, driver behaviour, urban and road planning, pedestrian risk-taking behaviours, vehicle design and health/trauma care.

In South Africa, most students (under 19 years) walk to school, and this is higher for lower-income households; the children usually attend schools within their neighbourhoods (Statistics South Africa, 2014). Data for 2003 estimate that in the age range 0–19 years, a total of 15 million weekday trips were undertaken; most were education related but there were also trips related to shopping, visiting and work (Statistics South Africa/Department of Transport, 2005). This shows that other activities are taking place which give rise to diverse transport patterns and mobility needs and problems. Other relevant issues were related to walking (non-motorized travel modes), head-loading, dependent versus independent mobility, accompanied travel for children, whom children travel with, and why they travel, but these nuances are unrecognized in survey data. The SANHTS data are collected using proxy reporting: an adult in the household provides the data on children's school travel. While these data were used in the 2009 National Scholar Transport Policy, children's voices are muted and their lived realities are obscured. There is limited focus on children's everyday mobility patterns and activities, and a bias towards adult, institutional and government priorities. Moreover, there is little critical discussion on whether such proxy reported responses reliably and validly reflect children's own travel and mobility experiences.

Independent mobility among older children (and youths), for example, shows that macro-sociological theorizations of the concepts of risk, danger and safety are limiting and narrow. Micro-level theorizations demonstrate that social stratification and differentiation in terms of social class, gender, race, disability, geography, space and place, or even age, produce powerful differences in some social group's perception, knowledge, experiences and management of risk, danger, safety and trust (Green et al., 2000). An examination of the knowledge and social construction of children's concerns, experiences and meaning-making about the places, spaces or locales they inhabit and traverse is invaluable. Interpretivist and critical conflict philosophies and qualitative methods (including participatory methodologies) produce insightful assumptions about, amongst others, everyday decision-making about travel, mobility, movement and activity participation and choice, including attitudes towards travel and travel modes, and the travel needs and constraints of some user groups (Clifton and Handy, 2001). This does not imply an outright rejection of the positivist mode of knowledge production and its mono-method. Qualitative and quantitative approaches to data collection are both essential for the monitoring of child rights, wellbeing and livelihoods (Committee on the Rights of the Child, 2000).

Children's sense of identity and belonging, meaning-making and development are influenced by when they travel, shop (consumption patterns), rest, socialize, work, or attend education or leisure activities; in addition, how they do this, if they can do this, who they do this with, what they do it for and how often they do it are also important influences (Rama, 2014). Children's mobility (or immobility) therefore extends beyond a reductive analysis of car-orientated travel, independent mobility, or chauffeuring, accompanying and escorting travelling practices and behaviours. Mobility (mobilities) and transport are embedded in the fabric of children's (and adults') everyday lives through the interactional, journeying, imaginative and social, civic or economic activities across the spaces and places they inhabit or traverse. Diverse or similar experiences, outcomes, lived realities, everyday life contexts, and livelihood and survival strategies for, on and about children will be produced. Mobility and transport characteristics and patterns will therefore be dependent on innate and biographical, as well as proximal (family) and distal (institution and community), influences. The study of children and childhood is therefore incomplete unless mobility and transport issues are also located in an understanding of their everyday complexities and diverse realities.

Bennet and Watson (2002) explain that in defamiliarizing the everyday, and in this context this includes everyday mobility and transport behaviours, choices and patterns, this renders the routine aspects of ordinary people's lives worthy of scholarly examination. Such studies show how social relations and practices inform individuals' or groups' experience and the organization of everyday life. It provides insight into the forms of power and power relations associated with daily roles and responsibilities, and the negotiation, contestation and reimagining of the sites or spaces where the activities take place. Works on micro-interactions and the focus on the everyday life experiences of individuals, and how the patterned interactions maintain social structures in society, can be equally illuminating to mobility and transport studies in general. What can we learn about peer, adult and institutional interactions with children and youth? What does it say about how the sexual division of labour operates in childhood? What does it illustrate about the importance and worth of the lives of less powerful social groups and classes? What does it say about the barriers to full participation in normative activities and access for different social and age classes of children within and across diverse social settings?

Additionally, the exclusive focus on children's daily educational journey-making is restrictive and problematic. This perspective usually draws on the scholarization, socialization, familiarization and institutionalization discourses (Edwards and Alldred, 2000; Qvortrup, 2007). The basis of this flawed assumption is that schooling is the dominant daily life experience of all children, and that all school-aged children attend an educational institution regularly. The UNESCO Global Monitoring of Education for All (EFA) report (2015) found that by 2012 more than half of the out-of-school youth of primary school age were living in Sub-Saharan Africa. Girls were more likely to never go to school.

In the region, children's irregular or non-attendance at school must be contextualized in terms of exogenous factors such as poverty, inequalities and conflict, and endogenous factors including gender differentiation, health status of family members and intra-household or intra-family decision-making and resource allocation. There is a failure then to acknowledge the reality that some children live outside the 'regulatory spheres of family and school' (Stephens, 1995: 12). The organization of the daily activities and lives of this group of children will produce diverse mobility and transport needs, experiences and challenges. Assumptions or generalizations based on adult or household activities, travel patterns, experiences and behaviours are therefore an inadequate proxy for children's activities, which excludes their mobility and travel patterns, experiences and choices. How useful then is the evidence base supporting the various policies and practices advocating for children's rights and wellbeing, including mobility and transport rights, if adult proxy responses are relied upon?

Professional planners, economists, traffic engineers and others in the transport and urban planning sector dismiss or do not productively engage with children (Whitelegg, 2010). Such social actions and behaviours are embedded in normative and traditional assumptions that children and childhood are homogeneous and/or universal. This generalized insight implies that children share similar experiences, circumstances, needs or problems, and that childhood(s) are comparable. This generates a passive, univocal, constrained and skewed portrayal of children and childhood. Such flawed assumptions are usually deployed to maintain, hierarchize or prioritize adultist needs. This bias results in the marginalized and subordinate social positioning of children within and across social groups, communities and societies, including the political economy. Affectual and traditional actions and behaviours become the basis of the value and instrumental rationalistic actions to exclude and mute even competent and able age classes of children. The persistence and reification of such actions and ideologies widen the theory-praxis-policy and rhetoric-versus-reality chasms.

In current theorizations and discourses there is an advocating for mobility and transport as a public good and as essential for a just society (Coggin and Pieterse, 2015; Tyler, 2004). This means recognizing, amongst others, physical or spatial inequalities and differences, as well as geographic exclusion through the lack of transport infrastructure and provision; this includes facilities and services across spaces, places and localities, economic costs and affordability, time-based constraints, psychological or emotional issues of fear, risk and personal safety, and personal capacities, particularly in terms of issues for persons with disabilities (Titheridge, 2004). When individuals', including children's, participation in everyday normative activities and in aspects that affect their lives and future outcomes is regulated, prohibited, limited, or subjected to conditions, they are deprived, and their rights, quality of life and wellbeing are compromised. Cass et al. (2005: 539) suggest that T.H. Marshall's clas-sification of citizenship into civil, political and social rights be extended to include mobility rights. The adoption and complementarity of the human rights and capabilities approach in contemporary mobility and transport discourses foreground issues of freedom, rights and duties, social justice, participation, equity and ethics, and, in terms of broader societal goals of development, wellbeing and quality of life.

The concepts of mobility and transport therefore have to be understood beyond their technocentric, automotive, androcentric, structural, macro-level, governance and bureaucratic or economic-political, metrocentric prioritizations and expositions. The mobilities (and spatial) turn in soci-ology and the social sciences has redirected normative and traditional theorizing and assumptions about mobility and transport. The shift includes examining, amongst others, people's multi-complex and diverse everyday activities, their sense of community and belonging, and identity con-struction (Sheller, 2014). It also includes how technological innovations mediate in social positioning, quality of life and wellbeing, construction of risk versus safety, by-products of increased travel and mobility, imagi-native travel and social networks (Urry, 2011). Conceptions of mobility and transport are now inextricably linked to knowledge and experiences of social change, problems and inequalities, spatial (dis)locations, and strati-fication and differentiation between and within individuals, social groups, communities and institutions.

Challenges for Theory and Practice

Dominant regimes of representation (Hall cited in Watson, 2009) oper-ate in all sectors and practices, including the private and public spaces, fuelling, reifying and perpetuating children's marginality and subordinate social positioning. To contest, disembed and reframe mainstream and parochial representations, discourses and attitudes that render children and their childhoods marginal, invisible and homogeneous means, amongst other aspects, acknowledging and activating children's agentic potential in terms of their evolving capabilities and competence. The complemen-tary principles embedded in the Sociology of Childhood, child rights and the 'new' mobilities/mobility rights approach give credence to such shifts in thinking. The discussion below broadly focuses on three intersecting tenets underpinning the shift in thinking: citizenship; age and competence; and children's participation and voice.

Citizenship encompasses complex relationships between the state, individuals and society; rights, liberties and responsibilities; and identity and nationhood. Usually, a person's nationality and citizenship are tied to the registration of their birth, but the practice of recognizing the rights of a citizen on this basis is more intricate than this. Yuval-Davis (1997), in citing T.H. Marshall's broad definition of citizenship as referring to 'a full member of a community', asserts that this produces a multi-tier construction of citizenship. Turner's (1997) sociological model of citizenship interlinks key citizenship components of identity, civil virtue, resources and community, with a sharp focus on the nature of inequality and access to socio-economic resources. These conceptions move beyond the political theorizations of the relationship between the state and individual to foregrounding social justice, social inclusion and equality. These elements, while significant to investigate, do not lend themselves to the broader focus of this chapter. The key emphasis here is that the contradictions, ambiguities and tensions in interpretation and understandings of the conceptual and lexical frames of 'citizen' and 'citizenship', including 'nationality', produce uneven and unequal treatment and access to resources, rights (including mobility), privileges, wealth, representation and power between and within social groups.

In South Africa, the Constitution and its Bill of Rights are the supreme law for, amongst others, the content and scope of citizenship and the range of rights, freedoms, dignity and protection to which a citizen is entitled (Republic of South Africa, 1996). In Section 3 of the Constitution, this is expanded on: All citizens are equally entitled to the rights, privileges and benefits of citizenship, and are equally subject to the duties and responsibilities of citizenship. In Section 9 of the Bill of Rights, there are specific stipulations on equality: 'The state may not unfairly discriminate directly or indirectly against anyone on one or more grounds, including race, gender, sex, pregnancy, marital status, ethnic or social origin, colour, sexual orientation, age, disability, religion, conscience, belief, culture, language and birth.' Section 28 of the Bill of Rights presents specific stipulations and obligations for the realization of children's rights, protection and care. The South African Constitution, in alignment with the United Nations Convention on the Rights of the Child (UNCRC) and the African Charter on the Rights and Welfare of the Child (ACRWC), notes that a child's best interests are of paramount importance in every matter concerning the child.

The stipulations in the Constitution and other legislation are not always clear cut; there are variations in interpretation. Carter (2013: 255) explains that 'there are those who regard children as "citizens in the making" whilst others see them as already citizens with rights and responsibilities'. These debatable disparities in conceptualization have a number of implications. For example, this invariably produces and contributes to the silencing, marginalization and constraining of children's voices, the lack of or limited opportunities for active participation, and loss of a sense of belonging and identity. Inconsistent understandings of key frames influence how children and childhood are reflected, represented and acknowledged in policy and legislation. Any obstacles and limitations to a citizen's full right to participate, have their voices heard, and for their rights, dignity and protection to be guaranteed are, however, unconstitutional. Section 2 of the South African Constitution notes that 'law or conduct inconsistent with it is invalid, and the obligations imposed by it must be fulfilled' (Republic of South Africa, 1996).

Despite these pronouncements, discrepancies persist around how children and childhood are understood, including in terms of practices translating them into implementation. A range of factors and forms of exclusion will reinforce and cushion each other, and engender stereotypes and attitudes across the private and public realms, where the lives of social groups intersect in a society. Embedded exclusionary rules or codes derived on the basis of politics, culture, class, race, gender, geography, disability, age and generation will determine how and to whom civil, political and social rights are endowed; this includes mobility rights. In contemporary society, there is no consensus on what or who constitutes a 'community'. This is shaped broadly by modernity, globalization, mobility and migration, and neoliberalism. Citizenship must also be viewed as gendered, racialized, and with varying intersectional understandings of age, disability, sexuality (Yuval-Davis, 1997), geography and space.

Age systems mediate in cultural inclusion and exclusion, and this has implications for groups and individuals within a society. Lower age groups are ascribed a subordinate position in the political, economic, social and power hierarchies in families, communities and society. Age remains a neglected force in the production and reproduction of varying forms of oppression and domination (Kirby, 1999). Yet, age differentials and stratification are hallmarks of all societies and have ramifications for some age classes and groupings. This institutionalized ageism or age prejudice results in adultist, idealized, unreflected and legitimized generalized insights about children and their childhood (Rama and Richter, 2007). Unless such differences and diversities are taken into consideration in developing policies and interventions, efforts towards the realization of rights, equity and transformation will remain largely ineffective. Age or age categorization or classes are striking examples of power differences within childhood, with consequences for survival, wellbeing, competencies and susceptibilities.

Euro- or Western-centric legal norms and rules usually dominate understandings of who a child is. The legal and political notions of 'child' and 'childhood' are, therefore, bound by rules, laws, regulations and policies of a state, and they depend on the child's age. The South African Constitution adopts an age-specific, legal definition of a child. Section 28 of the Bill of Rights defines a child as a person in the age range 0–17 years (Republic of South Africa, 1996). This delineation is in keeping with international rights-based treaties to which South Africa is a signatory: the UNCRC and ACRWC. Age, however, is not necessarily a significant marker for the acquisition of rights (Lister, 2008). Formal and legal rights may not necessarily match customary or community practices. Under African customary law, for example, the distinction between child and adult lies not in chronological age but in various life stages, initiations, ritual or rites of passage, as well as marriage and childbearing (Rama and Richter, 2007).

In Africa, there exists a paradoxical relationship between these legal obligations, cultural practices and paternal attitudes. Kaime (2005: 231) explains that, within African traditional societies, the adult–child relation and interactions are characterized by filial respect, and are reinforced 'by the ethic of domination'. Children are conceptualized within a dependency and protection framework, and as passive members of their societies. Even in culturally and socially progressive societies, the hierarchical adult–child relationships continue to produce power and status disparities (Moses, 2008). Consequently, international discourses and legal instruments do not improve children's participation in society, or give value to their voices. An-an'im (cited in Harris-Short, 2003: 133) suggests that national elites become signatories to these conventions on rights out of political expediency. In obliging states to subscribe to a Westernized norm of human rights, and Western values of competence and evolving capacities, this creates implementation, consensus and communication impasses at grassroots levels, particularly in the global South.

In the South African context, with its social and cultural diversity, there are implementation challenges too. In some communities and institutions, parents and adults may find the universal tenets embodied in the child rights discourse diametrically opposed to their own cultural and traditional practices, or indeed radically different from these practices (Moses, 2008). While children are recognized as valuable members of society in need of special care and protection, they are 'are normally considered to be deficient in their decision-making capabilities' (Chirwa cited in Kaime, 2005: 231). Depending on their age, children are often regarded as less trustworthy or are seen as not knowing as much as adults (Watson, 2009). Children's evolving capacities, however, have implications for the realization of their rights. The global marginalization, silencing and constraining of children's voices stem from concerns and questions about children's social competence and their abilities. Doek (2008) explains that the recognition of children as citizens and rights-holders lies in the concept of evolving capacities.

In UNICEF's report on evolving capacities, the view is that, as children acquire competencies, there is less need for guidance and more opportunity to take responsibility for decisions affecting their lives (Lansdown, 2005). Central elements include: ability to understand, ask questions and respond; ability to think and choose with some degree of independence; ability to assess the potential for benefit, risk and harm; and achievement of a fairly stable set of values. For those advocating and appealing for a generational mix in responsibility, decision-making and participation in the family, schools, institutions and local and national political processes, assessing the extent to which children have acquired these capacities is undoubtedly a highly complex process.

Birth order, gender, sex composition of the sibling group, and age or age group also mediate in children's level of participation and decision-making within private and public spaces (Boyden and Levison, 2000; Punch, 2001). In other words, communal and associative relationships can be 'open' or 'closed' in terms of who can or cannot participate, or whether a person's position permits participation, as well as the extent of participation (Weber, 1978). This implies that open and closed economic and non-economic relationships exist, including outside of the family, kin or household. The type of action, and the decisions to open or close a group, will depend on whether or not the 'dominant' group sees the participation of others as beneficial to them. The value of children's participation can be 'determined traditionally, affectually, or rationally in terms of values or of expediency' (Weber, 1978: 43–44). Depending on the viewpoints advocated by adults, this will then have implications for children's interaction with adults and their participation in adult-led activities; these implications include policy-making, research and programme implementation.

Drakeford et al. (2009: 248–249) argue that there is merit in adopting child-participatory (and emancipatory) approaches; it is an investment in children's future roles as active citizens, and their insights are likely to present adults with different strands of understanding and views. Alanen (in Mason and Fattore, 2005: 31–32), however, warns about the adoption of 'pseudo-inclusion', when the focus is on the institutional settings instead of the children and their contextual and lived realities. In this situation, children's voices become rhetorical devices rather than an empowering experience. Balen et al. (2006: 31–32) suggest that to acknowledge children as 'knowing subjects' means that 'children are epistemologically privileged in that they are better placed than adults to produce "situated" knowledges that prioritize the importance of their everyday experiences'. A programme or project must therefore be designed to maximize the opportunity for any child or youth to choose to participate at the highest level of their ability (Hart, 1992). Moyo (2015: 173) writes that '[p]articipation involves having a "voice" (control of the process) and having a "choice" (control over the decision)'.

Children's agency is a fundamental principle within the Sociology of Childhood discourse, and children's participation and voices within the children's rights discourse. These perspectives recognize children as participants, citizens and social agents or actors in society. For example, Article 12 of the UNCRC refers to age-appropriate participation (United Nations, 1990). Article 7 of the ACRWC states: 'Every child who is capable of communicating his or her own views shall be assured the rights to express his or her opinions freely in all matters and to disseminate his or her opinions subject to such restrictions as are prescribed by laws' (African Union, 1999). Children's right to participate, and to have their voices heard and acknowledged, is also enshrined in Principle 10 of Chapter 2 of the Children's Act No. 38 of 2005 of South Africa: 'Every child that is of such an age, maturity and stage of development as to be able to participate in any matter concerning that child has the right to participate in an appropriate way, and views expressed by the child must be given due consideration' (Republic of South Africa, 2010). A consultative process must therefore have *some* of the following characteristics: (1) children must understand what the process is about, what it is for and their role within it; (2) children must have the opportunity to contribute towards influencing outcomes; (3) allowing direct input from children and informing them of decisions taken; (4) enabling children to make independent decisions and direct outcomes (Lansdown, 2001).

Other South African legislative frameworks also do not prohibit the right and freedom to participate. Section 15 of the South African Constitution deals with freedom of expression, including freedom to receive or impart information or ideas and aspects relating to scientific research. The South African National Development Plan 2030 (National Planning Commission, 2012) also promotes the principle of an active citizenry, in order to strengthen development, democracy and accountability. The National Land Transport Transition Act No. 22 of 2000 (Republic of South Africa, 2000) and the National Land Transport Act No. 5 of 2009 (Republic of South Africa, 2009b) also include stipulations for public participation. For example, Chapter 2, Part 2 of the National Land Transport Transition Act stipulates that equitable and effective participation hinges on people's understanding, skills and capacity (Republic of South Africa, 2000).

Participation and consultation, then, are important strategies for sustainable development and the realization of democratic principles; yet young people are absent and dismissed from the decision-making spaces, processes and structures. The taken-for-granted assumption, that once legislation or policy has been formulated it will be implemented and have the desired developmental impact on the lives of the target group(s), no longer holds true. Inaction in itself can be viewed as a policy direction or 'act'. The lack of consultation with children, and the inaudibility of their 'voices' in mobility and transport research, and within the policy and decision-making processes, runs counter to the theoretical, rights- and capabilities-based, legislative and policy tenets.

The National Department of Transport, for example, has more than 300 stakeholder organizations (Musandu-Nyamayaro, 2007) which participate in policy-making and, while the issue of age and competency is given some consideration, this is not prioritized in practice. In drafting the National Scholar Transport Policy, about 100 stakeholders were consulted (Republic of South Africa, 2009a), namely, service providers and the contracted or non-contracted vendors of scholar transport in mainly urban centres. The right to participate of economically influential interest groups was legitimized, and was aligned to the policy's prioritization of business opportunities for economic growth and job creation. The absence of child participation implies that children are 'outsider' groups, having no legitimate status within this participatory and consultative process.

The above discussions show that core ideas underpinning the shifts in children and childhood studies are embedded in and across legislation and policy frameworks. In the transport sector in South Africa, there is a general protractedness in recognizing child rights or child-centred approaches, and in adopting a mobility rights framework. There is a misconception that any transport improvements will automatically benefit all citizens equally. This may also relate to the reluctance to view mobility and transport as basic human rights, and to acknowledge children's rights and citizenship.

Conclusion

Emerging empirical evidence (e.g. O'Brien and Tranter, 2010; Rivera and Santos, 2016) shows that promoting the active and effective inclusion of children in planning decisions shows commitment to seeing children as active agents, social actors and to recognizing them as rights-holders in society. The institutionalization of exclusionary practices and attitudes that are underpinned by gerontocracy, ageism, patriarchy and patrimonial domination, authority, power and control has no place in contemporary democratic, developmental and social justice agendas. Good governance and human rights are mutually reinforcing, with human rights informing the principles of good governance and good governance promoting human rights for all. Major characteristics include: being participatory, consensus-oriented, accountable, transparent, responsive, effective and efficient, equitable and inclusive, and following the rule of law (Sheng, 2007). If there is a genuine desire to put children first and act in their best interests, then children will be part of the policy and decision-making processes in all matters concerning their lives. In the transport sector there is a non-recognition and misrecognition of the impact that transport and mobility have on children's everyday activities and lives. The macro-level economic agenda overshadows the value of micro-level understandings of specific user, stakeholder and target groups. This suggests that we must challenge the generalizations, explanations and taken-for-granted assumptions about the broader child mobility and transport issues, if we are to improve the future, quality of life and wellbeing of children. This means that there must be political and social will in all spheres of society, not only to promote and encourage children's participation in consultative processes, but to ensure children exercise these rights.

References

African Union (1999) *African Charter on the Rights and the Welfare of the Child.* Available at: https://au.int/en/treaties/african-charter-rights-and-welfare-child

Alanen, L. (2011) 'Editorial: critical childhood studies?', *Childhood*, 18(2): 147–150.

Balen, R., Blyth, E., Calabretto, H., Fraser, C., Horrocks, C. and Manby, M. (2006) 'Involving children in health and social research – "human becomings" or "active beings"?', *Childhood*, 13(1): 29–48.

Bennet, T. and Watson, D. (2002) *Understanding Everyday Life (Sociology and Society)*. Oxford: Open University and Blackwell Publishing.

Boyden, J. and Levison, D. (2000) *Children as Economic and Social Actors in the Development Process*. Stockholm: Expert Group on Development Issues, Ministry for Foreign Affairs.

Carter, C. (2013) 'Children and the news: rethinking citizenship in the twenty-first century', in D. Lemish (ed.), *The Routledge Handbook of Children, Adolescents and Media*. Abingdon: Routledge. pp. 255–262.

Cass, N., Shove, E. and Urry, J. (2005) 'Social exclusion, mobility and access', *The Sociological Review*, 53(3): 539–555.

Clifton, K.J. and Handy, S.L. (2001) 'Qualitative methods in travel behaviour research', paper prepared for the International Conference on Transport Survey Quality and Innovation, Kruger National Park, South Africa.

Coggin, T. and Pieterse, M. (2015) 'A right to transport? Moving towards a rights-based approach to mobility in the city', *South African Journal of Human Rights*, 31(2): 294–314.

Committee on the Rights of the Child (2000) *Concluding Observations of the Committee on the Rights of the Child: South Africa. 2000/02/23. CRC/C/15/Add.122*. Geneva, Switzerland.

Doek, J.E. (2008) 'Foreword. Citizen child: a struggle for recognition', in A. Invernizzi and J. Williams (eds), *Children and Citizenship*. London: Sage. pp. xii–xvi.

Drakeford, M., Scourfield, J., Holland, S. and Davies, A. (2009) 'Welsh children's views on government and participation', *Childhood*, 16(2): 247–264.

Edwards, R. and Alldred, P. (2000) 'A typology of parental involvement in education centring on children and young people: negotiating familialisation, institutionalisation and individualisation', *British Journal of Sociology of Education*, 21(3): 435–455.

Green, E., Mitchell, W. and Bunton, R. (2000) 'Contextualizing risk and danger: an analysis of young people's perceptions of risk', *Journal of Youth Studies*, 3(2): 109–126.

Harris-Short, S. (2003) 'International human rights law: imperialist, inept and ineffective? Cultural relativism and the UN Convention on the Rights of the Child', *Human Rights Quarterly*, 25(1): 130–181.

Hart, R.A. (1992) *Children's Participation: From Tokenism to Citizenship*. Florence: UNICEF International Child Development Centre.

ICSU and ISSC (International Council for Science and International Social Science Council) (2015) *Review of the Sustainable Development Goals: The Science Perspective*. Paris: International Council for Science.

Jacobsen, M.H. and Poder, P. (2008) *The Sociology of Zygmunt Bauman: Challenges and Critique*. Farnham: Ashgate.

Joubert, A. (2017) '26 children crammed into unroadworthy taxi', *Netwerk24*, 5 May. Available at: www.news24.com/SouthAfrica/News/26-children-crammed-into-unroad worthy-taxi-20170505

Kaime, T. (2005) 'The Convention on the Rights of the Child and the cultural legitimacy of children's rights in Africa: some reflections', *African Human Rights Law Journal*, 5(2): 221–238.

Kirby, M. (1999) *Stratification and Differentiation*. London: Palgrave Macmillan.

Lansdown, G. (2001) *Promoting Children's Participation in Democratic Decision-making*. Florence: UNICEF Innocenti Insight.

Lansdown, G. (2005) *The Evolving Capacities of the Child*. Florence: UNICEF Innocenti Research Centre.

Lister, R. (2008) 'Unpacking children's citizenship', in A. Invernizzi and J. Williams (eds), *Children and Citizenship*. London: Sage. pp. 9–19.

Mason, J. and Fattore, T. (2005) *Children Taken Seriously in Theory, Policy and Practice*. London: Jessica Kingsley.

MasterDrive SA (2017) 'SA children at risk: overloading cars, bakkies and the law', *Wheels24*, 4 September. Available at: www.wheels24.co.za/News/Guides_and_Lists/sa-children-at-risk-overloading-cars-bakkies-and-the-law-20170904

Matzopoulos, R., Prinsloo, M., Bradshaw, D., Pillay-van Wyk, V., Gwebushe, N., Mathews, S., Martin, L., Laubscher, R., Lombard, C. and Abrahams, N. (2013) *The Injury Mortality Survey: A National Study of Injury Mortality Levels and Causes in South Africa in 2009*. Cape Town: South African Medical Research Council.

Mngadi, M. (2018) '20 children injured as KZN taxi crashes on the way home from school', *News24*, 23 November. Available at: www.news24.com/SouthAfrica/News/20-children-injured-as-kzn-taxi-crashes-on-the-way-home-from-school-20181123

Moses, S. (2008) 'Children and participation in South Africa: an overview', *International Journal of Children's Rights*, 16(3): 327–342.

Moyo, A. (2015) 'Child participation under South African law: beyond the Convention on the Rights of the Child?', *South African Journal of Human Rights*, 31(1): 171–184.

Murphy, R. (1983) 'The struggle for scholarly recognition: the development of the closure problematic in sociology', *Theory and Society*, 12(5): 631–658.

Musandu-Nyamayaro, O. (2007) 'Transport and the accelerated growth initiative in South Africa: have we mainstreamed?', paper presented at the 26th South African Transport Conference, Pretoria.

National Planning Commission (2012) *National Development Plan 2030: Our Future – Make It Work*. Pretoria: National Planning Commission Presidency.

O'Brien, C. and Tranter, P.J. (2010) 'Positive psychology, walking and well-being: can walking school buses survive a policy of school closures?', *World Transport Policy and Practice*, 15(4): 42–52.

Peden, M., Oyegbite, K., Ozanne-Smith, J., Hyder, A.A., Branche, C., Rahman, A.K.M.F., Rivara, F. and Bartolomeos, K. (eds) (2008) *World Report on Child Injury Prevention*. Geneva: World Health Organization and UNICEF. Available at: www.who.int/violence_injury_prevention/child/injury/world_report/en/

Pijoos, I., Raborife, M. and Silaule, Y. (2017) 'It will take a week to identify school kids burnt in taxi crash – MEC', *News24*, 24 April. Available at: www.news24.com/SouthAfrica/News/it-will-take-a-week-to-identify-school-kids-burnt-in-taxi-crash-mec-20170424

Porter, G. (2002) 'Living in a walking world: rural mobility and social equity issues in sub-Saharan Africa', *World Development*, 30(2): 285–300.

Punch, S. (2001) 'Household division of labour: generation, gender, age, birth order and sibling composition', *Work, Employment and Society*, 15(4): 803–823.

Qvortrup, J. (2007) 'Editorial: a reminder', *Childhood*, 14(4): 395–400.

Rama, S. (2014) *Child mobility, time use and social exclusion: reframing the discourses and debates*, PhD dissertation. Pietermaritzburg: University of KwaZulu-Natal.

Rama, S. and Richter, L. (2007) 'Children's household work as a contribution to the well-being of the family and household in South Africa', in A.Y. Amoateng and L. Richter (eds), *Families and Households in South Africa*. Cape Town: HSRC Press. pp. 135–169.

Republic of South Africa (1996) *Constitution of the Republic of South Africa*.

Republic of South Africa (2000) *National Land Transport Transition Act No. 22 of 2000*.

Republic of South Africa (2009a) *Final Draft: National Scholar Transport Policy*.

Republic of South Africa (2009b) *National Land Transport Act No. 5 of 2009*.

Republic of South Africa (2010) *Children's Act No. 38 of 2005*.

Rivera, R. and Santos, D (2016) 'Civic and political participation of children and adolescents: a lifestyle analysis for positive youth developmental programs', *Children & Society*, 30(1): 59–70.

Sheller, M. (2014) 'The new mobilities paradigm for a live sociology', *Current Sociology Review*, 62(6): 789–811.

Sheng, Y.K. (2007) *What is Good Governance?* Bangkok: United Nations Economic and Social Commission for Asia and the Pacific.

Statistics South Africa/Department of Transport (2005) *National Household Travel Survey 2003: Key Results – The First South African National Household Travel Survey 2003*. Pretoria: Statistics South Africa.

Statistics South Africa (2014) *National Household Survey Travel, 2013*. Pretoria: Statistics South Africa.

Statistics South Africa (2018) *Mid-year Population Estimates, 2018*. Statistical Release P0302. Pretoria: Statistics South Africa.

Stephens, S. (1995) *Children and the Politics of Culture*. Princeton, NJ: Princeton University Press.

Titheridge, H. (2004) *Social Exclusion and Transport Policy: Accessibility and User Needs in Transport, Scoping Study*. London: University College London.

Turner, B.S. (1997) 'Citizenship studies: a general theory'. *Citizenship Studies*, 1(1): 5–18.

Tyler, N. (2004) *Justice in Transport Policy*. London: School of Public Policy, University College London.

UNESCO (2015) *Education for All 2000–2015: Achievements and Challenge*. Available at: https://en.unesco.org/gem-report/report/2015/education-all-2000-2015-achievements-and-challenges

United Nations (1990) *Convention on the Rights of the Child*. Available at: www.ohchr.org/en/professionalinterest/pages/crc.aspx

Urry, J. (2011) 'Does mobility have a future?', in M. Grieco and J. Urry (eds), *Mobilities: New Perspectives on Transport and Society*. Farnham: Ashgate. pp. 3–20.

Watson, A.M.S. (2009) 'Children's human rights and the politics of childhood', in P. Hayden (ed.), *The Ashgate Research Companion to Ethics and International Relations*. Farnham: Ashgate. pp. 247–260.

Weber, M. (1978) *Economy and Society: An Outline of Interpretive Sociology*, G. Roth and C. Wittich (eds). Berkeley: University of California Press.

Whitelegg, J. (2010) 'Editorial', *World Transport Policy and Practice*, 15(4): 3–4.

WHO (World Health Organization) (2013a) *Make Walking Safe: A Brief Overview Of Pedestrian Safety Around The World*. Available at: www.who.int/violence_injury_pre vention/publications/road_traffic/make_walking_safe.pdf

WHO (World Health Organization) (2013b) *Pedestrian Safety: A Road Safety Manual for Decision-makers and Practitioners*. Available at: www.who.int/roadsafety/projects/ manuals/pedestrian/en/

WHO (World Health Organization) (2017) *Save LIVES: A Road Safety Technical Package*. Geneva: World Health Organization.

Yuval-Davis, N. (1997) 'Women, citizenship and difference', *Feminist Review*, 57(1): 4–27.

6

The Limits of Healthism

Understanding Children's Conceptions of Health

Tobia Fattore

Introduction

Children's health has been a site for establishing normative expectations as to what constitutes appropriate parenting and childhood behaviours. Because of the conflation between healthy lifestyle practices and well-being, children's bodies become the site of anxieties regarding the health of populations. The intention of this chapter is to explore children's understandings of health in relation to these anxieties. In particular I examine what children consider to be important to their health and to what extent children are agents in their own health promotion, based on a qualitative study with children about their wellbeing, undertaken in New South Wales, a province of Australia.

The chapter shows that when children discuss their health they invoke discourses associated with 'healthy lifestyles', which share many of the features of what Crawford (1980) has described as 'healthism': that is, the prioritization of pursuing healthy lifestyle practices as the primary focus for defining and achieving wellbeing. However, children problematize this discourse by calling upon more wide-ranging ideas regarding their health. The study demonstrates that children mediate between conventional healthism practices and other health practices which largely contrast with the healthism discourse. While healthism views parenting as the primary arbiter of children's health, children view their health as premised on a broader set of relationships. While healthism encourages choice within the market as the means to create healthy lifestyles, children envisage their health as located in multiple social sites. While healthism promotes a particular view of the body as signifying health, children emphasize the body as functional and sense-experiencing. And, finally while healthism emphasizes individual responsibility, advancing a limited view of children's agency, children discuss deploying their agency in order to be healthy, but acknowledge that their agency is intersubjectively constituted through important relationships.

The chapter proceeds by initially outlining the key features of healthism as an important discourse in understanding children's health. It then proceeds to present children's understandings of health. The chapter concludes by suggesting that children's standpoint on health provides important clues as to the limits of healthism, and offers a set of considerations to take into account in order to effectively engage children in the promotion of healthy practices.

Healthism and Children's Health

The emergence of biomedical sciences, epidemiology and developmental psychology in the late eighteenth and nineteenth centuries emphasized conditions under which children not only survive, but flourish. The expanded use of medical technologies and advances in public health meant that maternal and infant survival was no longer the baseline for child wellbeing. Rather, these advances created a space in which the 'new' psychological sciences could delineate markers of healthy child development. Not only was appropriate child development the object of scrutiny and the measure of successful health, these developments also provided a scientific rationale for social reforms aimed at improving maternal and child health.

In the late twentieth and early twenty-first centuries, there has been a shift in the character of these practices, with the increasing importance of what Crawford (1980) has described as 'healthism', defined as 'the preoccupation with personal health as the primary ... focus for the definition and achievement of well-being' (1980: 368). The term was initially used to describe holistic health and self-care movements; however, the tenets of healthism have become more generalized as lifestyle practices. Partly in response to changes in the nature of morbidity and mortality, from acute to chronic conditions (Nettleton, 2006), the focus on lifestyle and prevention rather than treatment and cure is a powerful public health priority.

While promoting a less medicalized concept of health than biomedical discourses, aetiological factors beyond individual behaviour do not feature prominently within healthism (Blaxter, 1997; Crawford, 1980). Rather, individuals are seen as responsible for maintaining their health through exercising the right kind of choices over an increasing number of health options (Henderson and Petersen, 2002; Murphy, 2003). Health outcomes are linked to individual choices, and poor health, then, is a result of inadequate knowledge or irresponsible health decisions.

It is in this context that several critics have illustrated that much of the discussion regarding children's health taps into deep sources of parental anxiety and concern about children's health, with poor child health posed as a failure of parental responsibility (Bell et al., 2009; Maher et al., 2010; Pike and Kelly, 2014). Health policy and healthy lifestyle campaigns evoke powerful responses of obligation regarding children's health, evident in concerns about whether children are eating the right foods, exercising enough or are overweight or underweight. These questions primarily focus on the adequacy of parental practices for maintaining children's health, and from this vantage we can see that health advice – as delivered by health professionals, through health pedagogy and the popular media – exists to rectify the potentially health-threatening behaviours of parents (Evans et al., 2011).

The normative framing of these issues also illustrates concerns about the future of, as well as concern for, actual children. For example, childhood obesity has attracted concern from policy-makers because of the long-term health burdens associated with childhood obesity (see e.g.WHO, 2012). Health prevention programmes are premised on the belief that, as parents obtain more knowledge about their children's health, this will translate into health-promoting habits that children will carry into adulthood (Pearson et al., 2012).

Additionally, a particular understanding of the relationship between the body and health are promoted by healthism discourses. Because healthism emphasizes physical activity as the 'primary predictor of health' (Wright and Burrows, 2004: 215), body shapes, weights and sizes are seen as denoting an individual's attitudes towards health. Furthermore, certain conceptions of the body are promoted as normal and healthy, reinforced through a consistent set of messages about good health that is reinforced through other sources of knowledge, such as popular film and television (Wright and Burrows, 2004).

As healthism discourses emphasize individual responsibility for health, it could be argued that a logical implication of healthism is that children should exercise agency over their health choices. However, children are the subject of health knowledge, acted upon through day-to-day health practices governed by their parents (Bell at al., 2009). For example, children are generally not responsible for the purchase and preparation of meals, for arranging family activities, for organizing health examinations, for their own immunization and so on. And it is assumed that children only have a limited understanding of health and can therefore contribute in a very limited way to decision-making about health practices. As Evans et al. (2011) point out, at most, children are envisaged as having certain roles to play: as transmitters of health information learnt at school to home; as challengers of parental authority about health practices, for example contesting parental authority at mealtimes; or as asserting 'pester power' to negatively influence parental decisions, such as purchasing fast food or sweets (Backett-Milburn, 2000; Colls and Evans, 2008; Horton and Kraftl, 2010; Warin et al., 2008).

Yet the extent to which children assert agency over their health has been extensively demonstrated in a range of studies involving children about their health and illness (e.g. Backett-Milburn et al., 2003; Bergnehr and Zetterqvist Nelson, 2015; Burrows et al., 2009; Clavering and McLaughlin, 2010; Jenkins, 2015; Place, 2000). These studies suggest that children occupy a complex set of roles in the construction of social relations, involving interactions and negotiations about the meanings of health and health practices and involving interactions with adults, both at home and at school, and with other children. Thus far, research has identified several tenets of healthism that are worth investigating from children's perspectives. These include:

- Health is an outcome of rational decisions, and therefore health outcomes can be associated with individual choices about, for example, consumption and physical activity. Within market economies, this essentially means that health is reliant upon individual choices within the market.
- Further, parenting practices are the primary determinant of children's health, and because it is parents, and not children, who are conceived as rational subjects, healthism ascribes a limited agency to children.
- Moreover, healthism promotes a particular view of bodies as signifiers of health (the body as slim and strong).

But are these tenets evident in children's discussions of health? Are children's priorities when discussing health similar to those within healthism discourses, and to what extent and in which ways do children enact agency over health practices?

Methodology: Researching Children's Understandings of Wellbeing

The findings presented here draw upon research on children's understandings of wellbeing and how these understandings relate to children's everyday experiences, undertaken in New South Wales, Australia (see Fattore and Mason, 2016). The research was conducted over three stages, with each stage involving either individual or group interviews, determined by participant preference.

In the first stage, we explored children's ideas about what wellbeing means to them; how wellbeing is experienced in the course of everyday practices; and what factors contribute to a sense of wellbeing. The interviews specifically examined whether wellbeing was a term that meant something to the participants; how wellbeing was experienced in different life domains (whether associated with particular people, activities, times or events, places and material objects); asked participants to recount a time in their life when they considered things were going well; and what participants would do to change a 'not wellbeing time' into a 'wellbeing time'.

The second stage explored in greater detail the main themes discussed by the participants in their first interview. Each transcript was analysed to identify key themes specific to each participant. These themes then formed the basis of the second interview. Each participant was asked whether these themes made sense to them and to elaborate on those themes that did, but also whether they would add themes or change the emphasis of the themes. In this way, the participants' interpretations of our initial analysis were built into the development of our analytical framework, extending, verifying or modifying the analysis that had been undertaken.

In the third stage, the children completed a project of their own design that explored a wellbeing theme or themes of interest to them. Combinations of photography, collage, drawing and journal-keeping were commonly used for these projects. We then sought children's interpretations of their own work and how it related to wellbeing. This continued to give prominence to children's own interpretations.

Children from both rural and urban locations participated in the research. Schools were initially selected and approached to participate in the research. Within each school that agreed to participate, a class group was selected in consultation with the principal, and children were invited to participate in the study. Twelve schools were selected from across the state representing a mix of areas characterized by levels of high, medium and low socio-economic disadvantage. The sample contained a marginally greater proportion of females (60%); approximately 40% of participants were from a migrant background; and approximately 40% of participants came from areas with high levels of socio-economic disadvantage, 40% from areas considered as having medium levels of socio-economic disadvantage and 20% of participants came from areas with low levels of socio-economic disadvantage.

Children's Understandings of Health: Mediating between Discourses

Children displayed knowledge about health consistent with broad guidelines associated with healthy behaviour. They talked about eating the right food and the importance of exercise. In discussing health, many of the participants chose photographs of fruit and vegetables or drew pictures of children being active, to describe wellbeing. Often the importance and efficacy of health-related behaviours were described in terms of identifiable signs associated with bodily appearance, as Deezee suggests in discussing the importance of swimming:

Deezee: Swimming, I'm pretty good at swimming, actually. It is the sport that I really enjoy and it is one that I am very good at. Because I want to have a pretty good body figure, yeah. And, my physical health is important to me as well as my mental health.

This knowledge of what is healthy included awareness of behaviours adverse to health, like avoiding foods high in saturated fats and sugars and the dangers of sedentary lifestyles. As Rosana describes, these foods should be avoided 'otherwise, like, you wouldn't be very healthy. If you like kept eating unhealthy food.' However, in discussing the balance between healthy and unhealthy practices, several children identified forces that promoted unhealthy practices, such as fast-food campaigns targeted at children. As Sarah and Beady demonstrate, in a typical discussion, parents and children are often confronted with conflicting messages regarding health that they are required to mediate:

Sarah: We are encouraged to eat a lot more healthy, but they go and advertise unhealthy products and stuff. I just think that it's like everything working in reverse. Like it is one step forward, two steps back kind of thing. 'Cause they say one thing, but then other people end up doing another and it just, it doesn't, something needs to be done to make everything balanced.

Beady: It is like one ad like saying do not smoke, eat healthy, exercise. And then the next ad is for a big block of chocolate or a fast food hamburger.

Sarah and Beady point out that health is a fraught issue, a topic where children are exposed to contradictory messages from powerful interests.

As Probyn (2010) points out, health discussions within the public sphere are saturated with messages about what is good and bad for us. Health messages play a central role in the school curriculum, and children can in fact be hyper-aware of health practices because of this exposure (Alexander et al., 2015). Yet many of these messages may have little resonance with children's desires and the practices of their peers and families. As Backett-Milburn suggests, the uncertainty about how health should be achieved means that the achievement of health is 'a complex and ongoing social accomplishment' (2000: 82). This was evidenced here when children discussed how difficult it is to mediate between healthy and unhealthy practices. The extent to which they are expected to mediate between the two is in contrast to how they are positioned as having limited agency in healthism discourses and also as consumers in marketing strategies.

It is perhaps unsurprising, then, that everyday relationships were prioritized in children's discussions of health. Very rarely did children discuss health professionals, and where they did, this was usually when discussing illness, which was a minor point of discussion (although see Mogensen and Mason, 2015). The lack of discussion of medical professionals is a notable finding, given the importance of health professionals in creating frames through which the body is understood. As Prout (2000) points out, medical discourse and practices construct bodies as passive, something to be regulated, disciplined, and of course also cured and remedied. Christensen (2000) describes this construction as the somatic conception of the body, seeing the body as something that can be diagnosed at a point in time and can therefore be objectified, interrogated technologically and subjected to clinical intervention. That this construction of health and the body did not feature significantly in children's discussions suggests that children understand and experience their bodies as something quite different. We return to this theme later.

Children instead emphasized that parents, mothers in the case of our research, as with Mayall's (1996) research, were primarily responsible for health. There was an explicit expectation that parents will actively ensure that children are healthy. For example, Sarah describes an appreciation for her mother's efforts to set new ground rules around diet:

Sarah: My Mum tries very hard for us. She is just starting to really concentrate on eating healthy. So she will only buy healthy things now. Now for me chocolates are being more like a treat to me.

In these discussions, healthcare revolved around the characteristics of parent–child relationships, rather than specific health practices. Stable and responsive relationships with parents were important, because these relationships provided consistent and nurturing interactions within which the provision of appropriate care was taken for granted by children. Overt dependence on parents was especially important where children felt unwell. It was in circumstances where children experienced illness that they emphasized the importance of parents and family. The following two extracts are typical examples of the importance of parental care. Illie emphasizes how parental instruction about eating well makes him feel safe, and Porscha suggests that knowing someone is there to care for you when you are unwell is important to wellbeing:

Interviewer: [Referring to a photo of fruit and vegetables] This one, the one about the food, number 6. What about this one?
Illie: I picked it because it makes me feel safe, because you get to eat healthy food and like my parents tell me to eat healthy food so I keep healthy. And I listen to them and I eat healthy food and it makes me feel safe.

Interviewer: Another thing you were telling me that has to do with wellbeing is about being healthy and not being sick.
Porscha: Like having someone there to give you medicine to help you. Maybe if you have medicine in the fridge, your parents give you some.

We can discern from these discussions that children have knowledge about what is healthy in ways consistent with dominant frameworks of healthism and developmental health, but in a general way. However, as mentioned earlier, many children discussed health as a contested issue and children have to mediate between conflicting messages about what is healthy and what is desirable, which can be a source of anxiety. These anxieties are mediated between parents and children at home, often by developing a set of 'reasonable habits', which represent a compromise between 'healthy practices' and 'unhealthy wants'. These themes are also played out in one of the two major themes that children discussed about health, eating.

Eating as Functional and Emotional

Eating was a major theme in children's discussions. As noted previously, children commonly made references to healthy eating, distinguishing between healthy and unhealthy foods. In these discussions, children sometimes employed somatic descriptions of the body, describing the body in a diagnostic manner. We saw some semblance of this when children discussed how particular types of food and exercise were associated with 'good' health outcomes. However, these discussions were only of a general nature. Rarely did children discuss the specifics of health practices (for example how much food or the regularity of exercise), nor the effects such practices might have on specific dimensions of health. For example, Angel and Apex identify the links between healthy eating and good health, but their descriptions are framed in instrumental terms. For Angel it meant strengthening her body:

Interviewer: What is it about food that you like?
Angel: Cereal, because when you have breakfast it gives you strength in your body.

For Apex it was about his ability to focus:

Apex: Yeah and food. Food helps you do that [focus]. You take, you drink a litre of Cola in the morning and you won't focus. You know. Yeah.

Children also expressed more nuanced understandings of health when they discussed their everyday practices, relationships and concerns. Of significance to children when discussing food was what could be described as 'food as a facilitator'. Children described food as important for undertaking the daily activities of being a child. Food was fuel, and many children made references to 'energy'. Again, this theme was discussed in terms of both positive and negative practices: healthy eating allows you to function well and unhealthy eating results in poor functioning:

Interviewer: Ah, you said food helps you live and it feeds you and makes your body healthy. Ah, what is it like to be healthy?
Angel: You can do lots of stuff. Um, and when you might get tired, no, when you like do something you don't get tired.

Prudence explicitly links functioning with energy, one precondition of which is healthy eating:

Interviewer: You talked about energy a couple of times. What does energy mean to you?
Prudence: Um, it means that you can do stuff. Like if you don't have energy, you can't do running or horse riding and stuff. So you've got the energy to do the things you want to do.

This included identity work associated with presentations of the self and the 'acceptable body'. For Nearly Ten, not having a healthy body can mark one out for ridicule. He emphasizes the importance of the healthy body in feeling happy:

Interviewer: So are happy and healthy linked together? To be happy, you have to be healthy?

Nearly Ten: Um, when you are healthy you feel more happier. I mean like when you are not healthy, I don't know, sometimes you feel, I don't know, like you don't feel well, because you get teased around and all that.

When asked to explain this further, Nearly Ten's response indicates that the healthy body is important to children in terms of sociability:

Interviewer: Mmm, so if you are overweight or not healthy, you might be teased?

Nearly Ten: Yeah, because people um, sometimes judge you about your looks and if um, you're fat, then I don't know if anybody will be your friend. That is pretty lonely. And upsetting.

Nearly Ten relates being overweight with the affective aspects of health, linked with acceptance by others and self-acceptance. The complex affective aspects associated with eating are also evident in children's discussions about eating being associated with self-care, involving a range of experiences including comfort, reflection, escape, a sense of managing anxiety and feeling 'normal'. As opposed to an active body, these discussions evoked images of the body in a more passive state. In the following quote, the participant is discussing a bodily and cognitive experience suggestive of ontological security, of having a sense of belonging to the world by being present to the experience of eating:

Interviewer: You said, food can be comforting. What do you mean by that?

Prudence: Like sometimes you are all worried about stuff and everything and when you eat you are concentrating on that and you just forget about everything else and it makes things seem normal and everything, like everything doesn't seem as hard.

Interviewer: Okay, so after you've done that, what difference does that make?

Prudence: Well, it makes it easier to stop thinking about it and worrying about it and worried about what you are going to do.

This sense of ontological security is critical in being able to engage in social practices, with their attendant risks and hazards, benefits that go beyond those typically emphasized within healthism. While children discuss some of their health practices in ways similar to healthism, eating well is also important not just because it promotes 'proper health' but because it makes you feel secure, good about yourself, and promotes a sense of autonomy by giving you 'energy' to do things.

Physical Activities and 'Doing Health'

The most recurrent theme in children's discussions of health was the active body. For children in this research, the healthy body was an active body. We have seen the importance of this already in children's discussion of food, but this was also demonstrated in children's discussions of physical activities. Children valued physical activities when they made possible a sense of freedom from organized time, including school and organized family time. These situations represent the 'practical enactments' of health knowledge. That is, they are the everyday contexts in which children practise healthy behaviours, and in so doing translate children's knowledge about health into 'doing health'.

The emotional and relational dimensions associated with physical activity and exercise were especially important in children's discussions. This is an important point of difference from healthism discourses, where physical exercise is an expression of a healthy lifestyle. However, in children's discussions, physical activity per se was not associated with wellbeing, but what these activities facilitate was associated with wellbeing. This includes, as Prudence points out, the expression of emotions through movement:

Interviewer: Okay, so just playing with others and doing it for fun.
Prudence: Expressing feelings. Yeah, sometimes when you are playing sports or something you are expressing your feelings through movement.

Or as Apex discusses, a state of general wellbeing:

Interviewer: Yep. Tell me about this a bit more. About exercising.
Apex: 'Cause your health is like, helps adjust your mind to something. You can focus and concentrate on what you are doing. You don't have to worry about it much. If you are not healthy, like you can't concentrate or nothing and it affects your studies and other parts of life.
Interviewer: Tell me about it?

Apex:　　　　You've got friends and relationships with friends and relationships with family. Um, and then there is physical sort of health,
which is exercise and food, and they are all interrelated. They all
go together. So the food comes back to health. Like I said before, it
is all interconnected ... So if you don't exercise, go out, you don't
make friends. If you are not making friends, you are bored.

Apex clearly links exercise with sociability. This was quite typical of children's discussions of exercise and fitness. As Valentine (2010) points out,
it is in interactions with other children that children learn how to differentiate their body from other children and to express a sense of individuality
and group membership. The discussion of physical activities as part of
routine social interactions with other children is quite different from how
health education campaigns attempt to promote exercise, as something
that an individual 'should make time for', 'fit in' or something that one
does as part of a health routine. These types of discussions might be typical ways that adults talk about the need to do more exercise, as an activity
that is an individual's responsibility (Backett-Milburn, 2000). But what
is evident from children's discussions is that exercise, because it is part
of their routine social interactions, often occurs spontaneously and thus
often as a 'natural consequence of their ways of living' (Backett-Milburn,
2000: 87).

This is important given how many public health programmes attempt
to enforce exercise routines without sufficient attention to the dimensions
of sociability and spontaneity that are central to children's discussions.
Schools enforce a certain discipline over children's bodies, and explicitly
so through physical education curricula. Rather than enforcing children to
undertake physical activity, children's discussions suggest that it would be
better to create environments within which children can freely associate
with each other and through which there may be opportunities to do physical activities as part of being sociable.

While these opportunities occur in children's autonomous spaces, it
was also apparent that such opportunities also arise in institutional spaces,
such as after-school care and organized sports. For example, Stella, in
discussing playing competitive netball, emphasizes feeling proud because
of her display of competence and winning:

Stella:　　　　One of the good things about playing netball is that you get to meet
new people. You get to meet friends outside of school and people
you play against. And um, also that it is good because you can feel
really proud like when you do well at it. And if you win especially.

Interviewer: Um, are there other things that are important about netball?
Stella: You are fit. You get fit and you get enough exercise.

These discussions are replete with images of the performing body, the body in motion and the body imbued with sensory experience, of the incarnate body as described by Christensen (2000), of the body as it relates functionally to its surroundings and engages in social interaction. Children's discussions of health are often focused on the context of their own actions and abilities, and on functioning in social contexts and physical environments. This is quite different to describing health in terms of diagnostic signs, such as muscle mass or the absence of illness, or particular body types. Therefore, physical activity is often associated with wellbeing where it facilitates certain affective states: autonomy, a sense of freedom through bodily movement, opportunities for fun and opportunities for obtaining social esteem and a sense of self-worth.

Discussion: The Limits of Healthism

Many of children's discussions about their health are consistent with healthism discourses. For example, children's views about eating and exercise were generally consistent with healthism. Eating the right types and amount of food, and regular exercise, were, in children's discussions, key to health. We might expect children to be well versed in these health behaviours if we were to specifically ask them about health. However, these views arose spontaneously as part of discussions about wellbeing. Apart from these few similarities, children in this research view health in quite different ways than suggested in healthism discourses. We can discern four key areas of difference: the relationship between health and wellbeing; how children's agency is understood; responsibility for health and the sites of health practice; and how the healthy body is conceptualized. These are discussed below.

The Health–Wellbeing Nexus

We have established that healthism discourses tend to reduce wellbeing to a set of values and practices that promote healthy living. However, children's discussion of health reverses this relationship, with health as one dimension of a broader experience of wellbeing. More specifically, health practices were especially important to children when associated with a sense of feeling safe, experiencing a positive sense of self and expressing agency.

Feelings of security and safety were emphasized when children discussed how health is embedded in stable loving relationships and in the importance of parents and carers in framing day-to-day health practices. This was associated not only with practices for maintaining the body, but also experiencing ontological security, especially through meals. Physical activities contributed to a sense of wellbeing where they provided opportunities for sociability and fun, the ability to express emotions through movement and in providing opportunities to obtain social esteem through achievements. Therefore, while healthism emphasizes individual lifestyle practices, in contrast children's discussion of health emphasizes that health is experienced as part of ongoing, but specific, social interactions, relationships and contexts.

Children as Health Agents

The relational constitution of health is especially important in children's experiences of agency in relation to health. While dominant frameworks attribute limited forms of agency to children, we see from children's discussions that agency is expressed in various health-related behaviours and activities: when children discuss food as a facilitator; of the body in motion; and a sense of wellbeing through positive sensory experiences. These expressions of agency are not so much about asserting 'choice' (that is, as a rational liberal subject), but are embedded in daily practices that may be taken for granted by children. These are quite different expressions of agency than that promoted in healthism discourses.

We find that even where children engage in health practices that are different to those of their parents, children nonetheless assume the existence of health rules set by their parents and often seek out such rules (Backett-Milburn, 2000). Children emphasized that parents established the parameters for health, through concrete measures such as buying healthy food. In so doing, there is at least an implicit recognition of the importance of the guidance and supervision over health provided by adults, even if children may disagree with such rules. Therefore, it would be inaccurate to say that children's agency can best be understood as 'performing health' separate from 'adult' contexts. Rather, health practices are constituted through ongoing intersubjective relations with other important and trusted people.

Responsibility and Sites of Health Practice

This leads to our next point, pertaining to how responsibility for health is understood. As noted earlier, healthism discourses perpetuate an ideology of the 'responsible parent', as having ongoing responsibility for children's health and responsibility for their children's health as future adults. Making the 'right choices now' becomes imperative. Therefore, how adults exercise choice in the market is of particular importance within healthism discourses, for the health of both children and the next generation of adults.

Children's discussions of health emphasize quite a different relationship between current activities and future health. Children actively mediate between conflicts that arise between healthism and food marketing, which can represent different expectations of how children should act in terms of their health. In mediating between the two, we see how children sometimes position themselves as responsible health agents.

Children also appear to prioritize present experiences as important to their sense of wellbeing. While discussions of the future were common, they were quite unlike health discourses that emphasize the long-term benefits from healthy practices. Much of what the children associated with health were immediately identifiable signs of healthy appearance, including physical, emotional and psychological signs and the functional outcomes of healthy practices, such as being able to focus or engage in physical activities competently. There was less emphasis on the long-term potential outcomes of health practices, such as prevention of ill health. Yet, many of the health experiences associated with a present sense of wellbeing are also likely to be preconditions for healthy development, for example eating to have energy is also likely to involve eating healthily.

Additionally, children's discussions of health emphasized that the sites of health practice are not only in the private sphere but include children's autonomous spaces within civil society. Intergenerationally, we see how responsibility for everyday care largely resides with parents and carers (Evans, 2005). Yet we also discern that, while adults are powerful arbiters of children's health, children also discuss the importance of intragenerational relationships. Relationships with peers were central to health practices associated with physical activity and recognition. These often occur outside the home, in children's autonomous play or in institutionalized spaces for children. Therefore, children also discuss the importance of their own social contexts for their health.

The Healthy Body

Within healthism discourses, bodies are considered in highly normative ways, with body shape and size signifying health status as well as a person's health practices. Children's discussions of health also emphasized a connection between eating the right foods and exercising and desirable or undesirable body types. But what was more often emphasized was the body's functional capacity and the body imbued with sensation.

Both function and sensation were important to children's discussions of health. The functional body is a competent body capable of engaging in everyday social practices (see also Valentine, 2010). But in discussing the body in action, a healthy body is a body imbued with sensation, which, from children's perspectives, is associated with internal states such as feeling calm or worthy. These were perhaps closer to states of pleasure, where a physical act, such as eating enjoyable food, could lead both to a bodily experience of pleasure and a psychological condition of contentment. Hence, children's discussions of health practices, while embodied, are also about affect and emotion.

Conclusion

Discursive, or representational, social forces are one component through which children understand and experience their health. However, while some elements of children's discussion of their health conform to the social ordering of health represented in healthism discourses, other elements contest it. In our research, children's discussions of their health reflect the salutogenic as opposed to the pathogenic approach to health. In part, the limits of healthism can be understood because it promotes a notion of self-responsibility as a moral practice that can alienate individuals. The need to constantly take responsibility for one's behaviour, a drive to self-improvement, the emphasis on individual choice and that poor health is a consequence of individual failings can leave little room for practices associated with pleasure, fun and a sense of wellbeing.

References

Alexander, S.A., Fusco, C. and Frohlich, K.L. (2015) '"You have to do 60 minutes of physical activity per day … I saw it on TV": children's constructions of play in the context of Canadian public health discourse of playing for health', *Sociology of Health & Illness*, 37(2): 227–240.

Backett-Milburn, K. (2000) 'Parents, children and the construction of the "healthy body" in middle-class families', in A. Prout (ed.), *The Body, Childhood and Society*. Basingstoke: Palgrave Macmillan. pp. 79–100.

Backett-Milburn, K., Cunningham-Burley, S. and Davis, J. (2003) 'Contrasting lives, contrasting views? Understandings of health inequalities from children in different social circumstances', *Social Science & Medicine*, 57(4): 613–623.

Bell, K., McNaughton, D. and Salmon, A. (2009) 'Medicine, morality and mothering: public health discourses on fetal alcohol exposure, smoking around children and childhood over-nutrition', *Critical Public Health*, 19(2): 155–170.

Bergnehr, D. and Zetterqvist Nelson, K. (2015) 'Where is the child? A discursive exploration of the positioning of children in research on mental-health-promoting interventions', *Sociology of Health & Illness*, 37(2): 184–197.

Blaxter, M. (1997) 'Whose fault is it? People's own conceptions of the reasons for health inequalities', *Social Science & Medicine*, 44(6): 747–756.

Burrows, L., Wright, J. and McCormack, J. (2009) 'Dosing up on food and physical activity: New Zealand children's ideas about "health"', *Health Education Journal*, 68(3): 157–169.

Christensen, P.H. (2000) 'Childhood and the cultural constitution of vulnerable bodies', in A. Prout (ed.), *The Body, Childhood and Society*. Basingstoke: Palgrave Macmillan. pp. 38–59.

Clavering, E.K. and McLaughlin, J. (2010) 'Children's participation in health research: from objects to agents?', *Child: Care, Health and Development*, 36(5): 603–611.

Colls, R. and Evans, B. (2008) 'Embodying responsibility: children's health and supermarket initiatives', *Environment and Planning A*, 40(3): 615–631.

Crawford, R. (1980) 'Healthism and the medicalisation of everyday life', *International Journal of Health Services*, 10(3): 365–388.

Evans, B., Colls, R. and Hörschelmann, K. (2011) '"Change4Life for your kids": embodied collectives and public health pedagogy', *Sport, Education and Society*, 16(3): 323–341.

Evans, R. (2005) 'Social networks, migration and care in Tanzania: caregivers and children's resilience in coping with HIV/AIDS', *Journal of Children and Poverty*, 11(2): 111–129.

Fattore, T. and Mason, J. (2016) *Children and Well-being: Towards a Child Standpoint*. Dordrecht: Springer.

Henderson, S. and Petersen A.R. (eds) (2002) *Consuming Health: The Commodification of Health Care*. London: Routledge.

Horton, J. and Kraftl, P. (2010) 'Time for bed! Children's bedtime practices, routines and affects', in K. Hörschelmann and R. Colls (eds), *Contested Bodies of Childhood and Youth*. Basingstoke: Palgrave Macmillan. pp. 215–231.

Jenkins, L. (2015) 'Negotiating pain: the joint construction of a child's bodily sensation', *Sociology of Health & Illness*, 37(2): 298–311.

Maher, J., Fraser, S. and Wright, J. (2010) 'Framing the mother: childhood obesity, maternal responsibility and care', *Journal of Gender Studies*, 19(3): 233–247.

Mayall, B. (1996) *Children, Health and the Social Order*. Buckingham: Open University Press.

Mogensen, L. and Mason, J. (2015) 'The meaning of a label for teenagers negotiating identity: experiences with autism spectrum disorder', *Sociology of Health & Illness*, 37(2): 255–269.

Murphy, E. (2003) 'Expertise and forms of knowledge in the government of families', *The Sociological Review*, 51(4): 433–462.

Nettleton, S. (2006) *The Sociology of Health and Illness*. Cambridge: Polity Press.

Pearson, M., Chilton, R., Woods, H.B., Wyatt, K., Ford, T., Abraham, C. and Anderson, R. (2012) 'Implementing health promotion in schools: protocol for a realist systematic review of research and experience in the United Kingdom (UK)', *Systematic Reviews*, 1(48). Available at: www.systematicreviewsjournal.com/content/1/1/48

Pike, J. and Kelly, P. (2014) *The Moral Geographies of Children, Young People and Food: Beyond Jamie's School Dinners*. Basingstoke: Palgrave Macmillan.

Place, B. (2000) 'Constructing the bodies of critically ill children: an ethnography of intensive care', in A. Prout (ed.), *The Body, Childhood and Society*. Basingstoke: Palgrave Macmillan. pp. 172–194.

Probyn, E. (2010) 'How do children taste? Young people and the production and consumption of food', in K. Hörschelmann and R. Colls (eds), *Contested Bodies of Childhood and Youth*. Basingstoke: Palgrave Macmillan. pp. 84–96.

Prout, A. (2000) 'Childhood bodies: construction, agency and hybridity', in A. Prout (ed.), *The Body, Childhood and Society*. Basingstoke: Palgrave Macmillan. pp. 1–18.

Valentine, G. (2010) 'Children's bodies: an absent presence' in K. Hörschelmann and R. Colls (eds), *Contested Bodies of Childhood and Youth*. Basingstoke: Palgrave Macmillan. pp. 22–37.

Warin, M., Turner, K., Moore, V. and Davies, M. (2008) 'Bodies, mothers and identities: re-thinking obesity and the BMI', *Sociology of Health & Illness*, 30(1): 97–111.

WHO (World Health Organization) (2012) *Population-based Approaches to Childhood Obesity Prevention*. Geneva: World Health Organization.

Wright, J. and Burrows, L. (2004) '"Being healthy": the discursive construction of health in New Zealand children's responses to the National Education Monitoring Project', *Discourse*, 25(2): 211–230.

Section Three

Identities and Social Transformation in Global Childhoods

Introduction

This section includes four chapters concerning children's experiences in different parts of the world, conditioned by the social transformations during the globalization process. The first two chapters concern two types of societal conditions limiting children's wellbeing in their own countries of origin, the following two are about different conditions limiting the wellbeing of children with migrant-background in Europe.

The first two chapters analyse different topics and social contexts, but they both deal with the structural presuppositions and illusionary solutions of children's problematic social conditions, respectively poverty and abuse.

The first chapter, 'Success: A 'Leitmotiv' of Kyrgyz Childhoods' by Doris Bühler-Niederberger, concerns the global educational presuppositions that influence the conditions of growing up in Kyrgyzstan, in particular focusing on families' expectations regarding children and young people's careers, and children and young people's ways of dealing with these expectations. The context of this chapter is the discourse of development organizations, experts, politicians and donors, who see childhood as a time of education, and thus promise investment opportunity for the future of children and society as a whole. This discourse is based on a general human capital approach, which encourages social and economic development in poor countries. The focus on successful education is very popular in Kyrgyzstan, both with the government and the people. In particular, many parents are convinced that education will help them overcome their difficult economic situation; therefore, a high percentage of young people are enrolled in the higher educational system and the number of private universities has grown. However, the labour market provides a very limited amount of jobs for graduates. The analysis of four studies undertaken since 2010, involving different age groups from kindergarten to university, shows that Kyrgyz children and youth are put under considerable pressure to succeed, and that little time remains for the realization of their personal preferences and talents. Therefore, this analysis leads to the criticism of education experts who are active and influential in Kyrgyzstan, for their insensitivity to the local conditions of life.

This chapter deals with the education system in a poor country and the influence of globalization on these education systems. These themes are also dealt with in the book; however, while that chapter focuses on children's agency, in Bühler-Niederberger's chapter the focus is on the structural conditions of children's success. The chapter claims that the adoption of global standards of education is illusory, for both children and their families.

The second chapter in this section, 'Child Abuse and Neglect in India: Locating Child Abuse in Fractured Indian Families through Children's Lenses', by Vinod Chandra, is based on a study of ten cases of child sexual and emotional abuse and neglect in fractured families in Lucknow City. The empirical part of the chapter investigates children's narratives. The point of departure of this chapter is the high incidence of child abuse in India, which happens at home or is perpetrated by family members. In the last few decades, Indian families have gone through structural changes due to economic and social factors, so that the extended family structure has been replaced by the nuclear family. In poor families facing economic hardship, children become extremely vulnerable, they are victims of neglect, emotional, physical and sexual abuse on the part of the adult family members. Indian families bring up their children to be submissive and obedient, and this creates the strong belief that parents and families in India are the sole caretakers of children. Against this background, the negative impact of broken families on a child's wellbeing has never been the concern of child protection laws and strategies. In 2012, the Indian Parliament introduced the Protection of Children against Sexual Offences Act (POCSO). Since its implementation, however, the reported cases of sexual abuse have increased. The high incidence of child abuse and neglect is a cause of concern for child protection activists, childhood researchers and child rights practitioners. The chapter focuses on several factors that can explain the reasons behind the high incidence of child abuse and neglect cases in India, such as poverty and family disruption, insensitivity to children's rights, and the discharge of responsibilities in addressing the issues of child abuse and neglect in childcare institutions.

In this chapter, the evolution towards the global standard of the family system (i.e. unstable nuclear family and frequent divorce) is considered as a relevant condition of abuse, and the adoption of a global standard of protection to contrast abuse seems to be illusory. Thus, the structural conditions that surround the problem of abuse contradict the apparent success of the process of globalization.

The following two chapters investigate the conditions of identity construction among migrant-background children. Both these chapters identify the structural conditions (and in the first one, the cultural conditions too) that influence children's experience of migration. The two chapters focus on different conditions of this experience. The first one focuses on ethnicity, immigrant status and socialization, the second one on social class. Moreover, the second chapter identifies opportunities for children's management of their conditions, which are not foreseen in the first chapter.

The first of these two chapters, 'Identity and Social Integration among the Children of African Immigrants in France', by Loretta Bass, draws upon in-depth retrospective interviews with 22 children and youths, aged 13–14, of Sub-Saharan African descent, some of whom are immigrants themselves and others who are second-generation French citizens. Qualitative methods, registering the voices of young people, are used to understand the identity formation and social integration experienced by immigrant and immigrant-descent children. This research highlights that young people find a sense of self-identification through ethnicity and immigrant status, despite their experience of French society and culture. Besides, it illustrates the dimensions of identity construction and experience of young people of African descent in France. On the one hand, identity construction depends on the structural dimensions of ethnicity, and assumed non-citizen status due to cultural markers such as a non-French-sounding name. On the other hand, identity construction depends on the cultural dimensions of family socialization and differential access to opportunity because of a lack of knowledge of French culture. Exclusion due to structural factors and isolation due to cultural factors frame the social integration experience and life opportunities perceived as possible for African-descent children.

The final chapter, 'Fluctuating Social Class Mobility of Filipino Migrant Children in France and in Italy' by Asuncion Fresnoza-Flot and Itaru Nagasaka, concerns the ways in which Filipino migrant children experience social class mobility and confront the class (im)mobility accompanying migration. The chapter is based on transnational families, which are characterized by solidarity despite family separation across geographical distance. There is social concern about the wellbeing of the children of transnational families, as these children grow up separate from one or both of their parents. These children become migrants when family reunification takes place in the receiving country of the migrant parents. The chapter focuses on ethnographic fieldwork about the generation of Filipino migrants' children who grew up partly in the Philippines and partly in Europe. These migrant children experience fluctuating social class (im)mobility differently from their parents. In particular, the chapter shows how social class belonging of these children changes from their country of origin to the country of migration. Before family reunification, these children enjoy a middle-class lifestyle in the Philippines, thanks to their migrant parents' remittances. When they migrate to join their migrant parents, they undergo downward class mobility in the receiving country. However, to confront these changes, they adopt strategies that demonstrate their agency and their ability to adapt to their social context.

The important reflection emerging from this section concerns the extent of successful experience of children in both poor countries where they stay and migration countries where they go. The chapters explore different structural (and cultural) conditions that can influence this experience. They show that the globalization of the promotion and protection of children's agency can fail, both when they live in non-Western societies and when they have a migrant-background in Western society.

7

Success: A 'Leitmotiv' of Kyrgyz Childhoods

Doris Bühler-Niederberger

Introduction: Global Educational Messages and Forgotten Children

A worldwide discourse composed of development organizations, experts, politicians and donors conceives of childhood as a time of education and, in this way, as a promising investment opportunity for the future of the individuals and society as a whole. According to the human capital theory that the World Bank and other important international organizations adhere to, education will be responsible for the end of individual and national poverty: education for all, early education and extended education (Mundy, 2002). 'Education changes everything' is the catchy formula used in calls for donations.[1] And this is what UNESCO promises among other things: 'In low income countries, universalizing upper secondary completion by 2030 would increase per capita income by 75% by 2050 and bring poverty elimination forward by 10 years'; 'universal upper secondary completion by 2030 would prevent up to 50,000 disaster-related deaths per decade by 2040–2050'; 'universalizing upper secondary completion for women in sub-Saharan Africa by 2030 would result in 300,000 to 350,000 fewer child deaths per year in 2050' (UNESCO, 2016: v).

This praising of education as a cure-all has received considerable criticism. Firstly, the way that the World Bank and other international organizations stick to neoliberal principles and a market-driven educational policy is said to contradict the goal of 'education for all', considering education only as an investment and not as a human right (Kamat, 2012). A second critique concerns the economic effect of education, arguing that this educational strategy is not a sound economic approach to development (Klees, 2012), and that the effects of schooling on the economic development of societies and on poverty eradication are overestimated. While human capital theory assumes that education is the basic tool to combat poverty on an individual and collective level, several studies have shown that this assumption is overly simplified. Education usually benefits the more-educated individual relative to the less-educated individual, but aggregate education gains do not necessarily translate into aggregate poverty declines, for a number of reasons. Believing in education as a central instrument to eradicate poverty underestimates the complex effects of educational expansion on income distribution and, not least, the effect that poverty has on education (Bonal, 2007; Wedgewood, 2005).[2]

Kyrgyzstan: a Fertile Soil for Global Messages

Kyrgyzstan is a Central Asian country of the former Soviet Union. It is a mountainous country with a continental climate. Therefore, although the country is sparsely populated, its agriculture is insufficient to nourish the population. And compared to neighbouring countries the natural resources are limited, too; what little gold, uranium and electricity (water resources) they have are virtually the only exports. There are severe infrastructural deficiencies in the country as well (traffic, drinking water supply and sanitation, medical care), especially in the many remote areas. After the collapse of the Soviet Union, industrialization remained weak, although considerable efforts were made in order to reform the economy, to privatize former state ownership, to support a competitive market, and to fight corruption to some degree. Several popular uprisings and inter-ethnic clashes in the last two decades weakened development efforts. Many men and women migrate to other countries of the former Soviet Union, especially Russia and Kazakhstan. Remittances of these migrants contribute considerably to the gross national income. In the ranking of countries according to their gross national income per capita, Kyrgyzstan is ranked 184th out of 230 countries, more or less equal with Lesotho, Côte d'Ivoire, or Kenya (CIA, 2017). Migrants' remittances constitute more than one third of this meagre gross national income per capita; there is only one country in the world, Liberia, where this amount is even slightly higher.[3] Kyrgyzstan depends heavily on foreign aid, and it cooperates intensively with international donors. The country has a democratic system; though this less autocratic development in comparison to other countries of the region is astonishing and not easy to explain – even for Kyrgyz sociologists (Yarkova, 2004). This may also be – together with the pressing economic weakness – one of the reasons for Kyrgyzstan's 'eagerness to accept foreign interference at the levels of both state and society' (Yarkova, 2004: 137).

The message of increased education as a strategy to eradicate poverty was readily accepted by Kyrgyzstan's government, which – considered in absolute amounts – was not able to invest much in education. This caused a constant underfinancing of the educational system. However, by investing almost 7% of GDP the relative contribution made to education is very high (CIA, 2017). A flood of reports, programmes and laws targeting education and services for children demonstrates the cooperation of the Kyrgyz government with developmental organizations (Aga Khan University, Institute for Educational Development, 2014; Ginsburg, 2009; UNDP, 2010; World Bank, 2013). Shamatow speaks of 'a myriad of international education assistance projects including international agencies, private foundations and philanthropists, and international nongovernmental organizations' (2014: 287) targeting curriculum development, teaching methods, inclusive education, assessments, etc. Since 2006, Kyrgyzstan has also participated in the Programme for International Student Assessment (PISA), an OECD programme that compares countries with regard to students' performance. However, Kyrgyz results were very disappointing: their students scored the lowest out of 57 participating countries (OECD, 2007).

The people of Kyrgyzstan welcomed the educational promise for the future, too. Many were convinced that education would help them overcome their difficult economic situation. The developments in higher education give proof of people's hopes: in recent years the number of universities in Kyrgyzstan has grown, from nine at the time of independence from the Soviet Union in 1991 to 52 today. In comparison, Denmark and Finland – two countries with roughly the same populations as Kyrgyzstan – have eight and 14 universities respectively (Sabzalieva, 2015). More than 50% of the relevantly aged portion of the population are enrolled in the higher educational system (Asian Development Bank, 2015). On the other hand, a study showed vocational education is of low prestige and generally disliked. If young people choose it, they do not justify this decision by their interest in the trade or skill, but with the lower costs and the short duration of the schooling (UNDP, 2010: 26). While one might object and say that higher education has just become a way to keep (otherwise unemployed) young people busy, high hopes come with such decisions, as families' expenses for education can be considerable. Student fees can be up to several thousand dollars per year at private universities, and even several hundred up to more than $1,000 at state universities – depending on the subject studied (Braunmiller, 2016).[4]

There is a sharp contrast between the efforts of the people and their yields. The labour market provides a very limited amount of jobs for graduates. The 'normal' path after education leads into an informal labour market or unemployment. The chances in the labour market of southern Kyrgyzstan are probably the worst, as borne out by a study by UNICEF. The respondents in this study were between 15 and 28 years old. If we exclude the ones who were still students (35% of the respondents), only 8% of the rest were in steady employment; 43% were in short-term, temporary, or seasonal employment – working in subsistence agriculture or similar jobs; 27% declared themselves unemployed; and 20% were housewives (UNICEF, 2011). Entrance into the labour market may also be difficult due to the fields of study that students prefer, which in most cases have little to do with the country's economic reality. Twenty-five per cent of students choose management and economics, 23% choose liberal arts and law, and only 4% study agriculture, while 26% of the GDP comes from agriculture (Dümmler, 2011; UNDP, 2010: 27). Therefore, education is no guarantee to overcome poverty. In addition, social networks and other informal mechanisms regulate access to the labour market: in the UNICEF survey, most young people, no matter what profession they aspired to be in, thought it would be necessary to pay a bribe in order to get a job (UNICEF, 2011: 29). Even excellent students cannot find jobs in their field of study. Only 30% of 5,000 scholarship students in tertiary education – selected according to their outstanding performances – found employment within a year of graduating from university, and most of them not in their field of study (UNDP, 2010: 27).

Research Questions and Data

While the discussion on global education – in particular its possible gains and biases – attracts a lot of scientific and political attention, children themselves are once again forgotten. Both global actors using the human capital approach and their critics, who are more aware of local and regional dynamics, are neglectful of children and their quality of life. While states are pressured to invest in education 'to transform today's young children into human capital assets' for their economic transformation – an example of the World Bank's rhetoric (2001) – the potential impact on children themselves is not considered. Children and juveniles are the ones attending kindergartens, primary schools, secondary schools and tertiary education; they are the ones who have to cope with the high expectations, whose educational performances and achievements may be projected onto their own future and the future of their countries – yet their voices remain unheard. These are, therefore, the guiding questions this chapter focuses on: How does the global educational promise influence the qualities and conditions of growing up in a poor country, i.e. Kyrgyzstan? And what are the expectations of children and young people especially from their families, and how do children and young people deal with them? Answers will be given on the basis of four studies undertaken by the author of this chapter from 2010 onwards.

Study I, 'Empowering Young Children', was realized with the support of the Aga Khan Foundation and UNICEF. The study asked for children's views on themselves and their contexts, their joys, their sorrows, and their wishes for the future. It aimed to collect information on persons that were important to them, mutual obligations, duties, and functional and emotional support. The parents were asked for their expectations concerning the child's future, situations in their daily life with the child, pleasurable moments and conflicts. A central part of the data collection were sessions in kindergartens with 117 children aged 3–6 years; with these children we conducted several exercises – drawing, playing, interpreting faces – according to the ideas of 'participatory research' (Gallacher and Gallagher, 2008; Punch, 2002). About half of the children were from the capital, or smaller towns and villages in the region of the capital, while the other half were from rural and remote regions. The study included interviews with 60 parents of these children and 30 home visits (see Bühler-Niederberger and Schwittek, 2014).

Study II, 'Self-Processes and Self-Oriented Learning', was carried out with primary school children and replicated and adapted a questionnaire which the research group developed and initially used for German children. The German part of the study was supported by the German Federal Ministry of Education and Research. The Kyrgyz part was realized by the support of university cooperation between Wuppertal University and several Kyrgyz universities, which was financed by the German Academic Exchange Service (DAAD). In this way, data collection and analysis was realized with the help of Kyrgyz exchange students. Children were mainly asked for their views on school and on the ways they got along with school demands. The questionnaire was meant for second graders, but as Kyrgyz children had more difficulties with reading and answering the questions than the German pupils of the same age, we changed our plans during data collection and addressed third graders as well, especially in rural areas. Questionnaires in the Kyrgyz and Russian languages (depending on children's preferences) were administered class-wise. The mean age of the 401 Kyrgyz pupils was 8.6 years. Twenty-nine per cent of the children were from the capital, 57% from smaller towns or villages and 14% from remote mountain areas. Their data were compared with 414 second graders in North-Rhine Westphalia, Germany, with a mean age of 7.7 years and who lived mainly in middle-sized cities and the agglomeration.

Study III, 'Children's Understanding of Wellbeing', is an ongoing project (worked on together with Ekaterina Chicherina). This project was made possible through Erasmus+, a European Union programme that supports university exchanges, which ensured we could rely once again on the cooperation of Kyrgyz exchange students. The study is based on a concept and set of questions developed by Fattore et al. (2015) that asks about children's life-worlds and their understandings of 'wellbeing' in a variety of countries – their experiences in school, family, with peers, in leisure time, their self-description, their hopes for the future, and their perspectives on what contributes to their quality of life. A multinational group of researchers is involved in the analysis of these data.[5] At the time of writing, the project has assembled data on 37 Kyrgyz children between 10 and 13 years old (with a mean age of 11.5 years). In our study we have used the 'lifestoryboard' (Chase and Diffey, 2010), a tool for interviews with children. By using this tool, the children can visualize their answers with stickers and modelling clay and configure a magnetic board that represents their narration. This makes the session more enjoyable for the children and gives them some control in the interviewing process. Originally developed to assess domestic violence, it is now used in interviews with children on a broad range of thematic issues. For this study we have made some comparisons with German data as well. Türkyilmaz (2018) conducted similar qualitative research in a qualitative family study and as an additional part of the project 'Self-Processes and Self-Oriented Learning' described above. The 28 children in Germany were asked for positive and negative experiences in their lives, their view of themselves, and their future aspirations. However, these children were somewhat younger, aged 7–10 years old.

Study IV, 'Three Generations – Changing Childhoods', is a study on university students in various countries who were asked to write short essays on their own childhoods, the childhoods of their mothers and fathers, similarities and differences between their parents' and their own childhoods, and finally the childhood which they want for their own future children. A questionnaire with closed-ended questions completed the data collection and mainly concerns the expectations of parents as perceived by students. It was realized without additional support and with just the university's resources. For Kyrgyzstan we analysed 40 essays and questionnaires, which can be compared with the information of 75 students in Italy and 69 students in Germany. In all three countries the data collection was done during lectures in university study programmes for social sciences and teacher education.

Basing the analysis on these four studies makes it possible to study the relevant questions for different age groups: from kindergarten children to university students. In addition, the results can be examined against the backdrop of data from other countries. This cannot be a comparative analysis in any strict sense: the sample sizes are too small and there are too many important differences between the contexts that influence the results. However, data for other countries can be taken as a point of reference when interpreting the findings and can cross-validate conclusions.

Results: The Urge to Succeed

Being Excellent Now and In the Future

The conditions of the local labour market are too well known in the country; however, and as the figures in the second section of this chapter make evident, this does not discourage people from investing in education. It is worth taking a closer look at people's hopes and strategies with regard to education; the expectations of parents and the ways children and young people accept or reject these expectations. In an ethnographic case study of a village in southern Kyrgyzstan, DeYoung et al. (2013) analysed the importance that people living in a remote valley give to education. The authors concluded that these people learned to consider education as important during the Soviet era, despite the many inequalities that existed during this period. And, while the utility of secondary and higher education in local and national labour markets has diminished since the collapse of the Soviet Union, as has the power and prestige of educators, the appeal of education still lingers. This is also definitely what characterizes our results: aspirations and hopes with regard to education which – given the situation of labour markets – may even be considered compulsive attempts to escape precarious situations. And most importantly, children and young people are supporting this illusory endeavour, even though it puts considerable pressure on them.

In order to take a closer look at the data that give evidence of this urge to succeed, one can start with the youngest children, those of Study I. Parents of the kindergarten children wanted them to achieve high positions. When they were asked what they wanted their children to become once they grew up, only two of the parents out of the 60 families mentioned occupations that did not require university degrees. Medical doctor was the most frequently mentioned professional aspiration, followed by engineer and then manager in business. One mother stated the following right away for her 4-year-old daughter: 'I think O. could be an ambassador'. Student fees are high (see the second section) and this may be the reason why parents want their children to excel at school – so that they might receive state scholarships. Parents tightly control the academic achievements of their children, even at this young age. When parents were asked to describe a recent situation in which the child made them angry, we got the following answers from different mothers of kindergarteners:

- One mother reported how her child makes her angry several times a day. When she forces him to learn and to read, he reads the wrong letters.
- Another mother recounted how her son had infuriated her two days previously as he did not want to do his homework.
- Another told how she had recently yelled at her child because she could not solve her maths exercise. The child used to be able to do that easily, but now she couldn't. The mother could not sleep at night because of this.

Young children showed the same orientation towards future success. Only very few children mentioned individual preferences or talents when talking about their wishes for the future. For instance, one boy wanted to become an artist because he liked to see his drawings on the wall, and two other children wanted to become singers or dancers and immediately started to perform for the researchers. Most often, however, the children said that they wanted to become doctors, engineers, or business people – very much like their parents had insinuated. And the pressure to succeed becomes even more evident in the following dialogue, in which a 6-year-old boy from a village where most inhabitants were farmers or animal herders explained what he would not like to be:

Researcher: What do you not want to be in the future?
Boy: I do not want to be a shepherd.
Researcher: Why?
Boy: I don't like to just wander around the mountains.
Researcher: Do you know shepherds?

Boy: Yes.
Researcher: Are they nice people?
Boy: Yes, but I want to be useful.

In Study II, when asking children for their orientation towards school (more than 400 in each country: Kyrgyzstan and Germany), it became evident that Kyrgyz children wanted to excel at school. 'At school I do want to know more than others' was a statement that 88% of Kyrgyz second and third graders declared to be 'exactly true' and only 1% responded 'not at all true'. To assess this finding it seems helpful to compare the German primary school children: 42% declared this to be 'exactly true', 46% to be 'a little bit true' or 'not really true' and 13% to be 'not at all true'. The same results were found for the statement 'At school I want to be the best'. Again, 88% of Kyrgyz children want that, while only 39% want it in Germany.

In Study III almost all (32 out of 37) of these children, aged 10–13, mentioned what they would like to be when they grow up. Their aspirations are mostly clear wishes to excel. Either children wanted to have prestigious and high-earning professions like medical doctor (8 children), lawyer and public prosecutor (3 children), business person, bank director, director of a company and economist (9 children), or they wanted glamorous careers as singers, dancers, actors, sports persons and film directors (7 children; some of them mentioned several of these wishes, like 'actor or film director', and 'actor or singer'). More modest wishes like baker, interpreter, police officer and car mechanic were astonishingly rare: only four children had these very normal plans for their future. Somewhere in the middle were the wishes of some children to become a journalist, an engineer, or a designer. Such were the wishes of five children, but most of them articulated these together with more ambitious ones.

The 28 German children in the qualitative family study showed clearly different orientations. Twenty-five of these children aged 7–10 who we asked what they want to be when they grow up already had ideas for their future professions. Their professional wishes do not show one clear direction for a prestigious, high-earning career; none of the children mentioned professions such as medical doctor or lawyer. Although their aspirations vary broadly and aim at different professional levels, only four children (all of them with a low socio-economic status, and three of them with a Turkish background) emphasized material desires in this context. Instead, the children referred primarily to their immediate preferences, interests, and abilities. While the Kyrgyz children mentioned parental advice and suggestions, the German children never did this. When talking about their ideas of their futures, some children described highly individualized plans that involved becoming a car engineer ('So that I can design my own car. Then I'll construct a motor with a rocket propulsion'), an astronomer ('So at some point I'll understand what came before big bang theory') or an author ('I think it would be awesome to make up stories all the time and continue them in a series'). Most frequently, though, the children articulated animal-related professions, based on their love of animals. Hence, the most frequently mentioned higher profession is veterinarian (4 children). Two children presented the idea of a business model that involves individual farm holding, while others wanted to become a zookeeper or riding instructor (4 children). Ten children mentioned rather ordinary or even modest wishes such as teacher, police officer, baker, flight attendant, carpenter and seller (Türkyilmaz, 2018). One might explain these more modest and self-oriented wishes with the children's younger age. However, Study I revealed the clear status orientation that Kyrgyz children (and their parents) already had in kindergarten.

Success is not only something that marks the future of Kyrgyz children, it is also a constant issue in their lives as children. While describing themselves and their pleasures or dismays, many children aged 10–13 in Study III refer to success or a lack of success. Bluntly and without any reticence, they may characterize themselves as a successful person; they base their self-esteem on success and explain pleasant and unpleasant feelings with regard to success or failure. This is what the following list of statements gives evidence of. All these statements are made by different children, boys as well as girls.

I have only A grades at school.

I have only A grades and I also take part in different school competitions.

I have always been an excellent student. I like to get A's.

I won first place in a dancing competition … I always receive excellent marks at school.

I took part in the school contest 'Miss Autumn'. I received a certificate for being the best in handicrafts.

And concerning failure:

I am very sad when I receive bad marks, because I am a very good student and usually I get A's.

I was working so hard for a test, but still I failed, I got an F. I was so upset about this.

No one likes our maths teacher. Once she gave me an F for a test. Actually for nothing. I checked this test one more time using the Internet and a calculator, and almost all my answers were correct. But still she gave me an F. Of course this made me sad.

I was a good student, but when I was in the third grade I became ill and had to stay almost one year in the hospital. After this my academic performance at school became worse ... I am very bad in maths. I'm attending some private lessons to improve my performance.

And they also mention being blamed for bad marks:

I am very sad when I don't receive an A. Even when I get B's, my grandmother becomes very upset.

I was so upset when I received a C in maths. It was a grade for the whole semester. I remember my mother scolded me for this bad result and I was crying.

Children's statements in Study III gave the impression that no school success less than the very best is good enough, which is very much consistent with the quantitative findings of Study II.

Success for Whom? Generational Hierarchy and Solidarities

Education sets people free, allows them to live independently – this is part of the rhetoric of the developmental organizations. International organizations' commitments to education are intertwined with a striving towards a more democratic, equal and individualized society.[6] Parent–child relationships in which children's talents and preferences matter should be part of such social development. In its country report on Kyrgyzstan, UNICEF admonishes families for not considering their children's individual wishes:

Some parents raise their children from an early age without taking into account wishes of the child as well as perspectives of child development in order to serve family interests. Over time these children fail to learn how to make decisions on their own, let alone know what kind of rights they have as a child. (UNICEF, 2007: 62)

However, UNICEF made this statement in the context of a discussion on child labour in the country. International organizations seem to ignore how education might also be functionalized by strong family interests, maybe even just as much so; hence it might lose the higher value of an individual right and entitlement.

Kyrgyzstan's generational hierarchy, and its solidarities which are organized along generational lines, are probably different from what Western experts imagine. In Kyrgyzstan, older people expect the youngest son to live with his wife in his parents' household, and for the daughter-in-law to be a help in the household. However, more than two thirds of young people would like to live in their own household (UNDP, 2010: 44).[7] But children who don't live in the household are expected to support their parents, too. In this way, children's success is not just for their individual profit. The current Constitution of the Independent Kyrgyz Republic declares that 'respect for the elderly … shall be the obligation of everyone',[8] while the former Soviet state had counteracted the power of the older generation for many decades with its own influence on education and young people's lives (Esengul, 2012: 38–39).

In Study I the item 'He/she should be a sustainer of the family' was ranked highly by more than two thirds of the parents of the kindergarten children; the children had evidently accepted this obligation themselves. They not only had very high aspirations for their future, but also they often explained that they were ambitious for the sake of their family. A selection of statements illustrates this, as they clearly contrast with the self-oriented professional aspirations of the German children quoted above.

> I will be a big girl. I want to be a bank officer. – Researcher: Why bank officer? – I will give money to my mother and father, I will buy a car, a Russian car.

> I want to be a doctor. I can take care of my mother.

> I will be a doctor. I'll treat parents, relatives, other people.

> I will be a doctor. I'll take care of my mother and other people. – Researcher: Is your mother sick? – No.

A mother's statement about her boy in kindergarten confirmed the generational obligations ('I hope S. will build a large house where we can all live together'). She added that she had adopted this child, since she had not had her own children after some years of marriage, and that, while he was not her own, all the same she did a lot for him and sometimes bought him fruit in the grocery store. She hoped that this investment in his education was not for nothing.

Study IV was the most explicit with regard to the generational obligations of young people. Students were asked about the expectations that parents had concerning their future. Young Kyrgyz people seemed convinced that these expectations were high. While the sample of this study is somewhat small for a quantitative analysis, the differences between the countries are nevertheless clear and consistent with the results of the other three studies. Table 7.1 shows the percentage of students who believe it's 'true' or even 'very true' that parents have certain expectations of them (while the categories 'not that true' and 'not true at all' are omitted from the table). The Italian students seem to feel the least burden from parental expectations, German students are somewhere in the middle, and Kyrgyz students have by far the heaviest burden on their shoulders. It is not enough that they will have a 'good position' – which is important for most parents in all three countries – but additionally young Kyrgyz people must become important, famous and rich. These are very high expectations that Italian and German young people only rarely have to struggle with.

Table 7.1 Parental expectations as perceived by students in Kyrgyzstan and other countries.

For my parents it is important that ...	German (*N* = 63)		Italian (*N* = 75)		Kyrgyz (*N* = 40)	
	Very true	True	Very true	True	Very true	True
I realize my own wishes	62%	35%	81%	16%	58%	25%
I will have a good position	44%	49%	27%	60%	60%	28%
I will be father/ mother of a family	44%	46%	19%	53%	63%	20%
I will be an important/ famous person	10%	6%	0%	8%	33%	20%
I will become rich	8%	13%	0%	20%	28%	36%

In the short essays on their own childhoods that the students wrote in Study IV, Kyrgyz students hardly ever complained about anything that characterized their childhood. Quite to the contrary, their statements were very respectful towards their parents, and they thanked them for the life, food and upbringing their parents gave them; thankfulness is what the rules of respect ask of them. This lifelong indebtedness of children for the life and upbringing their parents have given them can be found in many countries of the global South (Cole and Durham, 2007). However, some young Kyrgyz people's rebelliousness became apparent in their statements regarding what differences they wanted for their own children in the future, as can be seen in the following remarks made by different students:

I will allow them to choose their own speciality/occupation. Not like me. (Male, 24 years)

I want my children to have a different childhood from mine. I want them to study at a school which they want to study in. (Female, 18 years)

I want my children to have a different childhood. Also I want them to choose a profession which they would like. (Female, 18 years)

I will give to my children freedom of choice, i.e. I didn't have such freedom. (Female, 20 years)

Of course I want my children to live differently. Because now everything is developing. They have a chance to live differently. (Female, 25 years)

They gave me everything, never limited in anything. But they didn't give me an opportunity to make a decision about my studies by myself. (Female, 20 years)

While the pressure to succeed, and to succeed by playing the game according to the rules of the parents, is mostly accepted, it seems to be experienced as a constriction in several cases. It is remarkable that the complaints of the students focus so much on education and the freedom of choice with regard to education. Undoubtedly one of the promises that come with education is an entitlement to self-oriented decision-making. This also seems to be the promise for young people in a country where the urge to succeed is primordial, and where minors are compliant with adults' projects.

Conclusion: Children's Unheard Voices

Education is praised as a cure-all for poor and structurally weak countries by development organizations. This message finds fertile ground in Kyrgyzstan, where labour market opportunities remain more than limited and force people to emigrate and work in fields other than the ones they were educated in. Nevertheless – and it seems even a fortiori – parents expect their children and the youth in general to be most successful through education and to realize stunning careers; not only the children themselves, but also their parents should profit just as much from their success. Hence, Kyrgyz children and youth are put under considerable pressure to succeed. Little space remains for the realization of another promise also being structurally implicated in modern education: the chance to make one's own decisions according to personal preferences and talents. While children accept parents' demands and develop their plans and visions accordingly and in a compliant way, there seems to be some rebelliousness among young people. This is also shown by

Schwittek (2017), who speaks of 'double facework' to characterize the strategic attempts by young adults in Kyrgyzstan to realize at least some of their own wishes while still fulfilling their parents' expectations.

Of course, the results presented in this chapter are not meant to be interpreted as a request to diminish the efforts to improve and enhance education in the country. Rather, they are a critique directed towards education experts who are active and influential in the country. Such experts – most often consultants working for international organizations – are insensitive to local conditions. Their production of knowledge seems guided by a fascination with their inventory of techniques and terms, which they implement all over the world in a more or less uniform way. Hence, they attempt to improve teaching methods, curricula, school management and methods of assessment, trying to implement knowledge of the best educational strategies while assuming they are globally valid. When it comes to the impact this may have on children's lives, they often generalize based on experiences from completely different contexts. In this way, the World Bank is basing its prognosis of the worldwide return value of kindergartens on experiences in the underprivileged areas of US cities.[9] Meanwhile, they are rather ignorant of and disinterested in the perspectives and experiences of local people, especially of local children, and do not consider what their promises, recommendations and interventions might mean for children's lives in specific contexts. This is clearly a problem with regard to the pressures Kyrgyz children have to cope with. It is also a problem with regard to the possible quality of educational programmes in a long-term perspective. The inflated and compulsory aspirations of parents and children to be upwardly mobile, which are far beyond any structurally given opportunities, are neither a promising base for realistic personal horizons, nor for society's long-term development. Therefore, an adjustment to this bias is needed – for the sake of children and young people, but also for the development of a labour force in harmony with local opportunities and with goals of civic engagement and social cohesion. An adequate educational system would have to be in the service of a local society's many-faceted demands, rather than mere human capital accumulation and illusory promises.

Notes

1   See www.lessonsforlifefoundation.org/education-changes-everything
2   www.demos.org/blog/12/2/15/why-education-does-not-fix-poverty
3   World Bank Data: personal remittances; at: https://data.worldbank.org/indicator/BX.TRF.PWKR.DT.GD.ZS?year_high_desc=true)

4   In comparison: the gross national income per capita (GNI) is estimated at US$1,100 for 2016; http://databank.worldbank.org/data/download/GNIPC.pdf

5   For further information on the background to this project and the network of researchers, go to www.cuwb.org (last accessed 10 September 2019).

6   See e.g. the promises made in UNESCO (2016).

7   Somewhat more than half of Kyrgyz households are nuclear families meaning that old couples almost never live alone; there are mostly several siblings who might live with old parents once they are married (UNDP, 2010).

8   Article 37.2, Constitution of the Kyrgyz Republic, 2010; at: www.wipo.int/wipolex/en/text.jsp?file_id=254747

9   For instance, the World Bank referred on its homepage to the results of Carneiro and Heckman (2003), who were both economists working for the World Bank.

References

Aga Khan University (ed.) (2014) *In Search of Relevance and Sustainability of Educational Change*. Karachi: Aga Khan University, Institute for Educational Development. Available at: http://ecommons.aku.edu/cgi/viewcontent.cgi?article=1050&context=books

Asian Development Bank (2015) 'Assessment of higher education: Kyrgyz Republic'. Available at: www.adb.org/data/main

Bonal, X. (2007) 'On global absences: reflections on the failings in the education and poverty relationship in Latin America', *International Journal of Educational Development*, 27(1): 86–100.

Braunmiller, A. (2016) *Kirgisistan. Daten & Analysen zum Hochschul- und Wissenschaftsstandort*. Bonn: DAAD. Available at: www.daad.de/medien/der-daad/analysen-studien/bildungssystemanalyse/kirgisistan_daad_bsa.pdf

Bühler-Niederberger, D. and Schwittek, J. (2014) 'Young children in Kyrgyzstan: agency in tight hierarchical structures', *Childhood*, 21(4): 502–516.

Carneiro, P. and Heckman, J. (2003) *Human Capital Policy*. Working Paper 9495. Cambridge, MA: National Bureau of Economic Research. Available at: www.nber.org/papers/w9495

Chase, R.M.J. and Diffey, L. (2010) Life story board: a tool in the prevention of domestic violence. *Pimitisiwin: A Journal of Aboriginal and Indigenous Community Health*, 8(2): 10.

CIA (2017) *CIA World Factbook*. Available at: www.cia.gov/library/publications/the-world-factbook

Cole, J. and Durham, D. (eds) (2007) *Generations and Globalization*. Bloomington: Indiana University Press.

DeYoung, A., Zoldoshalieva, R. and Zoldoshalieva, U. (2013) 'Creating and contesting meanings of place and community in Ylai Talaa Valley of Kyrgyzstan', *Central Asian Survey*, 32(2): 161–174

Dümmler, J. (2011) *Ergänzungen zur Bildungsmarktanalyse Kirgisistan*. Bonn: DAAD.

Esengul, C. (2012) *Youth and Public Policy in Kyrgyzstan*. New York: International Debate Education Association.

Fattore, T., Fegter, S. and Hunner-Kreisel, C. (2015) 'Interview protocol and notes. Multi-National Qualitative Study of Children's Well-being. Stage 1 & 2'. Unpublished paper.

Gallacher, L.A. and Gallagher M. (2008) 'Methodological immaturity in childhood research? Thinking through "participatory methods"', *Childhood*, 15(4): 499–516.

Ginsburg, N. (2009) *Active Learning Pedagogies as a Reform Initiative*. Washington, DC: U.S. Agency for International Development (USAID).

Kamat, S. (2012) 'The poverty of theory: the World Bank's system approach to education policy', in S.J. Klees, J. Samoff and N.P. Stromquist (eds), *The World Bank and Education: Critiques and Alternatives*. Rotterdam: Sense Publishers. pp. 33–48.

Klees, S.J. (2012) 'The World Bank and education: ideological premises and ideological conclusions', in S.J. Klees, J. Samoff and N.P. Stromquist (eds), *The World Bank and Education: Critiques and Alternatives*. Rotterdam: Sense Publishers. pp. 49–68.

Mundy, K. (2002) 'Retrospect and prospect: education in a reforming World Bank', *International Journal of Educational Development*, 22(5): 483–508.

OECD (2007) *PISA 2006. Science Competencies for Tomorrow's World. Executive Summary*. Available at: www.oecd.org/pisa/pisaproducts/39725224.pdf

Punch, S. (2002) 'Research with children: the same or different from research with adults?', *Childhood*, 9(3): 321–341.

Sabzalieva, E. (2015) 'Challenges in contemporary education in Kyrgyzstan, Central Asia', *Perspectives: Policy and Practice in Higher Education*, 19(2): 49–55.

Schwittek, J. (2017) *Double Facework: Aushandlungsprozesse junger Erwachsen in Kirgistan zwischen Selbst und Kollektiv*. Opladen: Budrich UniPress.

Shamatow, D. (2014) 'Improvement of education quality', in Aga Khan University (ed.), *In Search of Relevance and Sustainability of Educational Change*. Karachi: Aga Khan University, Institute for Educational Development. pp. 282–289.

Türkyilmaz, A. (2018) *Zwischen 'Sich-Verbessern' und 'Selbst-Sein'. Ungleiche Familienprogramme*. München, Weinheim: Beltz Juventa.

UNDP (2010) *Successful Youth – Successful Country*. NHDR Report. Bishkek: UNDP.

UNESCO (2016) *Education for People and Planet: Global Education Monitoring Report* (2nd edn). Paris: UNESCO. Available at: http://unesdoc.unesco.org/images/0024/002457/245752e.pdf

UNICEF (2007) *Multiple Indicator Cluster Survey, 2006: Kyrgyz Republic. Final Report*. Bishkek: National Statistical Committee of the Kyrgyz Republic.

UNICEF (2011) *Youth, Livelihoods and Peace Promotion: A Knowledge, Attitudes and Practice. Study among Youth aged 15–28 in Osh and Jalal-Abad Provinces*. Bishkek: UNICEF.

Wedgewood, R. (2005) 'Education and poverty reduction in Tanzania', paper presented at 8th UKFIET International Conference on Education and Development, Oxford, 13–15 September. Available at: tdsnfp.org/wp-content/uploads/2013/06/Education-and-Poverty-Reduction-in-Tanzania.pdf

World Bank (2001) *A Directory of Early Child Development Projects in Africa*. Available at: www-wds.worldbank.org/external/default/WDSContentServer/WDSP/IB/2001/12/11/000094946_01110204011226/Rendered/PDF/multi0page.pdf

World Bank (2013) *SABER Country Report – Kyrgyz Republic: Early Childhood Development*. Washington, DC: World Bank.

Yarkova, T. (2004) 'Applying the concepts of legitimacy and trust in Kyrgyzstan', in C. Harrington, A. Salem and T. Zurabishvili (eds), *After Communism: Critical Perspectives on Society and Sociology*. Bern: Peter Lang. pp. 129–140.

8

Child Abuse and Neglect in India

Locating Child Abuse in Fractured Indian Families Through Children's Lenses

Vinod Chandra

Introduction

Child abuse and neglect in India is often a hidden phenomenon especially when it happens in domestic space by family members. It is generally presumed that the family is the safest place for children; however, in last few decades, Indian families are going through a transition stage where various structural changes are taking place. Earlier, Indian families were marked out as joint families which were later replaced by a nuclear family setup mainly in urban settings. Among these, the poor nuclear families that depend on daily wages for their subsistence face an acute crisis in case of the sudden demise of any of the earning members or the break-up of familial relationships. The economic hardship of such families hit the children and they become the most vulnerable unit in the family. In such circumstances, children fall into the trap of emotional, physical and even sexual abuse; and also ill treatment and neglect by the adult family members. The negative impact of these fractured families on child's emotional wellbeing has been neglected by child protection laws and strategies. Numbers of cases of child abuse in the family settings are hard to estimate because most of these crimes are hidden and prevailing social attitude about the safety net of children in family settings does not give a scope to legally protect children against abuse in these settings. Although, child abuses such as child marriage, child labour and exploitation, malnutrition, lack of education, poor health, neglect, etc., are duly recognised in various forms by the Indian legal system and Juvenile Justice System, the abuse of children in family settings has been largely unnoticed.

Incidence of Child Abuse and Neglect in India

India is home to almost 19 percent world's children. More than one third of the country's population, around 440 million, is below 18 years of age. In 2007, the Government of India's Ministry of Women and Child Development had released an exhaustive report on child abuse which drew attention towards the high incidence of child abuse in India. This report was based on a survey conducted in thirteen states. It reported that in the age group of 13–18-year-olds, 23.2 percent of children experience physical abuse who were not attending school, 26.5 percent of children experience some form of emotional abuse in their family settings and 30.5 percent of school-going children experience corporal punishment at school. More shockingly, 49.9 percent of children experienced sexual abuse in their daily lives (Kacker et al., 2007). In another study in India, the International Society for Prevention of Child Abuse and Neglect (ISPCAN) indicated that 29 percent of children face harsh physical disciplining methods by parents (Runyan et al., 2010). Seventy percent of children reported physical punishments and 35 percent of children experience neglect (Zolotor et al., 2009).

The National Commission for Protection of Child Rights (NCPCR), the Government of India's ombudsman of childrens' rights, published a report in 2012 based on the survey conducted in 2009–10 in seven states in which it was stated that 99.7 percent of children reported one or other form of punishment, 81.2 percent of children reported an outward rejection when on the ground of learning experiences. In the context of corporal punishment, 75 percent of children experienced physical punishment such as caning and 69 percent of children were slapped in school (NCPCR Report, 2012). A similar study conducted in Tripura, India revealed that 20.9 percent of children experience psychological abuse, 21.9 percent of children experience physical abuse and 18.1 percent of children experience sexual abuse (Deb and Modak, 2010). According to a recently held national survey by the Ministry of Women and Child Development, carried out by the NGO Prayas in association with UNICEF and Save the Children (2017), 50 percent of children in India are subjected to one or other form of physical abuse. The survey showed that among children, more boys are physically abused than girls. A considerable rise in the incidence of abuse and crime against children in India has also been reported in the last couple of years (*Handbook for Ending Violence Against Children* in association with Childfund in 2018). According to the report, 'during 2016, a total of 106,958 cases of crimes against children were reported in the country as compared to 89,423 cases during 2014, an increase of about 20 per cent' (NCPCR, 2018, Vol 1, page 31).

The National Institute of Public Cooperation and Child Development (NIPCCD) (1988) indicates that the lack of sensitivity to child abuse in India can be attributed to the widespread acceptance of corporal punishment and the belief in the right of parents to determine what is best for their children. Nevertheless, the privacy of the family is being questioned as human service professionals (Ashtekar, 1989; Mehta, 1982), social scientists (Nath & Kohli, 1988; Rane, 1988), and even media reporters (Menon, 1987; Srinivasan, 1989) are beginning to discuss the widespread prevalence of child abuse around the country.

The Indian Parliament had passed an Act in 2012 and made stringent laws to control sexual offences against young girls in India by introducing the Protection of Children against Sexual Offences Act (POCSO). Nonetheless, since the implementation of POCSO, the reported cases of sexual abuse has been increasing and according to daily newspaper *The Times of India* (July 9, 2015) eight cases of sexual abuse of young girls were registered every day in the previous two years. About 6,816 police cases were registered between November 2012 and March 2015. As per the records of National Crime Records Bureau (NCRB) the conviction rate is 2.4 percent out of total registered police cases of sexual offences and in 389 cases the accused were acquitted. Another survey conducted by the National Crime Records Bureau (NCRB) reported an increase in the number of child abuse cases registered under POCSO Act from 8,904 in the year 2014 to 14,913 in 2015. In 94.8 percent of POCSO cases, girls were raped by someone who was known to them. The highest numbers of First Information Reports (FIR) have been registered in Rajasthan followed by Maharashtra, Uttar Pradesh, Madhya Pradesh and Kerala according to data available from the National Commission for Protection of Child Rights (NCPCR). The number of convictions is only 166, that is 2.4 percent of the total cases registered, while in 389 cases the accused were acquitted. According to Government data, children are also subjected to gross abuses in the very sheltered homes that are made to protect them. There were 932 cases of abuses and violations registered in child care institutions in 2013–14, according to data provided by the National Commission for Protection of Child Rights. Of these, 532 cases were registered in Uttar Pradesh alone. In 2013–14, there were a total of 192 registered cases of abuse and 71 in 2014 alone. Apart from that, there were 481 registered cases against the young girls in 2013–14, and 54 cases in 2014 alone. In the last few months, gruesome cases of abuse in child care shelters have raised the question of safety in these homes.

Towards a Conceptual Definition of Child Abuse and Neglect

Finkelhor and Korbin (1988: 4) in their article on child abuse as an international issue, proposed a universal definition of child abuse as 'the portion of harm to children that results from human action that is proscribed, proximate and preventable'. This definition distinguishes it from the social, economic, and health problems and concerns, and allows its application to a range of situations and cultural contexts. In 1988, the National Seminar on Child Abuse in India defined child abuse as 'an intentional, non-accidental injury, maltreatment of children by parents, caretakers, employers, or others including those individuals representing governmental/ nongovernmental bodies which may lead to temporal or permanent impairment of their physical, mental and psychosocial development, disability or death' (NIPCCD 1988:10).

The National Centre on Child Abuse and Neglect (an agency of Federal Government of US) and The International Society for Prevention of Child Abuse and Neglect (ISPCAN) have given their definitions of child abuse and neglect. However, the most comprehensive and expanded definition of child abuse was proposed by World Health Organization (WHO) in 1999 in its report of the Consultation on Child Abuse Prevention which states that 'child abuse and maltreatment constitutes all the forms of physical and/or emotional ill-treatment, sexual abuse, neglect or negligent treatment or commercial or other exploitation, resulting in actual or potential harm to the child's health, survival, development or dignity in the context of a relationship of responsibility, trust or power' (WHO, 1999). In light of the Convention of Rights of the Child (CRC), child abuse is a violation of basic human rights of the child who is a person below the age of 18 years. Child abuse can result from physical, emotional, or sexual harm. According to UNICEF, violence against children can be physical and mental abuse and injury, neglect or negligent treatment, exploitation and sexual abuse. Violence may take place in homes, schools, orphanages, residential care facilities, on the streets, in the workplace, in prisons and in places of detention.

Child abuse which occurs in the form of an action is highly recognized; however, there is also evidence of inaction that cause harm that can be defined as neglect. Child neglect is an act of 'inattention or omission by the caregiver to provide for the child: health, education, emotional development, nutrition, shelter and safe living conditions' (WHO, 1999). Any act of the parent, guardian or any caregiver which harms the child's physical and mental health or affects moral and spiritual development is treated as child neglect.

Despite the fact that India has strong laws and legal instruments to check and control all possible forms of child abuse, the reported crime against children in India, both within and outside the family, is on the increase. The high incidence of child abuse and neglect is a cause of concern for child protection activists, childhood researchers and child rights practitioners. In the backdrop of the present scenario, the chapter explores the nature and form of child abuse in broken families. It also attempts to find out whether children consider poverty as the root cause of their abuse and neglect. The chapter highlights children's subjective understanding of 'abuse' and their 'parental relationship' in order to find out whether abuse and neglect in broken families dislocate children from the family relationship.

Family as a Site of Child Abuse: Literature Review

A substantive body of literature has documented various forms of child abuse in India in the last three decades. Child labour (Satyarthi, 1989), child prostitution (Ashtekar, 1989; Nath and Kohli, 1988), child marriage (Jabbi, 1986), and child beggary (Rane et al., 1986), are all forms of abuse that, though perhaps supported by families, are in fact perpetuated by society. Parental child abuse that occurs within the boundaries of the family has failed to elicit a similar response from proponents of child welfare. It appears that this may well be because, in addition to the general acceptance of parental supremacy, little is known about the magnitude of the problem, the causes of parental child abuse, or the short- and long-term effects of abusive behaviour on children.

Family environment and interpersonal relationship between father and mother play a significant role in the wellbeing and development of children. Early childhood settings are important in promoting health and a feeling of wellbeing for children, their families and ultimately their communities (Hayden and Macdonald, 2000). There is an increasing amount of research that indicates the role of family in individual functioning. Healthy family relations with happy marital relations and parenting behaviours, are conducive of well-functioning parents and children, while parental mental health problems, marital conflict, low quality parenting determine dysfunctions for children (e.g., low academic achievement, psychological problems, etc.; Robila and Krishnakumar, 2006). A family shares emotional relationships, common values, goals and responsibilities. These relationships are part of our daily lives and are central for human existence. Families have a pivotal role to care for their loved ones, and, in the case of children, ready them for healthy, happy and productive lives as active contributors to society. The capacity of parents to provide the key functions associated with optimal care for their children is absolutely central. Loving care, a secure attachment, sufficient structure for healthy growth and development, non-coercive discipline and an overall safe family environment characterized by empathic relationships are among the important factors needed to raise healthy and well-adjusted children. Healthy family relationships help all members of a family feel safe and connected to one another.

Strong positive relationships contribute to building a feeling of trust and support. A positive social environment and relationships also help in stress management when faced with difficult times. The foundation for healthy relationships and wellness develops from the family. Families provide a model from where to discover how to build relationships throughout lives. Children who have a model of healthy relationships from their families are better able to create these relationships outside their families, that is, with other children and adults in their lives. Additionally, family provides a sense of security to children, knowing their family members love and protect one another. A warm and safe family environment helps children learn, develop and experience what strong relationships look like.

Family relationships impact health and healthcare utilization as well. For example, evidence has shown that marital conflict negatively impacted health and healthcare utilization in older couples (Sandberg et.al., 2009) and that family and marital support were associated with better treatment adherence and illness adaptation (e.g. Trief et al., 2003). Family support is also significant in mental ill-health treatments, determining better outcomes and fewer remissions. The WHO report (2004) on *Prevention of Mental Disorders: Effective Interventions and Policy Options* indicated that 'individual and family related risk and protective factors can be biological, emotional, cognitive, behavioural, interpersonal or related to the family context' (2004: 22). These factors have strong impacts at different moments in the lifespan and could be transmitted from one generation to another (e.g., depression, anxiety, alcohol abuse).

There is large body of literature on the adult population exploring the link between subjective wellbeing – 'a person's cognitive and affective evaluations of his or her life' (Diener et al., 2002: 63) – and social relationships (Diener and Seligman, 2002; Lewis and Lyo, 1986; Michalos et al., 2001; Ganglmair-Wooliscroft and Lawson, 2008). Happy people tend to have stronger social relationships than less happy people (Diener and Seligman, 2002). Findings from these studies on adults suggest that social relationships influence individuals' psychological wellbeing by providing love, intimacy, and guidance.

Over the last few decades researchers have become increasingly interested in children's subjective wellbeing (Bradshaw et al., 2007; Cummins and Lau, 2005; Fattore et al. 2007), with an emphasis on the relational aspects. For example, Huebner (1991a, 1991b, 1994) suggested that child's relationships with family and friends are two important domains of their wellbeing. There has been an increasing focus on relating child abuse and neglect to family dysfunction.

The *World Report on Violence and Health on Child Abuse* (Krug et al., 2002) has linked certain characteristics of the caregiver as well as the features of the family environment to child abuse and neglect. While some demographic factors are related to variation in risk, others are related to psychological and behavioural aspects of the family environment that may compromise parenting and lead to child maltreatment.

Physically abusive parents are more likely to be young, single, poor, and unemployed. In both developing and industrialised countries, poor, young, single mothers are among those at greater risk for using violence towards their children (National Research Council, 1993; Sariola and Uutela, 1996; Straus et al, 1998). Size of family also relates to the abuse of children: a study from Chile (Larrain et al., 1997) found that families with four or more children were three times more likely to be violent towards their children than parents with fewer children. Unstable family environments, in which the composition of the household frequently changes as family members and others move in and out, are a feature particularly noted in cases of chronic neglect (Dubowitz et al., 2001; National Research Council, 1993). Another major factor impacting child abuse in households is related to intimate partner violence. Data from studies as geographically and culturally distinct as China, Colombia, Egypt, India, Mexico, Philippines, South Africa and the United States have all found a strong relationship between these two forms of violence (Frias-Armenta and McCloskey, 1998; Hunter et al., 2000; Klevens et al., 2000; Madu and Peltzer, 2000; National Research Council, 1993; Tang, 1997; Youssef et al., 1998). A study in India also showed that the occurrence of domestic violence in the home doubled the risk of child abuse (Hunter et al., 2000).

In the mid- to late 1980s, a few researchers speculated that family transitions experienced by children can have harmful effects on their adjustment (Brody, et al.,1988; Furstenberg and Seltzer, 1986). Transitions include parents' separation, cohabiting romantic partner's move into, or out of, the home of a single parent, remarriage of a single (non-cohabiting) parent, or disruption of marriage. A growing body of literature suggests that children who experience multiple transitions in family structure may fare worse developmentally than children raised in stable two-parent families (Fomby and Cherlin, 2007). For instance, in a study by Barnow et al. (2001), researchers reported that parenting behaviour including harsh punishment and emotional rejection and separation at an early age affected the child's behaviour in terms of aggressiveness, depression, delinquency, sexual abuse, physical abuse and social problems. Wilson et al. (1980) reported that abuse and neglect were both maximal in father-only homes and minimal in two natural parent homes. Mother-only households exceed those with one natural and one stepparent in incidence of neglect. Also, the study discussed the evidence of an unrelated adult filling a parental role.

The vast literature on the subject, thus portrays light on the matter and highlights the impact of domestic violence and child abuse on children's health, development, academic performance, etc. Scholars with a child protectionist viewpoint have done extensive research on issues like insecurity and anxiety, depression and drug abuse, cognitive and behavioural problems among children. However, there is a dearth of literature on child abuse from the children's perspective. Only limited research has appeared on children's views of their abuse and neglect in broken families and/or single families, which has explored how these children locate themselves in an environment of abuse and neglect in fractured or broken families (e.g. Aktar, 2013; Chan, et al. 2011; Masson and Falloon, 1999; 2001; Ney et al., 1986; Sharma and Sharma, 2016).

Methodology and Data Collection

The research design I selected for this study was an exploratory-cum-descriptive research design, in which I selected seven cases of *child abuse* and neglect in fractured families that were produced before the Child Welfare Committee (CWC) of Lucknow, India, from 2014 to 2016. The operational definition of a fractured family for the purpose of study entails any family where parents are separated or have strained relationships which disrupt the normal life of all the members of the family. In this type of family, crises may have arisen due to any misconception, misunderstanding, unacceptance, mishappening, etc. These crises may even lead to divorce of parents, discarding of children by parents, ignoring the care of children and abandonment of other family members.

The study was conducted by the author of this chapter who happens to be the member of Child Welfare Committee (a statutory body constituted under the Juvenile Justice Act 2007) of Lucknow. In the data collection process, a research assistant who worked as counsellor under Integrated Child Protection Scheme (ICPS) in Lucknow, had helped me. Standard ethical code of conduct was adhered to and permission from the Child Welfare Committee Lucknow and from other gatekeepers (parents and care-takers) was attained. My understanding and knowledge of the issues related to Juvenile Justice Act and handling of conversation with children in difficult circumstances and children in need of care and protection were effective and facilitated the development of strategy of building relationships with participants. In the course of data collection, I was not only open and neutral but also particular about inclusion of children as respectful participants in the study.

The research engages a qualitative analysis approach, which is the examination, analysis and interpretation of personal interviews of children and their family members. Group interviews were also conducted with children and their families to discover underlying meanings and patterns of child abuse and children's relationships with their parents as well as abusers. The children included in the study were aged seven to eighteen. The total sample for this study was made up of ten children of both sexes from seven case studies.

The instrument for data collection was an interview schedule made up of ten probing questions. The items in the interview schedule included personal data, family status – whether an intact or broken family, socio-economic status of family, level of education, number of persons living in their homes and family attachment (e.g., family activities, vacations, love, affection, bonding and communication). The specific inquiry was made regarding the form and nature of abuse experienced by the child.

Children's Narratives of Abuse and Neglect in the Family: Case-I

Zoya: They are there to look after you, but suddenly you get to know that they're not rather they abuse you, it's very painful…

Zoya Khan was a resident of Sitapur. She was wandering near Lokbandhu hospital when the helpline volunteers found her. After questioning her about her identity, no satisfactory answers were reported. She was then taken to Balgrih and after staying there for one day, she was taken for counselling. When the counsellor met her, she started the therapy sessions.

During the therapy sessions she revealed:

I am Zoya and live in Sitapur with two little sisters and my mother and father. My father is a carpenter and mother is a part-time worker in a sewing factory, she also works as [a] domestic help at some places. I have to look after my sisters and do most of the household work. I am 14 years old and used to go to school. I loved my school and my friends' company. But I was forced to leave the school and do the housework.

My father loves me, but he is an alcoholic due to which there is often a quarrel between my parents. He often beats my mother when he comes back from work. My mother gets fed up and she beats me a lot. You can see the mark on my face, two days back she hit me with *Chimta*.[tongs] Earlier I used to visit some of my friends living nearby, but now with all the housework and taking of care of my sisters, I do not get time to go out. There is not a single moment of happiness and enjoyment. All work and no play.

Two days back, I wanted to go my cousin's wedding at my aunt's place. She only lived in Sitapur, but my mother refused to let me go. I was feeling very trapped, I wanted to meet my cousin with whom I played in childhood. I thought what is the point of staying in such a house where no one cares about my feelings. So when my mother left home for her work, I escaped from the house. I took a bus where I met a lady who was kind to me and offered to take me to my aunt's house. But she came to Lucknow and when the policeman got suspicious and started asking about me, she left me near the hospital.

I was roaming about here and there as I did not know anybody. I was very hungry and tired also. After two days of roaming, I could not understand where to go. Then I met two boys who have brought me to this home.

The counsellor asked her again, 'Do you want to go back home?' 'I will die, but won't go back home', Zoya replied.

She stayed in a girls' shelter for one week. A week later when the next meeting of the CWC was held and her father and mother were called in to meet Zoya, she broke down in tears but asked the Committee to give her more time to decide whether she would go back with her parents. In the next couple of days the counsellor had another opportunity to talk to Zoya and explored the experiences of abuse and how Zoya has seen abuse in the relationship within the family. Specific acts such as 'pushing', 'smacking', 'slapping', 'pulling hair', etc., were common abuse by her parents. She informed us that sometimes the parents don't provide her food for hours, just for a small mistake. Zoya's father was abusive to her mother and in return her mother was abusive to her. She says:

> My father normally comes back home in a drunk state and demands food of his choice. Most of the time my mother provides him all those, which he asks for, but sometimes when she fails to provide ... she was abused by him ... I don't like all this.

> In fact, abuse is a normal feature of my family. My father is the boss and he wants his orders only [to be followed] ...

> When I was younger, I didn't care [about] all those things but as I grew up and started going out and mixing with my friends, I realized that whatever happened to my mother was not good, but as you know ... I didn't have a say in my family so I always kept silent ...

> Even my mother never complains about the attitude of my father to anyone. So we have taken all this as normal.

Children's Narratives of Abuse and Neglect in the Family: Case-II

Savita: I pray to god [that] no one should have father who is *unlike father*... [who] has no respect for daughters or wife.

A girl of 16, Savita was brought by a teacher from her school to the CWC, where her case was represented by the teacher. 'She has been continuously crying since morning', the teacher said. '"I don't want to go home", are the only words she's uttering. We kept asking her, but she did not utter a single word. So we decided to bring her here. I think she needs a good counsellor.'

The CWC then decided to offer her counselling. The counsellor, Sangeeta, asked, 'What is wrong my dear? Tell me, I won't let anybody know.' After about two hours, Savita started to speak.

I was very happy with my father, mother and elder brother. But then about four years back my father died in an accident. For about a year my mother worked in houses and tried to feed us. But soon she got fed up of her work and decided to marry again to run the family smoothly. It was my father's friend with whom she got married to. Earlier he used to visit us and was very kind to us. But things changed after he became my father. For some time everything was fine. My mother was happy that she got a bread winner and she had to work less then. But after a year or so, my stepfather changed his attitude. When [he] used to come back home mostly he used to be irritated and shout at us. We were scared. But eventually I got used to this kind of routine. Everything was again in a routine way when I noticed some change in my father's attitude. He became sympathetic and [a] little soft with me. I was a bit surpris[ed], but I liked that he was caring for me. Three months back, when my mother was working as a domestic help in other houses and my brother had gone to his friend's house, I was alone in the house. My father came back a bit early from work and I made tea for him and was going back to do my work. Just then he held my hand and asked me to sit near him. At first I was happy because he was giving attention to me. But then …

She started crying again. The counsellor said, 'don't worry my dear, you can tell me everything'. She said 'he held me tightly here', as she pointed at her breast, 'and he started kissing me here and there, leave me, leave me! I said, but he said don't worry dear I won't do any harm, you are my good girl. I felt like running from there, but he made me sit on the bed forcibly, I was very scared and didn't know what to do. Then he removed my clothes, and then and then', she started weeping again.

I can't tell you anymore, he did a very bad thing. I was very uncomfortable. Don't tell anyone about this, not even your mother, he told me, otherwise she'll beat you. I'll get you nice clothes for Diwali, you are my darling.

I ran from there, and went to the park. I sat there and cried for long. It became dark when I came back. My mother asked me what was wrong, looking at my face. I didn't speak a word. Then she became busy. In the night, when my stepfather went to his friend's house, I told everything to my mother.

'Keep quiet, completely silent, don't tell to anyone', she said and I had to be silent. Next day when I went to school I was very serious. My favourite teacher asked me 'what is wrong my dear', looking at my face and I burst into tears, she got really worried and brought me here.

After an hour her mother came running into the committee. Since the counsellor had told the whole story to the members, they were very angry. They asked her to call her husband as he should be jailed. But the woman begged in front of the CWC members and said, 'Sir, please save him, if my husband goes to jail, how will I run my family?'. However, a case was lodged against him and he was sent to jail for his crime.

With regard to discord between a father and mother and its impact on the child with reference to abuse, Savita had this to say:

If you have the right man as a father then it is fine, otherwise it is not good to live with anyone who pretend[s] to be your father ... anyone can't be your father, whether your mother accept[s] him as husband ...

My step-father is not a good man... he used my mother for his own sake. He keep abusing her but I don't understand why mother is still living with him ...

She should have left him and saved our lives too.

I don't like anyone who abuses or touches me whether it is my family member or a friend.

Children's Narratives of Abuse and Neglect in the Family: Case-III

Raj: After the loss of my mother my father lost interest in us and we started feeling so lonely. We [both] are so scared of my father and don't want stay with him...

Another case, of Raj, 13 years old, and Renu, 16 years old, brother and sister, was presented before the CWC in which the custody of the boy Raj was to be decided by the CWC: whether to award it to the child's grand-mother or to the father. The parties were in complete opposition. They were shouting and blaming each other. Raj was taken to the counsellor and after a few sessions he spoke:

My *didi* [elder sister], I and my mother and father were a happy family. My mother was a Christian and my father is Hindu. About a year ago my mother was travelling by a rickshaw and a mini bus pushed the rickshaw so badly that she fell [out]. She hurt her head and became unconscious. She was taken to hospital by some people who notified my dad and *nani* [maternal grand-mother] later. The treatment started but there was no improvement in her condition. She was getting worse and after four days' she left us. I was there in the hospital when I heard that she is no more. I cried. My *nani*, my 16-year-old sister and my *mausi* [mother's sister] were there. My sister was also crying. My *nani* and my *mausi* consoled us. They took us to their house. My dad was also sad. The next day my mother was cremated according to her wish in [a] Christian crematorium. We stayed at *nani*'s house for [a] few days. Then my father took us. My father was a busy person. He used to spend most of his time in his office. We started going to school again, life was coming back to normal, but without mom everything was so quiet that we didn't like it anymore. Most of the time we two were alone at home. Then my father decided to send my sister to [a] hostel. I didn't like the idea. But he was strict so I couldn't say anything. We went to drop her to [the] hostel. Now I was very lonely. So my father sent me to *nani*'s house for some days. I went to school from there only. In a week's time I came back. When my *nani* dropped me at home, I saw a lady sitting in my house and chatting with my dad. My dad introduced her as my mother's friend. Then I also recalled her, she also used to teach in my school. Then I found her coming every day to my house. When I next talked to *nani* and my sister I told them about this lady. My *nani* told me to stay away from her. Soon I noticed that aunty was getting close to my dad. I didn't like it, but I couldn't do anything about it.

Whenever my dad used to come late from work, he used to ask my aunt to pick me from school and take me home. I didn't like aunty but I had to come with her. She was very rude. She never used to ask me to eat anything. As soon as we reached home she used to go to rest and I was left to change my clothes and eat whatever I could take on my own. I missed my mom every day and cried a lot. When my sister got to know about all this she was very angry and asked my *nani*, 'Who's this lady? I have a feeling that she is trying to take my mom's place, which we both will not allow.'

Nani tried to talk to my dad regarding this. But my dad always avoided the situation. Things were getting worse day by day. Now the lady sometimes used to stay also at my house and sleep in my mom's room. She used to wear my mom's clothes and used her makeup. And my dad was the one who was giving [her] all this. I hated all this.

One day I was passing through my father's room when I heard her saying, 'Your son is becoming very naughty, and he doesn't listen to me. He wants to play all the time, doesn't want to study or do any housework. I think I should be a little strict with him otherwise he will cross his limits', and my dad said, 'it's up to you my dear, do whatever you think is good for him'.

I was stunned. Is this my dad? Mummy where have you gone? Why have I [got] to face all this? *Didi* has also gone to [a] hostel. What will I do now, I'm all alone. I wept till late at night. Next day my *nani* came home and I told her the whole story. She said she will talk to dad and she had a word with him. But when she came out of his room she was disappointed and was shouting, 'I will not tolerate this, first you have ditched my daughter and now you're troubling my grandchildren. I will not let them stay with you. It's good that Renu has gone to [the] hostel, at least she doesn't have to face all that this poor little boy is facing. I am going to take my boy with me, you live with your friend and stay away from him.'

She took me to her house. In the evening my dad came to *nani*'s house. He wanted to take me back but she refused. They both had a verbal fight. She said that she will file a case against him and request keeping me with her. So she filed a case.

During the case proceedings, Renu and Raj both were presented in front of the CWC members and were asked whether they wanted to go to their father's house or *nani*'s house. Renu said, 'I would rather stay in the hostel and whenever I'll have holidays I would like to go to *nani*'s house.'

The members of CWC asked her, 'Why don't you want to be with your father?' She replied, 'he is more of a friend of that lady than our father. It seems rude but it is true. It looks as if he was never married to our mom. He has completely forgotten her. Neither has he any love towards my brother nor for me. He doesn't even bother about paying my fee[s] and hostel charges. It is my *nani* who is taking care of us and our expenses.' 'How is it possible?' one of the members asked.

Of course it is possible, you won't believe when Raj was with him, one of his important books was torn and he had [a] unit test next day. He kept asking dad on [the] phone to buy a new book. My dad said he will but he completely forgot because he was at some party with the lady while Raj was alone at home, crying for the book. He could not perform well on his test for which he was punished at school. This would never have happened if my mom was there. Also, he has to sit hungry for hours because there is no one to give him food and they don't buy anything that he can eat on his own. And also last week when he reached school he was having [a] high fever. After an hour when the teacher realized it and got to know about it, she called my *nani*. My *nani* then came there and took him along with her because my dad was not bothered at all. My brother is so young that at times one has to ask him about his needs. Whereas the situation is completely in contrast. My dad is very strict and the lady is also rude, so Raj is so scared that he doesn't tell anything. His personality has changed and he has become very silent now, he rarely talks to anyone, let alone me. The teachers noticed this and told us; now how can you expect us to go to that house, where my brother has faced such a trauma?

Later, Raj was also asked where he wanted to live, and he also wished to go to his *nani*'s house. Renu informed us that she wasn't comfortable with her father as he had started neglecting both of them under the influence of his new lady friend. Neither of the children accepted the new partner of their father as their new mother and this was the main reason. On exploring further the parent–child relations in the family, Renu shared:

> We have seen that our mom and dad fight [with] each other on several times and my *nani* used to intervene in between to resolve the issues.

> My dad is a short-tempered person and used to shout [at] my mom when she was alive.

> Dad was thinking that my mom wanted us to be practising Christian[s] under the influence of my *nani*, which was not true. My mom never stopped us to attend *Puja* [worship] in [the] Hindu Temple during festivals.

> My mom was open minded and allowed us to wear all type of clothes while father is an orthodox Hindu and doesn't allow us to wear such clothes, he believes that we were becoming too modern and too Christian.

> When my mom was alive my dad wasn't so cruel and he was only strict, but after her death he became so cruel and started abusing us both physically and mentally.

Major Findings and Analysis of Case Studies

The above reported cases show that children are abused or harmed in their respective families in many ways and the most common types of abuse they have experienced are physical, emotional and sexual. They are ill-treated frequently, neglected or deprived of proper care and love for various reasons. Children are not able to differentiate between love and care and the punishment is perceived in a positive light; however, with the stress in the family environment and strained relationships between parents and their children, the positive punishment takes the shape of abuse and neglect towards the children. This neglect gradually converts into physical and emotional abuse and the children come to identify it when they compare their situation with their peer group's or compare their old experiences of love in the family.

Children's Conceptualization of Their Abuse in the Family

The foundations for wellness and healthy development are based on the relationships a child develops in the early stages of his or her life. Parents are the ones who give birth to a child and are responsible for their upbringing. Developing a positive relationship with children inculcates positive thoughts and feelings about one another and mutually respectful behaviours towards each other. A healthy parent–child bond leads to a functioning and appropriate level of development of the child and contributes to his or her wellbeing. The parent–child relationship is not a static one but is dynamic and develops over a period of time; it is influenced by factors like the child's characteristics, parents' characteristics and the family context in which they coexist.

Effective parenting involves warmth and affection and at the same time some amount of control and disciplining. It is the family environment and the parental behaviour that set the tone for the child's emotional and moral development from early childhood. The punishment or disciplining procedure hence becomes an integral part of the process and is viewed in a positive light, contributing to the effective development of the child. However, a healthy and warm parent–child relationship and family context is considered a prerequisite for the disciplining or controlling practice to be effective.

Family discord or an unstable family environment can lead to problematic and testing parent–child relationships. In the present study it was found that children experienced maltreatment and neglect in their familial environment. Initially, this maltreatment was taken by children as routine and a normal way of life in their families; however, gradually in the name of positive disciplining their parents become abusive. As reported by Zoya:

When my mother started beating me regularly, I thought that this is the way children are brought up, so I took it so casually… I have not told anyone about this. Once my mother had beaten me so ruthlessly [for] one of [my] silly mistakes, I felt too bad and complained to my friend. She [friend] consoled me and said she will talk to my mother, but I stopped her. I thought my mother will not be happy if [an] outsider will talk [about] my complaint.

Initially whatever happened to me was not hurting me but gradually when I knew that my friends are not getting the similar treatment [from] their parents, rather they are more cared and loved by their parents, then it pinched me and I was hurt …

… it is worse when you come to know that children in other families are loved and cared [for] by their parents and you are not…

What I feel [is] that my parents also love each other and me too, but their way of caring is not good at all, they are very dominating and never listen to each other or to any one of us, most of the time they order us and scold us, which is not good …

Another 14-year-old girl reported:

… both my mother and father fight with each other on petty issues, their anger come to us and most of the time they beat us without any good reason, this is really an abuse, they have [the] right to scold but not to abuse unnecessarily.

In another case, a 16-year-old boy said:

… when my father scold me or beat me without listening [to] me under the influence of my [step]mother, it hurts me and I believe this is an abuse.

Zoya came to understand the meaning of abuse when she compared herself with her friends. Similarly, in the other two cases the children were able to discern the act of beating as an 'abuse' and not discipline after interacting with other agencies. Children's subjective understanding of abuse begins as they come away from their family environment and find the care and protection from other agents.

The fractured family context is found to be a common theme in all the cases in the study. The family environment creates a space for abuse and neglect of the children at the hands of their parents in a disturbed or fractured household. The disharmony in the environment leads to a decreased focus on the child and his/her upbringing and hence also contributes to the abuse.

Economic Hardship and Child Abuse

Another important finding is that the children link the family's poverty and economic hardships with the abusive conditions they are subjected to. In their narratives the children associate the economic status of their parents with the family's wellbeing and happiness. A stable domestic economy is essential to provide the necessities and comforts of the family and its members. It caters to the basic needs of health, education and hence maintaining a good and productive livelihood. Our study finds that the children's academic functioning as well as their physical health was affected due to the poor economic conditions of the parents. However, in contrast to this there are two case studies in which child abuse and neglect were found in economically stable and well-off households as well. Therefore, our case studies inform us that poverty and poor economic circumstances act as a risk factor for child abuse but not necessarily a prerequisite. Stress caused by poverty and low income can increase the likelihood of abuse and neglect. Additionally, limited access to basic necessities and resources due to lack of money can lead to neglect and the inability to provide appropriate care for the children.

Our study also corroborates the fact that poverty perpetuates child abuse and neglect. In addition to economic hardship, there are other factors such as excessive use of alcohol, social pressure to get remarried after the demise of the spouse, less quality time for the family, the particular difficulties in single-parent families, strained relations between divorced partners, etc., which lead to child abuse and neglect.

In the present study, based on cases of children coming from divergent income backgrounds, the interpersonal compatibility of mother and father is another important factor as a determinant of child abuse and neglect. In some cases, it superseded poverty as a cause for child abuse. The parental relationship and family environment was found to be the prominent theme emerging in all the cases, affecting the wellbeing and development of the child.

Abused Children's Subjective Meaning of Family Relationships

The present study has discussed cases of children in which familial abuse became an integral part of their lives, subsequently overshadowing their childhood. The burden of domestic chores and the responsibility of feeding and serving as well as maintaining the household, leave these children bereft of their playful years.

In some cases, the children's narratives inform us that they are doubly victimized by the family. The mother being a victim of domestic violence further victimizes the children due to frustration or discord with their husband. For example, Savita (Case study II) describes that:

> ... for me the family is not a pleasant place as my mother and father both are living to meet their [own] demands. They even fight with each other to settle their scores. They also defend each other before me when they abuse me... So

tell me for what reason I should stay back [with] my family when I have no place in their life.

Another important theme that emerged in the present study was the children's detachment from family members and their unwillingness to live with them. As reported by Savita:

My family is no family. For me, my friends are good and I want to live with them, but I can't as they are in their [own] families.

In Case III, Renu also stated that she did not want to live with her father as he had moved another lady into the house who was unknown to her. She narrates her discomfort with her father and she refused to stay with him. She distanced herself from the family where she and her brother were emotionally abused and she preferred to stay in the girls' hostel and later on with her *nani* (maternal grandmother) who not only looked after them but also provided them with protection from their own father who had severely abused them.

Children and their worlds revolve around their parents and their families. It is the family relationship which is the primary source of safety, security, love, understanding, nurturance and support for the child. But our case studies of fractured families inform us that the maltreatment and neglect of children, which sometimes amount to abuse, changed the perception of the family relationships in the children's mind. Insecurity and constant threat to children in such families are unpleasant life experiences in the domestic space. Narratives in the case studies reveal that these children construct their own meaning of the family relationship. They describe 'family' as a place where they feel free and acknowledged as a unit. The present cases find that children who have experienced disturbed relationships with their parents are marked with incidences of abuse and severe neglect. Children demonstrated a sense of distrust and feelings of anger and anguish towards their parents. Some children also showed anxiety and depression as a result of the abuse and disillusionment with the family relationships, especially the parent–child relationship.

To sum up, child abuse and neglect is a reality in most of these fractured families. Family is an essential unit for the foundation of happy and healthy relationships, however, where relationships have broken down and marital partners are separated or divorced, the family relationship between the single parent and the child becomes unpleasant. Economic hardship, excessive use of alcohol by parents, remarriage of a parent and less quality time spent with children are the main reasons for the break-down of relationships within the family. This fractured relationship can lead to a range of abuses – from emotional to sexual. As children are those who suffer the consequences in a fractured family, they develop different notions of 'family' and 'abuse' and their construction of meaning differs from adults' understanding. They are unable to experience the 'conventional family' as their experiences are rugged and negative. For some children in fractured families, the conventional family is a jail and they want to run away from it. The subjective meaning of 'family' and 'abuse' constructed by these children affects their social, emotional and educational functioning.

References

Aktar, S. (2013) 'Effects of family breakup on children: a study in Khulna City', *Bangladesh e-Journal of Sociology*, 10(1): 138–152.

Ashtekar, A. (1989) *'Profile of victimised girls'*, paper presented at the National Seminar on Research on Families with Problems, Bombay, Tata Institute of Social Sciences.

Barnow, S., Lucht, M. and Freyberger, H.J. (2001) 'Influence of punishment, emotional rejection, child abuse, and broken home on aggression in adolescence: an examination of aggressive adolescents in Germany', *Psychopathology*, 34(4):167–173.

Bradshaw, J.P., Hoelscher, P. and Richardson, D. (2007) 'An index of child well-being in the European Union', *Journal of Social Indicators Research*, 80: 133–177.

Brody, G.H., Neubaum, E. and Forehand, R. (1988) 'Serial marriage: a heuristic analysis of an emerging family form', *Psychological Bulletin*, 103: 211–222.

Chan, Y., Chung, G., Lam, L.T. and Shae, W.C. (2011) 'Children's views on child abuse and neglect: findings from an exploratory study with Chinese children in Hong Kong', *Child Abuse & Neglect*, 35(3): 162–172.

Cummins, R.A. and Lau, A.L.D. (2005) *Personal Well-Being Index – School Children (PWI-SC) Manual* (3rd edn). Melbourne: Deakin University.

Deb, S. and Modak, S. (2010) 'Prevalence of Violence against Children in families in Tripura and its relationships with socio-economic factors', *Journal of Injury and Violence Research*, 2: 5–18.

Diener, E. and Seligman, M.E.P. (2002) 'Very happy people', *Association for Psychological Science*, 13(1): 81–84.

Diener, E., Oishi, S. and Lucas, R.E. (2002) 'Personality, culture and subjective well-being: emotional and cognitive evaluations of life', *Annual Review of Psychology*, 54: 403–425.

Dubowitz, H., Papas, M.A., Black, M.M. and Starr, R.H. Jr (2001) 'Child neglect: outcomes in high-risk urban pre-schoolers', *Pediatrics*, 109(6): 1100–1107.

Fattore, T., Mason, J. and Watson, E. (2007) 'Children's conceptualisation(s) of their well-being', *Social Indicators Research*, 80: 5–29.

Finkelhor, D. and Korbin, J. (1988) 'Child abuse as an international issue', *Child Abuse & Neglect*, 12(1): 3–23.

Fomby, P. and Cherlin, A.J. (2007) 'Family instability and child well-being', *American Sociological Review*, 72(2): 181–204.

Frías-Armenta, M. and McCloskey, L.A. (1998) 'Determinants of harsh parenting in Mexico', *Journal of Abnormal Child Psychology*, 26(2): 129–139.

Furstenberg, F. and Seltzer, J.A. (1986) 'Divorce and child development', in P. Adler and P.A. Adler (eds), *Sociological Studies of Child Development*. Vol. I. Greenwich, CT: JAI Press. pp. 137–160.

Ganglmair-Wooliscroft, A. and Lawson, R. (2008) 'Applying the International Wellbeing Index to investigate subjective wellbeing of New Zealanders with European and with Maori heritage', *New Zealand Journal of Social Sciences*, 3(1): 57–72.

Hayden, J. and Macdonald, J.J. (2000) 'Health Promotion: A new leadership role for early childhood professionals', *Australasian Journal of Early Childhood*, 25(1): 32–39.

Huebner, E.S. (1991a) 'Initial development of the Students' Life Satisfaction Scale', *School Psychology International*, 12: 231–240.

Huebner, E.S. (1991b) 'Correlates of life satisfaction in children', *School Psychology Quarterly*, 6(2): 103–111.

Huebner, E.S. (1994) 'Preliminary development and validation of a multidimensional life satisfaction scale for children', *Psychological Assessment*, 6(2): 149–158.

Hunter, W.M., Sadowski, L.S., Hassan, F., Jain, D., De Paula, C.S., Vizcarra, B. et al. (2000) 'Training and field methods in the WorldSAFE collaboration to study family violence', *International Journal of Injury Control and Safety Promotion*, 11(2) Accessed on October 6, 2019

Jabbi, M.K. (1986) 'Child marriages in Rajasthan', *Social Change*, 16(1): 3–9.

Kacker, L., Varadan, S. and Kumar, P. (2007) *Study on Child Abuse India 2007, New Delhi: Ministry of Women and Child Development, Government of India 2007*. Also Available on http://wcd.nic.in/childabuse.pdf

Klevens, J., Bayón, M.C. and Sierra, M. (2000) 'Risk factors and context of men who physically abuse in Bogotá, Colombia', *Child Abuse & Neglect*, 24(3): 323–332.

Krug, E.G., Dahlberg, L.L., Mercy, J.A., Zwi, A.B. and Lozano, R. (eds) (2002) *World Report on Violence and Health*. Geneva: World Health Organization.

Larrain, S. et al. (1997) *Relaciones familiars y maltrato infantile*. Santiago, Chile: UNICEF.

Lewis, S. and Lyo, L. (1986) 'The quality of community and the quality of life', *Sociological Spectrum*, 6: 397–410.

Madu, S.N. and Peltzer, K. (2000) 'Risk factors and child sexual abuse among secondary school students in the Northern Province (South Africa)', *Child Abuse & Neglect*, 24(2): 259–268.

Masson, J. and Falloon, J. (1999) 'A children's perspective on child abuse', *Children Australia*, 24(3): 9–13.

Masson, J. and Falloon, J. (2001) 'Some Sydney children define abuse: implications for agency in childhood', in L. Alanen and B. Mayall (eds), *Conceptualizing Child–Adult Relations*. London: Routledge Falmer. pp. 114–128.

Mehta, M.N. (1982) 'Physical abuse of abandoned children in India', *Child Abuse & Neglect*, 6(2): 171–175.

Mehta, M.N., M.R. Liokeshwar, S.S. Bhatt, V.B. Athavale, and B.S. Kulkarni (1979) 'Rape in children', *Child Abuse & Neglect*, 3(3): 671–677.

Menon, R. (1987) 'Child abuse: tragically widespread', *India Today*, 31 January, 116–119.

Michalos, A.C., Hubley, A.M., Zumbo B.D. and Hemingway, D. (2001) 'Health and other aspects of the quality of life of older people', *Social Indicators Research*, 54: 239–274

Nath, N. and Kohli, M. (1988) 'Child abuse in India: some issues', *Report on the National Seminar on Child Abuse in India*, 22–23 June. New Delhi: National Institute of Public Cooperation and Child Development. pp. 137–151.

National Research Council (US) (1993) 'Panel on Research on Child Abuse and Neglect: Understanding child abuse and neglect'. Commission on Behavioral and Social Sciences and Education, National Research Council.

NCPCR (2018) Ending Violence against Children-I- Situational Analysis of India (2018), Report of NCPCR and Childfund, Available at: https://www.ncpcr.gov.in/index1.php?lang=1&level=1&&sublinkid=1678&lid=1681.

Ney, P.G., Moore, C. McPhee, J. and Trought, P. (1986) 'Child abuse: A study of the child's perspective', *Child Abuse & Neglect*, 10(4: 511–18.

NIPCCD (National Institute of' Public Cooperation and Child Development) (1988) 'Introduction', in *Report on the National Seminar on Child Abuse in India*, 22–23 June 1989. New Delhi: National Institute of Public Cooperation and Child Development. pp. 1–10.

Rane, A.J. (1988) Approaches to prevention and management of child abuse in India. *National Institute of Public Cooperation and Child Development: National seminar on child abuse in India: A report* (pp. 71–83). NIPCCD New Delhi.

Rane, A.J., Naidu, U.S. and Kapadia, K.R. (1986) *Children in Difficult Situations in India: A Review*. Bombay: Tata Institute of Social Sciences.

Robila, M. and Krishnakumar, A. (2006) 'Economic pressure and children's psychological functioning', *Journal of Child and Family Studies*, 15(4): 435–443.

Runyan, D.K., Vishanathan, S., Hassan, F., Hunter, W.M., Jain, D., Paula, C.S., et al., (2010), 'International variations in harsh child discipline', *Pediatrics*, 126: 701–711. Available at: http://dx.doi.org/10.1542/ped.2008-2374

Sandberg, J., Miller, R.B., Harper, J.M., Robila, M. and Davey, A. (2009) 'The impact of marital conflict on health and health care utilization in older couples', *Journal of Health Psychology*, 14(1): 9–17.

Sariola, H. and Uutela, A. (1996) 'The prevalence and context of incest abuse in Finland', *Child Abuse & Neglect*, 20(9): 843–850.

Satyarthi, K. (1989) 'Child bonded labour in South Asia: an overview', paper presented at the South Asian Seminar on Child Servitude, New Delhi, India, 30 June–4 July.

Sharma, S. and Sharma, A. (2016) 'Unmasking the mask: childhood realities of victims of child abuse', in V. Chandra (ed.), *Childhood Realities: Working and Abused Children*. Delhi: Kalpaz Publications. pp. 243–258.

Srinivasan, S. (1989) 'No one talks about it', *Eve's Weekly*, 8–14 July, 50–53.

Straus, M.A., Hamby, S.L., Finkelhor, D.W., Moore, D.W. and Runyan, D. (1998) 'Identification of child maltreatment with the Parent–Child Conflict Tactics Scales: development and psychometric data for a national sample of American parents', *Child Abuse & Neglect*, 22(4): 249–270.

Tang, C.S. (1997) 'Psychological impact of wife abuse: experiences of Chinese women and their children', *Journal of Interpersonal Violence*, 12(3): 466–478.

Trief, P.M., Sandberg, J., Graff, K., Castronova, N., Yoon, M. and Weinstock, R.S. (2003) 'Describing support: a qualitative study of couples living with diabetes', *Families, Systems & Health*, 21(1): 57–67.

World Health Organization (1999) *Report of the Consultation on Child Abuse Prevention* (document WHO/HSC/PVI/99-1) (29–31 March). Geneva: WHO.

WHO (World Health Organization) (2004) *Prevention of Mental Disorders: Effective Interventions and Policy Options*, summary report. Geneva: WHO.

Wilson, M.I., Daly, M.and Weghorst, S.J. (1980) 'Household composition and the risk of child abuse and neglect', *Journal of Biosocial Science*, 12(3): 333–340.

Youssef, R.M., Attia, M.S. and Kamel, M.I. (1998) 'Children experiencing violence. I: Parental use of corporal punishment', *Child Abuse & Neglect*, 22(10): 959–973.

Zolotor, A.J., Runyan, D.K., Dunne, M.P., Jain, D., Peturs, H.R., Ramirez, C., et al., (2009) 'ISPCAN Child Abuse screening tool children's version (ICAST-C): instrument development and multi-national pilot testing', *Child Abuse and Neglect*, 33: 833–841.

9

Identity and Social Integration Among the Children of African Immigrants in France

Loretta E. Bass

Introduction

The children of immigrants represent almost 20% of all children in France today, and of these children, 12.5% have one or both parents of Sub-Saharan African origin (Kirszbaum et al., 2009). Indeed, a substantial number of children are first- or second-generation immigrants with Sub-Saharan African origins. Historically, immigration has increased from African countries since the 1950s (Fassmann and Munz, 1992). The Sub-Saharan African population tripled between 1982 and 1990 (Tribalat, 1999), then doubled from 1990 to 2000, and then tripled again between 2000 and 2010 (Institut National Etudes Démographiques [INED], 2013). Even prior to this unprecedented number of African-origin individuals living in France, social scientists (de Rudder et al., 2000; Poiret, 1996) had made the case that social integration of those of African origin into French society is distinctive and stunted, because of discrimination due to ethnicity and race characteristics.

Immigrants from Sub-Saharan Africa in France typically come from countries that are former colonies of the French colonial empire in West Africa, which largely dissolved in 1960, when many West African countries asserted and gained their political independence from France (Bass, 2014). Immigrants coming from Sub-Saharan Africa include many ethnic groups with distinct cultures, varied beliefs including Islam, Christian and African religions, and the common thread of the French language, which facilitates international migration to France.

Increasingly, young people of immigrant origin have been associated with social unrest and a lack of social integration in the French popular press. In October 2005, six weeks of rioting broke out in the Clichy-sous-Bois suburb of Paris after children of North and Sub-Saharan African immigrant origin had been killed while being pursued by police. In 2012, riots again broke out for nearly two weeks north of Paris in Amiens, as young people of immigrant descent attacked official and city buildings, or symbols of the French government. Wieviorka (2005) pitched these protests as immigrant communities contesting their social and economic marginalization and discrimination by police and government institutions. More recently in public discourse, youth of Muslim immigrant descent largely in the second generation have been associated with terrorist attacks. First- and second-generation youth, who claimed allegiance to the Islamic State fighting in Syria and Iraq, attacked Paris twice in 2015, first with the January killing of writers of the satirical political magazine *Charlie Hebdo*, and second in November with the massacre of 90 concert goers in the Bataclan Concert Hall. In July 2016, another terrorist attack by an immigrant of North African origin claiming allegiance to the Islamic State killed 86 people at the Bastille Day celebrations in Nice. In the period since 2005, there has been a great deal of public discourse focused on the lack of social integration of immigrant and second-generation youth in France.

Scholarly research on the social integration and inclusion of immigrants in France focuses on different types of barriers. Chapman and Frader (2004) and Thomas (2007) contend that race and ethnicity are visual cues that lead to discrimination and exclusion for immigrants and those of immigrant descent in France. Research by Ribert (2006) showed how the term *étranger* or foreigner often refers to immigrant-origin populations more generally, even beyond the first generation. Therefore, appearing foreign, or *étranger*, or coming across as foreign because of the sending-country culture, translates into immigrant status. Adding to this, transnationalism can be viewed as a coping mechanism, or response, to a lack of social integration or acceptance in the receiving country, and this lack of social integration may be felt even though migrants may spend many years in France and even have legal citizenship (Beauchemin, 2015; Bruneau, 2004). These studies highlight race, ethnic cultural markers such as having a foreign name or a foreign accent, and citizenship as potential factors that shape identity and social integration. At the same time, these studies do not focus on the experience of young people, so there remains a need to include the social integration experiences of youth.

Examining the transition to adulthood, Safi (2006, 2010) finds lower labour market outcomes and poorer life satisfaction for the children of immigrants compared to the children of the native-born in France.

In agreement, other research (Silberman, 2011; Silberman and Fournier, 1999; Simon, 2012) finds that children of immigrants in the first and second generations fare worse in labour market participation as adults than children of native-born individuals in France. Similarly, Ferrari and Pailhé (2017) find that among children of immigrants, those from Southern Europe are more likely to forge a similar path to employment in adulthood as native-born children, whereas the children of North African immigrants experience greater difficulties in becoming economically self-sufficient. Moreover, Silberman et al. (2007) find that compared with the children of native-born French, those in the second generation, with origins in former French colonies or countries with dominant Muslim populations, are more disadvantaged. Further, their results show that while just 8% of the French report labour market discrimination, Sub-Saharan African origin men in the second generation report the highest level of 'perceived discrimination' in the job market: 41.5%, compared with 40.8% for those of North African origin, 23.6% for those of Turkish origin and 20.1% for those of Asian origin. Altogether, these studies of the transition to adulthood highlight the lower life chances of the children of immigrants from North and Sub-Saharan Africa as well as the importance of employment and Muslim religion for social inclusion and life satisfaction.

Moreover, Muslim religion arouses a negative reaction in France and in other European countries. Many countries in Sub-Saharan Africa have majority and substantive minority Muslim populations. Religion is part of a sending country's culture, and in the French context, Muslim religion can be a barrier to socio-economic success (Foner and Alba, 2008). Religion provides a frame in which children are named either Modou or Fatou as Muslim children or David or Marie as Christian children. With the terrorism related to the Islamic State in recent years in France, the French government has emphasized the values of the Republic and secularism (Foner and Simon, 2015).

This research focuses on African-descent young people in France, and examines identity and social integration using the voices of young people. In the next sections, I first discuss the sample, the data gathered and the methods used in this analysis. After this, I present the results of this research, first taking on the question of identity, and second examining the relative influence of the differentiating factors of race, ethnicity and citizenship on the one hand, and religion on the other, as conferring a foreign, or *étranger*, or immigrant status.

Data and Methods

Sample

For this project, I gathered in-depth interviews of 22 children and youth of Sub-Saharan African immigrant descent in the suburbs of a city in southwestern France. Of these, 12 were female aged 15–23 years old, and 10 were male aged 14–23 years old. All participants were born in France or had spent five or more years in French public schools. In terms of religious make-up, three identified as Catholic, 11 as Evangelical Protestant and eight as Muslim. I also collected expert interviews with social workers, teachers and administrators at the city government level.

To generate a representative sample of the Sub-Saharan African resident population, I used a combination of convenience and snowball sampling techniques. I used methods outlined in Strauss and Corbin (1990) to secure individuals' informed consent and protect anonymity. Similar to prior studies (Matute-Bianchi, 1986; Tribalat, 1999), I included the experiences of child migrants, native-born children of naturalized parent(s) and second-generation, native-born children. Culturally similar pseudonyms are used in the presentation of findings.

Methods

I gathered and transcribed the data. I met with respondents and was able to observe other relevant information, such as appearance and self-presentation. Face-to-face interview research also enabled me to observe facial expressions, attitudes and feelings that may add meaning to the respondent's words in their answers (Berg, 2007).

I used open and axial coding in the analysis of these qualitative interview data, using respondent voices throughout the data analysis process to inform the research questions at hand. First, I used open coding to delineate and inform each category (e.g. relative import of religion in daily life) (Berg, 2007; Neuman, 2006). Other themes emerged during the initial coding of the data. I categorized and coded the data from these emergent categories. I then organized the codes into analytic categories (i.e. axial coding) (Glaser and Strauss, 1967; Neuman, 2006). I examined the data several more times, repeating this open and axial coding process until I was satisfied with the coding and the categorization frame. The resulting frame points to the usefulness and appropriateness of qualitative research methods for this type of analysis.

Identity: 'French on the inside, African on the out'

To explore identity formation, I asked young people of migrant descent, 'Where do you fit in French society?' An overwhelming majority, 18 of 22 young people, identified more with French culture when pressed to identify with either being African or French; culturally they report feeling French. This finding for my sample is similar to Simon's (2012) finding for immigrants in general in France, of which most identify as feeling French. However, at the same time, the individuals in my sample then explain how they are culturally different and hold some divergent values when compared to their French peers of non-immigrant descent. Adding to this, they point to social structures – such as race, citizenship and immigrant status – that additionally influence or constrain where they fit in French society. They voiced both agreement and some ambivalence between their values and both those of their parents and those of their French peers of non-immigrant descent. Social identity theory holds that self-assignment and attachment to a group are key components of identity formation (Killian, 2006; Tajfel, 1981; Turner, 1985). The following young people's voices illustrate how they negotiate and construct a French self, both within their minds and in their daily interactions, despite being constrained by an immigrant outsider status.

For example, Juana, who is in her first year at university, identifies as French using citizenship and culture. She explains:

> I am French, but I have two passports … one from Centreafrique … but I have French mentality. I don't know the customs of Centreafrique. It is like being French on the inside, African on the out. (Juana, age 19, female, first generation from Central African Republic, Christian, citizen)

While she is a citizen of both the Central African Republic (CAR) and France, she migrated with her mother to France at age 4, received all of her formal education in France, and spent most of her life in France. She feels French, not African, and identifies with having French identity and values. Culturally, she is largely French in attitudes and outlook. She was raised in a family that regularly attended Christian worship, and this aligns with the majority cultural history of Europe. Juana also has French citizenship, so structurally she has more access to French institutional life and support. In other research on North African, Portuguese and Turkish immigrant young adults in France (Ribert, 2006), having French citizenship was found to be a key component for the construction of self-identity, because having the identity card makes daily living easier in France.

There is an ambiguity at play, because with the 'Republican model' of integration, French education endeavours to socialize immigrant children. Historically, the secular French public school has served as the key instrument to integrate a diverse population into a unified nation. Bourdieu and Passeron's (1979 [1964]) classic study of French school children illustrates that French cultural values by social class are reproduced and transferred to the next generation of that social class. Because of French educational socialization – offering secularism or *laïcité*, along with the French principles of equality, fraternity and liberty – many young people identify with a French perspective rather than the African perspective of their parents.

Similarly, Cedric, a third-year student at university who identifies with European culture, indicates that he identifies with Europeans because of his exposure to French education during childhood. Even though he was born in Cameroon, he migrated to France in early childhood, and he completed elementary school in France. He explains:

> I am much like Europeans because I have a European education. It is the same for me as it is for children with [native-born] French parents, however, I respect my parents a lot. (Cedric, age 21, male, first generation from Cameroon, Christian, citizen)

Note how Cedric first identifies with being European, but then he qualifies that there exists an African form of respect felt by African-descent children towards their parents in family life, and that this is different from that of their European counterparts. Specifically, he suggests that children in Sub-Saharan African immigrant families respect their parents more than children of native-born French parents. Moreover, there is a sense from these data that socialization of children is qualitatively different, in terms of values taught to children, within African immigrant families compared with French children generally.

Similarly, Ramatoulaye affirms that her childhood as a second-generation African provided her with a different set of values than the children of French parents.

> I am different than a French girl with French parents. I respect my parents ... older people. You need to put your head down a bit and listen. I am more natural ... not the same. As a child, we do not have the same rights as French kids. We [Africans]

> do not look our children in the eyes ... like you do. (Ramatoulaye, age 20, female, second generation, Senegalese descent, Muslim, citizen)

Even though she is a French citizen, she considers herself as holding different family values from her French counterparts because of her African cultural education in the home. Even while reporting being *French* on the inside, over two thirds (15 of the 22 youth) of the first- and second-generation African youth identified as having different family values to their French counterparts', and these values are more closely aligned to the values of their immigrant parents and by extension their home-country societies. Youth of African descent view themselves as being different from youth of native-born French parents, because of parental expectations based in African cultures. As one second-generation male youth of Central African Republic origin explained, 'We don't do everything with the kisses and everything in my family. A lot of things depend on your customs ... whether you're Swedish or Canadian or African.' Affection in African families in the second generation typically resembles African customs and not French ones.

While African-descent youth does not wholly identify with the dominant socio-cultural norms of French society, these young people may not completely comprehend and practice their parent's sending-country social and cultural norms. A few, like Modou, aged 15 and Muslim, from Guinea, may report speaking an African language within the family, yet may not know what the language is called. In Modou's case, he reports speaking 'Guinean' but does not know the ethnic group in Guinea corresponding to this language. Guinean could be any one of the over 25 languages spoken in Guinea (Leclerk, 2011).

Some children of African immigrants further vocalize an alienation and distance from their parents' African cultures.

> I do not know my ethnic group in CAR. The ethnicity is not important. My mom speaks to me in Sango ... I respond in French. I visited Africa four times. The nationality is just crazy. I don't care ... African or what. (Jessy, age 19, female, second generation, CAR descent, Christian, citizen)

And Jessy's mother independently explained in an interview: 'My daughter is ashamed to speak in our local language in public, but she understands.' Other mothers similarly commented on the language issue with their children. For these children, their speaking French is part of their French identity as they assert it.

The idea that these young people are 'French on the inside, African on the out' holds true. While they have taken on 'French' values and ideals, they are perceived and treated by the larger society as outsiders. This sentiment of French on the inside through school socialization and African on the outside because of physical or ethnic markers runs parallel to Sayad's (2004 [1999]) discussion of being in a new country but at the same time being excluded or ignored. Sayad (2004 [1999]: 259) describes this ambiguity for Algerian-descent individuals in France:

> I am Algerian despite my French papers; I am French despite my Algerian appearance ... I was not born in Algeria, I was not brought up in Algeria, I'm not at home in Algeria (or I don't have Algerian habits), I don't think like an Algerian ... but I feel Algerian all the same.

Across the interviews, youth of Sub-Saharan African origin expressed this same type of ambiguity – feeling French and at the same time not being treated as French – not feeling as African as their parents and at the same time being treated as an African outside by the larger French majority culture. Moreover, these immigrant-descent youth inhabit a liminal or in-between space at the boundary of French mainstream and their parents' sending-country culture. Similarly to the liminality documented for asylum seekers in the Netherlands (see Ghorashi, de Boer, and ten Holder 2018), young immigrant-descent people in France are able to reflect and find agency within their marginalized position. They are on both sides of these cultures as they negotiate their identity and place in French society.

Black Race, Muslim Religion and Citizenship

For some youth, it is the intersection of two or more statuses, such as having black skin, Muslim religion and no French citizenship papers, that translates into diminished opportunity in France. This multifaceted construction of a constrained self is summarized succinctly by Khadi, an 18-year-old woman from Mauritania, who was educated since age 6 in France. She explains:

> Racism and integration are the same ... hard for us. We are outsiders. We do not have the same education as a European. We don't have the same opportunities. We were different as children culturally. (Khadi, age 18, female, first generation from Mauritania, Muslim, non-citizen)

Khadi is able to situate her constrained position today in terms of her statuses: because of her black race and being an immigrant outsider, she does not have the same access to the dominant French society's education and cultural knowledge. She perceives that these factors coalesce and offer a diminished trajectory of opportunity for immigrants. Her upbringing within a Muslim family points to a cultural difference for Khadi, and her biography of not having French citizenship points to an additional structural constraint that limits her ability to seek an internship or position in the labour market. Her ability to realize social inclusion appears to be blocked by lack of citizenship, being culturally different because of her family's Islamic cultural orientation, and due to her perceived race and assumed immigrant status.

The scholarly research (see Beamon, 2015; Keaton, 2006) on North African immigrant youth in France highlights that even when one may appear native-born French, having a Muslim-sounding name is a powerful marker of immigrant-origin status. In my interviews, African youth described North African Muslims as suffering from discrimination, because they are associated with terrorism and polygamy. They are viewed as foreign, too, even though their family may have been in France for several generations. For them, it is appearance and name that translates into immigrant status or *étranger* (i.e. foreigner).

The Intersection of Race and Immigrant Statuses: 'We are different ... not French'

Structural factors such as race status and immigrant status largely shape the parameters for social interaction for young people of African immigrant descent in France. Overwhelmingly, youth point to skin colour as a powerful marker of their immigrant status, because they are perceived by French society as immigrants due to the black colour of their skin. This intersection is important for understanding the black African experience as distinctive from that of the North African (i.e. Arab) experience in France, and a world apart from that of youth with an appearance that is white or stereotypically native-born French in descent. Madia explains:

> It is both the colour of the skin and racism. Because of skin colour, they assume we are all immigrants. I only know France. (Madia, age 25, female, first generation from Togo, Muslim, citizen)

Like Madia, these young people may hold citizenship in France and have a *French* mentality, yet because of an 'outsider' appearance, they are cast into an immigrant role by the native ethnic majority population (i.e. *French-French* as they describe it) and then come to 'feel' this 'outsider' status. In this way, Sayad (2004 [1999]) would contend that they then carry a stigma of an 'outsider' class of people.

When I asked Sub-Saharan African youth what matters more, race or immigrant status, they heavily sided with race, but then qualified the response with acknowledgement of other immigrant groups, which points to the weight of both race and immigrant statuses independently, and at their intersection, as being poignant social structures that regulate behaviour.

In interview after interview, young people of African descent recounted being treated as second-class citizens while taking public buses and trams. Jessy explains:

> There is racism on the tram with the old women. They don't like us. They don't accept us. There is racism ... with the whites ... it is the dark colour of my skin. It happens on the street ... Then, they have taken the racism and turned it into discrimination. (Jessy, age 19, female, second generation, CAR descent, Christian, citizen)

Young people attribute their mistreatment to racism and/or immigrant status. For example, Cedric explains the importance of race both structurally and in individual interactions in everyday living in France:

> There is racism. It is something against the immigrants. And it is racism, because race marks immigrants, and then they are treated poorly. I think it is the French system, and it is the people, too. (Cedric, age 21, male, first generation from Cameroon, Christian, citizen)

Altogether, young people explain how black race is associated with holding immigrant status in France. This intersection of black race and immigrant status is intertwined and provides the filter through which to comprehend how their childhoods take a different trajectory of education, both inside and outside the immigrant-descent home, in France. Throughout these interviews, this intersection of race status and immigrant status is profound and delineates a lower set of life opportunities.

Names Matter, Sub-Saharan African or Muslim

For some, having a Sub-Saharan African name marks an individual as an immigrant and therefore not acceptable. One male youth explains, 'It is the first name ... your name ... too. Not just racism.' Certain names can flag an individual's African immigrant-origin status, such as having an African name like Mbankou, Ndiaye or Diop. Similarly, religious affiliation provides cultural clues: we know that Marie or Matthieu are likely to be Christian, and that Fatou or Mohammed are likely to be Muslim. Amadieu's (2004) research tested and found lower labour market prospects for resumés submitted with foreign-sounding, North African names compared with historically French-sounding names in France. And similarly, recent research (Alba et al., 2013) notes that discrimination against North African descent immigrants in France often takes the form of targeting their names when applying for jobs. While immigrant descent youth may have difficulty accessing internships in professional occupations due to their having less developed social networks in France, this does not explain why immigrants with traditionally European-sounding names, such as those of Portuguese-descent youth, have a disproportionally and markedly higher placement rate in professional internships compared to children of non-European descent.

Indeed, young people of Sub-Saharan African descent report that their foreign-sounding names create barriers to opportunities in general terms, because they are perceived as being immigrants. For Jessy, all immigrants are considered together to be unacceptable because they are not French. She explains:

> All immigrants are in the same sack. Fatima or Aisha or Mohammed ... you have a first name that does not work. This [non-French] name is not accepted. (Jessy, age 19, female, second generation, CAR descent, Christian, citizen)

When we consider names like Madir or Mohammed, they are not only non-French-sounding names, but they are Muslim names. Other research has established that there is higher unemployment among immigrant groups in France that have substantial Muslim populations (Silberman et al., 2007). Cedric, from Cameroon, maintains that having a foreign-sounding name is a flag in interactions with the government, noting: 'Most of the time, though, we immigrants are in the same boat vis-a-vis the government. They know us by our foreign-sounding names.' And one youth described being black and immigrant as a 'double-damned condition'.

Across the interviews, youth of African immigrant descent express with much frustration that they are not included or allowed the same opportunities as their counterparts of native-born French parents. These young people of Sub-Saharan descent understand that skin colour and a perceived immigrant status through one's name are symbols that are readily misinterpreted to mean that they do not hold true French cultural norms.

Conclusion: Negotiating an 'Outsider' Status

Exclusion due to structural factors and isolation due to cultural factors come together to frame the integration experience for immigrant and African-descent youth in France. My research finds that young people find a sense of self-identifying through the prism of their black race and immigrant statuses: 'I am French on the inside, African on the out.' Black race and cultural markers, such as dress or name, serve as structural dimensions by which a non-citizen or immigrant status is placed on these young people. Cultural differences and socialization translate into differential access to opportunities because of a lack of knowledge to successfully navigate the majority French culture. This exclusion and isolation due to structural and cultural factors coalesce the social integration experience and trajectory of life opportunities perceived as possible for immigrant and African-descent young people in France.

These young people do not share a common identity (i.e. culture) with either their parents or other young people with native-born French parents, yet they identify with French Republican or civic ideals. Typically, young people of African immigrant descent have only a vague idea of their African cultural roots through the family socialization that they have received in France (i.e. respect for elders, respect for others). However, they feel French culturally, or 'French on the inside'. Their full integration is blocked due to their immigrant status and racism (i.e. working as a social structure) imposed by French mainstream society. In this way, they are being assimilated while they continue to face racial exclusion, which is analogous to the coexisting assimilation and ethnic exclusion documented in the US context for Mexican Americans (Ortiz and Telles, 2008) or the French context for North Africans (Sayad, 2004 [1999]). At the same time, this liminal state between cultures is a constrained state yet it also creates a space for young people to negotiate their identity and place in French society.

There is a dissatisfaction among the Sub-Saharan African young people that I interviewed which is consistent with Safi's (2010) finding of lower life satisfaction for immigrants in a study of 13 European countries.

This dissatisfaction is not diminished by the second generation or with time in the country. The voices of young people within my interview data evidence similarly unequal and bifurcated life chances – and therefore a segmented assimilation pattern rather than a straight line – for those of Sub-Saharan African immigrant descent. And the riots and protests by young people on the streets in France's communities with high concentrations of immigrants provide additional support for this conclusion. My interviews indicate that young people protest in the street not because they want to remain an ethnic minority, but rather, because they want to be recognized and treated as full French citizens.

These first- and second-generation children of African descent feel culturally isolated, and because immigrant status carries a stigma, they are not allowed full access and participation in French society as protected by the Constitution and Republican model. This discrimination and social marginalization experienced by African descent youth do not bode well for an egalitarian France.

References

Alba, R., Silberman, R., Abdelhady, D., Brinbaum, Y. and Lutz, A. (2013) 'How similar educational inequalities are constructed in two different systems, France and the United States: why they lead to disparate labor-market outcomes', in R. Alba and J. Holdaway (eds), *The Children of Immigrants at School: A Comparative Look at Integration in the United States and Western Europe*. New York: Social Science Research Council and New York University Press. pp. 160–203.

Amadieu, J. (2004) 'Enquête testing sur CV', Enquête réalisée pour l'Observatoire des discriminations, May, Université Paris-I. Available at: www.observatoiredesdiscriminations.fr/images/stories/presentation_du_testing_mai2004.pdf

Bass, L. (2014) '*Black immigrant youth in another France*', paper presented at the International Sociological Association Congress, July.

Beamon, J. (2015) 'Boundaries of Frenchness: cultural citizenship and France's middle-class North African second-generation', *Identities: Global Studies in Culture and Power*, 22(1): 36–52.

Beauchemin, C. (2015) 'Migration between Africa and Europe (MAFE): looking beyond immigration to understand international migration', *Population*, 70(1): 7–11.

Berg, B.L. (2007) *Qualitative Research Methods for the Social Science* (6th edn). Boston: Pearson.

Bourdieu, P. and Passeron, J.-C. (1979 [1964]) *The Inheritors: French Students and their Relation to Culture*. Chicago and London: The University of Chicago Press. (Originally published in French as *Les Héritiers: les étudiants et la culture*, 1964).

Bruneau, M. (2004) *Diasporas et espaces transnationaux*. Paris: Anthropos.

Chapman, H. and Frader, L. (2004) *Race in France*. New York and Oxford: Berghahn Books.

de Rudder, V., Poiret, C. and Vourc'h, F. (2000) *L'Inégalité raciste: l'universalité républicaine à l'épreuve*. Paris: PUF.

Fassmann, H. and Munz, R. (1992) 'Patterns and trends of international migration in Western Europe', *Population and Development Review*, 18(3): 457–480.

Ferrari, G. and Pailhé, A. (2017) 'Transition to adulthood in France: do children of immigrants differ from natives?', *Advances in Life Course Research*, 31: 34–56.

Foner, N. and Alba, R. (2008) 'Immigrant religion in the U.S. and Western Europe: bridge or barrier to inclusion?', *International Migration Review*, 42(2): 360–392.

Foner, N. and Simon, P. (2015) *Fear Anxiety and National Identity*. New York: Russell Sage Foundation.

Glaser, B.G. and Strauss, A.L. (1967) *The Discovery of Grounded Theory: Strategies for Qualitative Research*. Chicago: Aldine.

Ghorashi, H., de Boer, M. and ten Holder, F. (2018) 'Unexpected agency on the threshold: Asylum seekers narrating from an asylum seeker center,' *Current Sociology*, 66(3): 373–391.

INED (Institut National Etudes Démographiques) (2013) *World Migrations, Discrimination, Integration*. Available at: www.ined.fr/en/, and specifically, www.ined.fr/en/grands-themes/world-migrations-discrimination-integration/.

Keaton, T.D. (2006) *Muslim Girls and the Other France*. Bloomington and Indianapolis: Indiana University Press.

Killian, C. (2006) *North African Women in France – Gender, Culture, and Identity*. Stanford, CA: Stanford University Press.

Kirszbaum, T., Brinbaum, Y. and Simon, P., with Gezer, E. (2009) *The Children of Immigrants in France: The Emergence of a Second Generation*. Innocenti Working Paper 13. Florence: Innocenti Research Centre.

Leclerk, J. (2011) 'Guinée-Conakry', in *L'Aménagement linguistique dans le monde*. Available at: www.tlfq.ulaval.ca/axl/afrique/guinee_franco.htm

Matute-Bianchi, M.G. (1986) 'Ethnic identities and patterns of school success and failure among Mexican-descent and Japanese-American students in a California high school', *American Journal of Education*, 95(1): 233–255.

Neuman, W.L. (2006) *Social Research Methods: Qualitative and Quantitative Approaches* (6th edn). Boston: Pearson.

Ortiz, E.E. and Telles, V. (2008) *Generations of Exclusion*. New York: Russell Sage Foundation.

Poiret, C. (1996) *Familles africaines en France*. Paris: L'Harmattan.

Ribert, E. (2006) *Liberté, égalité, carte d'identité – Les jeunes issus de l'immigration et l'appartenance nationale*. Paris: La Découverte.

Safi, M. (2006) 'Le processus d'intégration des immigrés en France: inégalités et segmentation', *Revue Française de Sociologie*, 47(1): 3–48.

Safi, M. (2010) 'Immigrants' life satisfaction in Europe: between assimilation and discrimination', *European Sociological Review*, 26(2): 159–176.

Sayad, A. (2004 [1999]) *The Suffering of the Immigrant*. Malden, MA: Polity Press. (Originally published in French as *La Double absence – des illusions de l'émigré aux souffrances de l'immigré*. Paris: Éditions du Seuil, 1999).

Silberman, R. (2011) 'The employment of second generations in France: the republican model and the November 2005 riots', in R. Alba and M.C. Waters (eds), *The Next*

Generation: Immigrant Youth in Comparative Perspective. New York: New York University Press. pp. 283–315.

Silberman, R. and Fournier, I. (1999) 'Les enfants d'immigrés sur le marché du travail: les mécanismes d'une discrimination sélective', *Formation Emploi*, 65: 31–55.

Silberman, R., Alba, R. and Fournier, I. (2007) 'Segmented assimilation in France? Discrimination in the labour market against the second generation', *Racial and Ethnic Studies*, 30(1): 1–27.

Simon, P. (2012) *French National Identity and Integration: Who Belongs to the National Community?* Washington, DC: Migration Policy Institute.

Strauss, A. and Corbin, J. (1990) *Basics of Qualitative Research.* Newbury Park, CA: Sage.

Tajfel, H. (1981) *Human Groups and Social Categories.* Cambridge: Cambridge University Press.

Thomas, D. (2007) *Black France: Colonialism, Immigration, and Transnationalism.* Bloomington and Indianapolis: Indiana University Press.

Tribalat, M. (1999) *De l'immigration a l'assimilation. Enquete sur les populations etrangeres en France.* Paris: La Decouverte/INED.

Turner, J. (1985) 'Social categorization and the self-concept: A social cognitive theory of group behavior', in E.J. Lawler (ed.), *Advances in Group Processes: Theory and Research.* Vol. 2. Greenwich, CT: JAI Press. pp. 77–121.

Wieviorka, M. (2005) *La Violence.* Paris: Hachette Littératures, Pluriel.

10

Fluctuating Social Class Mobility of Filipino Migrant Children in France and in Italy

Asuncion Fresnoza-Flot and Itaru Nagasaka

Introduction

Studies on family reunification in the context of migration illuminate the various implications of this family event on the lives of migrant children. Previously 'left behind' in their country of origin, these young people later on become part of the '1.5 generation', the members of which immigrated to their receiving country at the age of 18 or below after spending part of their childhood or adolescence in their country of origin (Nagasaka and Fresnoza-Flot, 2015; Rumbaut and Ima, 1988). In recent years, these childhoods spent in two or more different societies have been the object of several analytical enquiries analysing the children's identity (re)construction, school incorporation and intergenerational relationships, among others (Bartley and Spoonley, 2008; Danico, 2004; Harklau et al., 1999). However, one experiential dimension that remains understudied in the life of these young migrants is their social class mobility during the migration process. In what way do these migrants experience and confront their social class (im)mobilities accompanying the serial migration(s) in their transnational families? How different are their social and class experiences from those of their parents?

When addressing these questions, we need to take into account the fact that the members of the 1.5 generation are themselves migrants. Unlike the members of the 'second generation' who were born and grew up in the receiving country of their migrant parents, these migrant children have undergone two or more different experiences of childhood in the course of their mobile lives. On the other hand, their lives in the place of origin were significantly affected by the transnational ties that their migrant parents (the so-called 'first generation') had constructed (Fouron and Glick-Schiller, 2002; Levitt and Waters, 2007; Nagasaka and Fresnoza-Flot, 2015).

Put differently, in order to address the main questions of the present study, we need to be attentive to the complex and shifting relationships between their own spatial, social, and class mobilities and those of their families (Nagasaka and Fresnoza-Flot, 2015).

Social class encompasses here young migrants' economic, cultural, and symbolic capital in a Bourdieusian perspective, as well as their subjective views concerning the 'prestige' in a Weberian sense attached to their migration situation. We pay attention to their experiences of immobility and upward or downward mobility along social class lines, both before their migration in their societies of origin and after their immigration to their destination country. As a case study, we analyse the experiences of 1.5-generation children of Filipino migrants in France and in Italy. These migrants arrived in these countries before the age of 18 to reunite with their migrant parents and experienced two school systems. We argue that these migrant children experience social class (im)mobilities differently from their adult counterparts, who, in many cases, undergo 'contradictory class mobility', meaning upward social mobility in one country and downward social mobility in another at the same time (Parreñas, 2001).

The empirical data we examine here originated from ethnographic fieldworks we separately conducted in the Île-de-France region in France and in Rome, Italy. In France, one of us (Asuncion Fresnoza-Flot, AFF), interviewed 21 children (10 male and 11 female) aged between 15 and 36 years old of Filipino migrants. Eighteen of them were single, two were married, and one was divorced. Eight respondents were employed full-time, five had part-time jobs, and the others were unemployed. Most interviewees (15 out of 21) lived with their parents. The six exceptions included three who already had children, one college graduate who worked full-time in a French company, and two women who lived with their boyfriends and worked in the service sector, one as a hotel receptionist and one as a nanny. In short, a majority of the respondents were not yet completely financially independent from their parents. Most of them had arrived in France at the beginning of the 2000s and had been residing in this country for an average of eight years.

For the cases in Italy, one of us (Itaru Nagasaka, IN) interviewed 22 children of Filipino migrants, aged 12 to 26, either in the Philippines or in Italy between 2010 and 2013. Almost all of them had their origins in rural Philippines. Fourteen of them had immigrated to Italy at age 17 or younger and experienced the two school systems of the Philippines and Italy. Half of these 1.5-generation interviewees had roots in the villages of the northern Philippines with a long history of overseas migration to the United States of America and Italy, where one of the authors (IN) has conducted fieldwork since the 1990s. Of the 14, 11 were single, two were married, and one was separated. Seven were students at the time of their first interviews, four had regular jobs (one as a babysitter, one as a sales-person, one as a cleaner of buildings, and the last one as a factory worker). One worked on an irregular basis and two had recently stopped studying. While their living arrangements in Italy were characterized by the fluidity of having two dwelling spaces (one in their employer's house and another in their apartment, which is quite common among Filipino domestic work-ers), most of them (12 of 14) lived in the apartment rented by their parents. Two women lived with their partners and their partners' families. All of them had immigrated to Italy after 1999 to be reunified with their parents.

Before examining the experiences of these young migrants, we briefly review the literature on migration to see how migrants experience mobility in terms of social class. We also take a look at the recent trends regarding child and youth migration from the Philippines. In the discussion sec-tion, we highlight the fluctuating social class mobility of 1.5-generation migrants in France and in Italy, as well as the strategies they used when confronting social class issues. We conclude by reflecting on the similari-ties and differences of their experiences and by proposing one possible research direction concerning the study of childhoods in migration.

Social Class Mobilities in the Context of Migration

The question of mobility in terms of social class has been invoked in many studies of adult migratory movements. In this context, social class is more often associated with the economic resources of migrants (Fresnoza-Flot and Shinozaki, 2017): in many cases, resources accumulation means upward social class mobility. However, taking into account the 'transna-tional social spaces' of migrants (Faist, 2000), social class mobility appears more complex than some scholars of migration previously thought.

In the logic of the 'push–pull' framework, individuals migrate to escape their difficult life condition (push) and proceed to countries where they expect economic possibilities (pull) to improve their life. Their upward social class mobility appears to be the recompense for their geographical movement: a mobility resulting from gaining access to eco-nomic resources. Through remittances, migrants of working-class origin are able to afford socially valued possessions in their countries of origin and to support their children's education (Aguilar, 2014; Oliveira, 2013).

These facilitate the upward mobility not only of themselves but also of their whole family unit in the social class hierarchy of their societies of origin. In the case of individuals with privileged class background, their migration most often ensures their family's upper social class belonging. This is, for example, the case of 'parachute children' who are sent abroad to study, opening opportunities herein for social class mobility and for their parents' businesses (Zhou, 1998).

Nonetheless, not all migrants' experience upward social class mobility – notably if we take into account their cultural capital that is usually not recognized in their countries of immigration (Erel, 2010). In many cases, migrants with tertiary-level education undergo downward social class mobility, as they engage in precarious and low-paid jobs. Guo (2013) attributes this to a 'glass gate' that keeps migrants away from professional communities, a 'glass door' that impedes their access to professional employment, and 'glass ceiling' that prevents them from moving to managerial positions. This may subsequently affect these migrants' health and wellbeing (Nicklett and Burgard, 2009). To make sense of their deskilling and to redefine themselves, many migrants focus on their countries of origin where they can experience upward mobility in the social class hierarchy there, thanks to their economic benefits obtained from migration.

In her study of Filipino women migrants working in the domestic service sector, Parreñas (2001) observes that these women experienced 'contradictory class mobility': a downward mobility in their country of immigration due to their deskilling and domestic work, at the same time as an upward mobility in their country of origin because of their elevated economic status thanks to their earnings in their country of immigration. Some migrants resort to a 'transnational expenditure cascade' by sending remittance to their relatives (Thai, 2014), whereas others forge a successful image of themselves by offering gifts and wearing fashionable clothes during their visits in the country of origin (see Suksomboon, 2007).

To sum up, migrants' social class position changes in space and time due to their geographical movement. As we can observe in the studies above, the experiences of adult migrants unveil the complexity of social class (Fresnoza-Flot, 2017b), which poses the question of how this can be applied to migrant children, whose experiences of social class mobility remain largely underexplored. Given that these young people's socio-demographic characteristics (age, level of education at the time of migration, and so on) are distinct from those of adult migrants, their mobility in social class terms in their transnational social spaces is also probably different from that of the latter. To find out, we examine in the following sections the case of 1.5-generation children of Filipino migrants in France and in Italy.

Childhood Migration from the Philippines: A Brief Overview

Since the 1960s, the Philippines has been a major sending nation of international migrants. According to the Stock Estimate of Overseas Filipinos released by the Commission on Filipino Overseas (CFO, 2013), over 10 million Filipinos, approximately 10 percent of the total population of the Philippines, live and work in over 200 countries. One of the significant trends in Filipino migration is the increasing number of migrant children.

During the 36-year period from 1981 to 2016, over 700,000 emigrants, aged 19 or younger, left the Philippines. The number of these children has fluctuated, but since 2000, the number has increased steadily. Since the year 2005, over 20,000 emigrants of this age group left their home country every year, and this number reached 30,000 in 2015 (CFO, 2016). The destinations of these migrant children have multiplied since 2000. During the 1980s and 1990s, the US and other 'classical countries of immigration', (Castles and Miller, 2009) such as Canada and Australia, were their main destinations. These children were either brought into these countries by their parents through family reunification programs or migrated together with their parents.

While child and youth emigration from the Philippines to these countries has continued to be significant, the recent trend shows that newly emerging destinations of Filipino overseas migrants, notably Italy and Japan, have become the major destinations of young emigrants. From 2008 to 2012, the top four destination countries of emigrants aged 13 to 19 were the US, Canada, Italy, and Japan. The numbers of registered Filipino emigrants of this age group were 26,302, 17,603, 4,259 and 3,244 respectively (CFO, n.d.). The rise in the number of migrant children to Italy and Japan in this period can be explained by the increase of Filipino immigrants in these countries who are eligible to sponsor their minor children. While migratory patterns of children to these countries show a marked variety (Nagasaka, 2015b), they share the notable life experience of being 'left behind' by their migrant parents for a prolonged period. Having said this, in what follows, we will start the illustration of migratory experiences of 1.5-generation Filipinos to these new destination countries from the time they were 'left behind' by their parents and taken care of by their close kin and others.

The 1.5-generation Filipinos in France

Background to Their Migration

The migration to France of Filipino children has been happening since the early 1980s. It mainly results from family reunification, that is, children joining their migrant parent(s) in the receiving country. The French migration policies shape such migratory movement.

The 1980s witnessed many cases of family reunion between Filipino migrants and their children due to the regularization of undocumented migrant workers in the country between 1981 and 1982 (Fresnoza-Flot, 2017a). As the years passed, family reunification became harder and harder, as the French government tightened its control over migratory inflows in its territory. In fact, the last amnesty for irregular migrants took place between 1997 and 1998. Aside from this, conditions for family reunion became difficult to satisfy for many Filipinos who mainly work in the domestic sector (Fresnoza-Flot, 2017a). As a result, more and more Filipinos, regardless of migration status and economic condition, had their children come to France using unofficial channels of family reunion, which has resulted in intergenerational irregularity in Filipino migrant families (Fresnoza-Flot, 2017a).

Young Filipinos arrive therefore in France through *de jure* or *de facto* family reunion channels (Fresnoza-Flot, 2017a). In 2010, for instance, there were 595 Philippine-born immigrants who were aged between 0 and 17 years old (INSEE, 2010). Taking into account those who entered the country using a *de facto* family reunion channel, the number of Filipino migrant children is probably more than the French official statistics report. Since adult Filipino migrants earn modest income from their domestic work, providing a comfortable life in France for their children is particularly challenging. This has an important impact on their offspring, who have positive expectations of the life waiting for them in their new country.

Changing Class Positions in Space and Through Time

The migration of the parents of the 21 respondents triggered a familial separation that ended when their parents managed to have them come to France. In this case, parental migration appears to be an important precursor of the migration of young Filipinos to this country. Successive geographical movements first by parents and then by their offspring engendered fluctuations in the latter's social class mobility during their childhood years.

> Gino[1] was 6 years old when his parents decided to work in the Middle East. Although his mother was a school teacher and his father was employed in a private company, their monthly income was not enough to support the needs and schooling of Gino and his four siblings. Gino described their life prior to migration as 'economically difficult' (*naghihikahos*) and remembered his challenging pre-school life: 'I was enrolled in a private [kindergarten].[2] It was private at that time. I remembered I had no packed meal [in a] private school of people with money. During break, recess time, the teacher circulated a basket in the class and those who would put money in it would go to the canteen. You know what I used to do? … I would pretend that I was writing something, that I was busy. I would entertain myself. I would pretend not seeing anything, the basket would pass in front of me, then nothing anymore'.

Gino undeniably acquired at a young age an awareness of his social class belonging and what it meant. He demonstrated his agency by confronting the contradiction in his life at that time: economically deprived but enrolled in a private kindergarten. Unlike him, a few respondents had comfortable lives when they were very young, either because some family members (one or both of their parents, aunts, or grandmothers) were already working abroad prior to their birth or because their family had stable economic resources from the beginning.

> Linda was born into a middle-class family in the Philippines: her mother was running a restaurant, whereas her father was managing his own car workshop. Her father worked in the Middle East when Linda was a baby, and when he returned he bought a big house for his family. When Linda was 6 years old, the income from her family's businesses was starting not to meet their needs. In 1986, her mother therefore decided to go and work in France in the domestic sector, and the year after, her father followed. Linda told me her parents' reason for leaving: 'My siblings and I were in a private [school], and then while growing up, with many expenses, my mother and father could not afford them anymore'.

The migration to France of Linda's parents was rooted in the desire of ensuring the continuity of the family's middle-class lifestyle that was attained through the initial migration of her father. When children are growing up, an economically challenging situation often prompts parents like those of Gino and Linda to migrate abroad, either to sustain or achieve a comfortable life for their offspring. This transforms children's lifeworld, not only emotionally due to separation from parents, but also in social class terms. The remittances of their parents allowed the respondents in the study to live an economically privileged childhood, including education in reputable institutions. When family reunification took place in France, these respondents experienced another change in their social class position, which in many cases was characterized by a downward mobility.

> Tina grew up under the care of her maternal grandmother after her mother migrated to France when she was 5 years old, followed by her father three years later. Thanks to her parents' remittances, her family was able to buy a house in a middle-class area, to sustain Tina's private schooling and that of her sibling, as well as to accumulate lands. When Tina moved to France when she was 15 years old, she needed to adjust to living in a small apartment and to doing household chores: 'when I arrived here [France], I did not know how to cook rice, and I learned that here. I was lazy according to them [her parents]. This is because it was my grandmother who was doing all for me. We had also a house helper in the Philippines, and here no. I learned to work, to work at home here.'

Aside from learning to do things by themselves, the respondents in our study also adopted other strategies to confront their downward social class mobility. Some respondents, mostly male, decided to concentrate on their studies, whereas others focused on presenting themselves as successful and trendy in photos or during visits to the Philippines. Gino shared his strategy: 'You pretend that you are very happy. Then you ask somebody to take a picture of you in a beautiful [place], and then in front of a car pretending that it is yours'. Image management could also be observed when some respondents returned for a visit to the Philippines. For instance, Harold remarked how his entourage in the Philippines was surprised to see the changes in him: 'They seemed surprised. Before I was not neat, then now I am. I know now how to dress up. … My cousins, my friends were also surprised. They looked at me differently, as if I had become superior [to them].' Pursuing a socially valorizing job is another strategy that a few respondents adopted, like the case of Linda below.

Linda: I told to my friend to study. She studied [cooking]. She told me [that she spent] 22,000 [euros]. I told her, 'Maria I would like to study pastry-making'. She said, 'okay, I will inquire'. She inquired and she told me, '17,000 [euros]'. Oh my God.

AFF: After you obtain your diploma, you can apply then for a job in a bakery?
Linda: Yes, in a bakery. My friend [Maria] and I would like actually to open a restaurant after our studies.

AFF: You will save for it [the pastry-making course]?
Linda: Yes, I will save.
AFF: Do you think that next year you can start attending the course?
Linda: Yes, this September I can already go to the class.

Linda and other study respondents mainly focused their attention on their life in France, building their professional career, and forming their own family in the country while maintaining contacts within the Philippines. In contrast, their parents, in many cases, underwent 'contradictory class mobility' (Parreñas, 2001) and intended to spend their old age in their native country.

At the time of their interviews, most of the respondents were over 18 years old and six of them had already completed tertiary or higher education. These six respondents had experienced in their transnational social spaces fluctuating mobility in social class terms: an upward mobility in the Philippines thanks to their parents' remittances, a downward mobility in France at the beginning of their migration, and later on an upward mobility as they gained cultural and social capital in their country of settlement. Three respondents who decided not to pursue higher education but instead to work maintained their initial social class position. However, from their point of view, their life in France was much better than what they had experienced in the Philippines, both economically and socially. Their cases underline the importance of the subjective, psychological perspectives of individuals on social class (Reay, 1998), which is central to comprehend the evolving meanings of it in time and space.

The 1.5-generation Filipinos in Italy

Background of Their Migration

Filipino migration to Italy has been increasing since the 1970s. During this period and the following decade, most Filipinos entered the country (most often without proper documentation) and found jobs in the domestic service sector through their kin or friends who were already working in Italy. Since the 1980s, there has been a growing demand for foreign domestic workers in urban Italy (Andall, 2000; Zontini, 2010) due to the combination of several factors such as the decreased interest of rural Italian women to become domestic workers, the increasing labour participation of Italian middle-class women, the insufficient public support for care-related work, and the ageing of the population. Partly due to their high level of schooling, Filipinos have gained a reputation as capable and trustworthy workers in this sector (Nagasaka, 2015a).

In contrast to the case of Filipinos in France, a sizable number of Filipino workers during the 1980s through the 2000s had acquired a residence permit through legalization programmes of the Italian government. In 1986, a family reunification provision for documented foreigners was introduced in the country. While many Filipino workers with regular status brought in their spouses during the 1990s, they usually either left their children in the Philippines or sent them back to their homeland, due to the difficulty of working full-time with small children (Aguilar, 2009; Parreñas, 2001). These children of migrants were in many cases taken care of by their close relatives, such as grandparents and siblings of their parents. According to the survey conducted by one of the authors (IN) in the villages of the northern Philippines in the late 1990s, 32 of the 39 couples who worked in Italy with their spouses and who had at least one child under the age of 18 years had left their children in the Philippines (Nagasaka, 2016).

After the 2000s, largely due to the improvement of their living conditions in Italy, many Filipino parents started to bring in their children through the family reunification programme. In 2011, 43,561 (32%) of 136,597 registered Filipinos in Italy were aged below 30 years (ISTAT, 2011). A significant proportion of these young Filipinos were thought to have spent part of their childhood in the Philippines. While the Stock Estimate of Overseas Filipinos by the Commission on Filipinos Overseas suggests the presence of undocumented Filipinos workers in Italy, the ratio is much lower than that in France: 20% and 79% respectively (CFO, 2013). Their relatively stable settlement has allowed them not only to keep their concrete ties with their family and kin in the homeland, but also to facilitate their children's migration to Italy.

Different Class Belongings 'Here' and 'There'

When their children were taken care of in their homeland, Filipino migrant parents working in Italy had sent regular remittances to their children and their foster parents. Because all the respondents have rural origins in the Philippines, such regular remittances have in many cases dramatically elevated their family's class positions in the local community (see also Aguilar, 2014). As for their offspring, the regular remittances have allowed them to have a lifestyle closer to that of urban middle-class children than that of children from non-migrant households in rural and urban labour class communities (Nagasaka, 2015a). The life experience of Jacky, a daughter of a female migrant who migrated to Italy in 1980 and was separated from Jacky's father, illustrates this well.

> Jacky was born in Italy and lived there until she was 5 years old. Because it was difficult for her mother to care for an infant while working, she decided to send Jacky to the Philippines to be cared for by her grandparents. She lived with her brother and cousins in her grandparents' house that was newly constructed by her mother. When it was time to begin elementary school, her mother sent her to a prestigious private girls' school located in the provincial capital. Traditionally, only elite families in the province could send their daughters to the school. In the provincial capital, Jacky and her brother lived with a carer, usually a relative or co-villager, in rooms rented for them. She described her daily life at that time: 'every day, our *yaya* [hired carer] sent me to and picked me up from the school. She cooked for us'. With a good allowance given to her every week, she habitually went out for snacks and shopping in the provincial capital. While Jacky was in the Philippines, she recalled that her mother gave her 'everything' she wanted. She migrated to Italy when she was 13 years old.

As shown in her case, with regular remittances, these youngsters usually lived with their close relatives in a concrete-built house that was constructed by their parents. Many of them studied in a reputable private school in the cities. During their school days, with generous daily allowances, they often went out for snacks in the fast-food shops and shopping in business establishments in the cities. These experiences observed in their children's lives were not seen in the pre-migration lifestyles of the parental generation. The first-generation migrants with rural origins repeatedly mentioned a 'difficulty of life' in the Philippines as a reason for their migration to Italy. In contrast, many of these migrants' children, particularly those whose parents were already working in Italy when they were infants, mentioned that they did not experience 'difficulty of life' when they were in the Philippines. However, it should be noted that one respondent did emphasize his 'difficulty of life' in the Philippines due to his foster parents' misuse of remittances.

After migrating to Italy, some children related their feeling of change in their social class position by saying 'we don't have a help here' as in the case of their counterparts in France. Some of them further elaborated on how they felt when they observed the lives of their parents and other Filipinos. A male migrant who came to Italy when he was 12 years old said, 'I urged my mother to buy things I wanted' when he was a small child. But after he came to Italy and observed his mother's job, he realized that 'her job here is like this. All [they did for me] came from their sacrifice'. Another male migrant, Brian, who also came to Italy when he was 12, described his impression of the lives of Filipinos working in Italy as follows:

> Because we had no class on Saturday, I went with my mother when she went to work. Then I saw many Filipinos here [in Italy] and looked at their faces … I felt their faces are, somewhat like being tired out … I did not have such image of life here. I then realized how difficult the life here is … I realized how they [his parents] had built a large house in the Philippines… When I was in the Philippines, my mother bought things I wanted. Like toys, and they then sent a parcel to us … Anything and everything … When I wanted to go to Jollibee [fast-food chain], we went. Our life was like that. So when I was a small child, I wondered what my mother's job was. But when I came here, I came to know how she had worked. They have really sweated for us.

In this way, after migration, some of them realized how their middle-class lifestyle in the Philippines was made possible and reflected on their family's class positions 'there' and 'here'.

When they narrated their experiences after their migration, they emphasized their difficulty in adapting to their family and school in Italy. Largely due to their lack of proficiency in Italian, their perceived gap of school education and their occasional experiences of discrimination from their Italian classmates, only one of the 11 1.5-generation interviewees who had left secondary school was studying at university after finishing a technical school education and two had passed the national school-leaving examination (*esame di maturità*) (Nagasaka, 2015a). Responding to these difficulties, they have built their networks with their cousins and fellow young Filipino immigrants and created their own social spaces (Nagasaka, 2015a). Such networks were actively utilized when they searched for jobs after leaving school. A male migrant mentioned that his Filipino friend whom he came to know in a computer game arcade introduced him to the director of a restaurant. However, when they search for a job beyond the reach of their own networks and those of their parents, they usually face immense difficulties. A young female migrant, who graduated from the higher secondary school in Italy, related her employment experience as follows:

> My parents' job is 'job of the house', right? I graduated here, so I wished to get a different job from theirs. But I fell to the job of the house. How many months I was stuck in my house when I submitted my resumé to many. Even a sales lady, a worker in the call centre, I wanted to be. But nothing …

In addition to their scarcity of social capital outside their ethnic niche in the domestic sector, increasing employment insecurity notably among unskilled young workers since the 1980s (Bernardi and Nazio, 2005) as well as the fact that young people have been disproportionately affected by the recent economic crisis in Italy (Bonizzoni, 2017) has made it harder for these young Filipino immigrants to find employment outside their niche, even if they graduate from the upper secondary school in Italy. As a consequence, many of the 1.5 generation also started to work in the domestic sector.

Through their migratory experiences, they came to be well aware of the interrelation between their lifestyle in the Philippines and their parents' jobs in Italy, as shown in Brian's narrative. However, for those who have not experienced 'difficulty of life' and who hence did not feel a sense of economic and social marginalization in their homeland so much as their parents' generation with rural origins did, their feelings of social and economic marginalization in Italy are thought to be more intense than their parents' generations.

The question of how they have responded to such feelings of marginalization and lowered class positions after migration remains to be seen, partly due to the fact that many of them were still studying or had recently left school at the time of the interviews. But we may point out some emerging tendencies observed during the research period. One is to create and reaffirm their own transnational ties with their society of origin. They usually return to their communities of origin regularly, but some have started their own transnational engagement such as building a house, investing in retail business and sending remittances to their cousins to cover the cost of their cousins' children's education. Their regular returns to their original communities provide them with opportunities to reaffirm their ties with kin, neighbours, and friends there, and firmly place them into intimate circles that stretch across borders. These returns also make it possible for them to reconstruct their social identities as returnees, *balik-bayan*, who are able to enjoy earning opportunities that are not available within or around the homeland communities. Although the nature of their transnational ties is varied and may shift, for some of them, their places of origin seem to be emerging as an important 'point of social reference' (Kibria, 2009) as they have been for the first generations.

Another tendency is to utilize their existing social capital as well as skills acquired in the immigrant community to secure their employment and economic base. A young female migrant, who worked as a salesperson for a well-known brand, lost her job because of the sudden closure of the shop. She then acquired a babysitting job through her kin networks. She explained that having skills in doing domestic work is very important for their survival in the time of 'crisis'. She added that they could quit their jobs outside the domestic sector when the working conditions worsened, and if they have skills necessary for domestic work. We may say that, by making use of opportunities in the ethnic niche that the parental generations have constructed since the 1980s, she has secured her economic base and simultaneously explored job opportunities beyond this niche amid the increasing casualization of the labour market as well as the economic 'crisis' that has disproportionally affected youth employment in Italy.

Discussion and Conclusion

The migration experiences of 1.5-generation Filipinos in France and in Italy indicate how children in transnational families undergo (im)mobilities not only in space and time, but also in social class terms. Their fluctuating social class mobilities are characterized by several upward/downward movements, and also include phases of immobility.

First, they experience an elevated social class position when their parent(s) migrate and send remittances back home. Second, they move down on the social class ladder when they reunite with their parents in their receiving country, where their parents are mostly employed as domestic workers. And third, they move up again in the social class hierarchy when they become incorporated in their new society through schooling and employment outside of the domestic work sector. They go down anew on the social ladder when they lose their job outside of the domestic work sector and subsequently engage in domestic work. This suggests that migrant children/youth's position in the social class hierarchy is unstable and not static at all during their childhood or young adulthood lives, due to their migration and that of their parents. Their social class mobilities also appear contingent on their parents' social class position and on the value of the monetary benefit of their domestic work in different countries. Remittances from migrant parents allow stay-behind children to live a comfortable life in the Philippines, but the same amount of money has a lower impact on the material aspects of their lives in their receiving countries, France and Italy, where the standard of living is higher than that in their country of origin.

To face their downward social class mobilities, migrant children often resort to varying strategies. In France, 1.5-generation respondents learn to be independent, concentrate on their studies, manage their self-presentations in photos or the virtual world as well as during visits to the Philippines, and try to pursue socially valorizing employment. They also maintain ties with their country of origin, but they tend to focus on their lives in France, which sets them apart from their migrant parents. On the contrary, 1.5-generation Filipinos in Italy follow their parents' example by reinforcing their transnational ties with the Philippines while living in Italy. Some of them attempt to find a job outside of the domestic work sector with their academic records and their proficiency in Italian. If they encounter difficulties to do so, they take refuge in the domestic work sector, ending up doing the same job their parents' generation has engaged in. In this case, they undergo social class immobility, a temporary condition partly dependent on Italian labour market forces after the economic crisis. These (im)mobilities in social class terms of 1.5-generation respondents point to the importance of the influence of space on migrants' lives, as changes in spaces of living most often entail changes in spaces of being. This is important to take into account in rethinking the concept of social class and belonging.

Acknowledgements

We extend our gratitude to all the migrants who agreed to be interviewed for these case studies. The Japan Society for the Promotion of Science supported these studies under grants JP21402032 (2009–2012) and JP24401039 (2012–2015) to Itaru Nagasaka (Hiroshima University). The previous version of the French case study was presented by Asuncion Fresnoza-Flot during the 'Research Profile Seminar' of the Department of

Sociology and Work Science at the University of Gothenburg (Sweden, 20 March 2019).

Notes

1 All names of the respondents are pseudonyms to protect their privacy.
2 Pre-schooling was not compulsory in the Philippines until recently, and kindergartens in Gino's time were privately run.

References

Aguilar, F.V. (2009) *Maalwang Buhay: Family, Overseas Migration, and Cultures of Relatedness in Barangay Paraiso*. Quezon City: Ateneo de Manila University Press.

Aguilar, F.V. (2014) *Migration Revolution: Philippine Nationhood and Class Relations in a Globalized Age*. Kyoto: Kyoto University Press.

Andall, F.V. (2000) *Gender, Migration and Domestic Service: The Politics of Black Women in Italy*. Aldershot: Ashgate.

Bartley, A. and Spoonley, P. (2008) 'Intergenerational transnationalism: 1.5 generation Asian migrants in New Zealand', *International Migration*, 46(4): 63–84.

Bernardi, F. and Nazio, T. (2005) 'Globalization and the transition to adulthood in Italy', in H. Blossfeld, E. Klijzing, M. Mills and K. Kurtz (eds), *Globalization, Uncertainty and Youth in Society*. London: Routledge. pp. 349–374.

Bonizzoni, P. (2017) 'Challenging the social reproduction crisis: young Italian middle-class families in London', *Journal of Family Studies*, 24(1): 25–40.

Castles, S. and Miller, M.J. (2009) *The Age of Migration: International Population Movements in the Modern World* (4th ed.). London: Macmillan.

CFO (Commission of Filipino Overseas) (2016) 'Number of registered Filipino emigrants by age group: 1981–2016'. Available at: https://www.cfo.gov.ph/downloads/statistics/statistical-profile-of-registered-filipino-emigrants.html

CFO (2013) 'Stock estimates of overseas Filipinos as of December 2013'. Available at: www.cfo.gov.ph/downloads/statistics/stock-estimates.html

CFO (n.d.) 'Number of registered Filipino emigrants by country of destination and age group (13–19)'. (Unpublished Statistics).

Danico, M.Y. (2004) *The 1.5 Generation: Becoming Korean American in Hawai'i*. Honolulu: University of Hawai'i Press.

Erel, U. (2010) 'Migrating cultural capital: Bourdieu in migration studies', *Sociology Compass*, 44(4): 642–660.

Faist, T. (2000) *The Volume and Dynamics of International Migration and Transnational Social Spaces*. Oxford: Oxford University Press.

Fouron, G.E. and Glick Schiller, N. (2002) 'The generation of identity: redefining the second generation within a transnational social field', in P. Levitt and M.C. Waters (eds), *The Changing Face of Home: The Transnational Lives of the Second Generation*. New York: Russell Sage Foundation. pp. 168–08.

Fresnoza-Flot, A. (2017a) 'Beyond migration patterns: understanding family reunion decisions of Filipino labour and Thai marriage migrants in global reproductive systems', *Migration Studies*, 6(20): 205–224.

Fresnoza-Flot, A. (2017b) 'Gender- and social class-based transnationalism of migrant Filipinas in binational unions', *Journal of Ethnic and Migration Studies*, 43(6): 885–901.

Fresnoza-Flot, A. and Shinozaki, K. (2017) 'Transnational perspectives on intersecting experiences: gender, social class and generation among Southeast Asian migrants and their families', *Journal of Ethnic and Migration Studies*, 43(6): 867–884.

Guo, S. (2013) 'Economic integration of recent Chinese immigrants in Canada's second-tier cities: the triple glass effect and immigrants' downward social mobility', *Canadian Ethnic Studies*, 45(3): 95–115.

Harklau, L., Losey, K. and Siegal, M. (eds) (1999) *Generation 1.5 Meets College Composition: Issues in the Teaching of Writing to US-educated Learners of ESL (English as Second Language)*. Mahwah, NJ: Lawrence Erlbaum.

INSEE (Institut National de la Statistique et des Études Économiques) (2010) 'Répartition des immigrés par pays de naissance'. Available at: www.insee.fr/fr/themes/tableau.asp?ref_id=immigrespaysnais

ISTAT (Istituto Nazionale di Statistica) (2011) 'Cittadini on comunitari regolarmente presenti per classe di età, area geografica e principali paesi di cittadinanza, per sesso, al 1 gennaio 2011'. Available at: http://demo.istat.it/altridati/noncomunitari/index.html

Kibria, N. (2009) '"Marry into a good family": transnational reproduction and inter-generational relations in Bangladeshi American families', in N. Foner (ed.), *Across Generations: Immigrant Families in America*. New York and London: New York University Press. pp. 98–113.

Levitt, P. and Waters, M.C. (2007) 'Transnational migration studies: past developments and future trends', *Annual Review of Sociology*, 33: 129–156.

Nagasaka, I. (2015a) 'Immigrating into a segregated social space: the case of 1.5-generation Filipinos in Italy', in I. Nagasaka and A. Fresnoza-Flot (eds), *Mobile Childhoods in Filipino Transnational Families: Migrant Children with Similar Roots in Different Routes*. Basingstoke: Palgrave Macmillan. pp. 87–116.

Nagasaka, I. (2015b) 'Migration trends of Filipino children', in I. Nagasaka and A. Fresnoza-Flot (eds), *Mobile Childhoods in Filipino Transnational Families: Migrant Children with Similar Roots in Different Routes*. Basingstoke: Palgrave Macmillan. pp. 87–116.

Nagasaka, I. (2016) 'Growing up in a transnational family: experiences of family separation and reunification of Filipino migrants' children in Italy', in K. Um and S. Gaspar (eds), *Southeast Asian Migration: People on the Move*. Eastbourne: Sussex Academic Press. pp. 8–39.

Nagasaka, I. and Fresnoza-Flot, A. (eds) (2015) *Mobile Childhoods in Filipino Transnational Families: Children of Immigrants with Similar Roots in Different Routes*. Basingstoke: Palgrave Macmillan.

Nicklett, E.J. and Burgard, S.A. (2009) 'Downward social mobility and major depressive episodes among Latino and Asian-American immigrants to the United States', *American Journal of Epidemiology*, 170(6): 793–801.

Oliveira, G. (2013) 'The consequences of maternal migration on education aspirations of Mexican children left behind', in L. Bartlett and A. Ghaffar-Kucher (eds), *Refugees, Immigrants, and Education in the Global South: Lives in Motion*. New York and Abingdon: Routledge. pp. 226–239.

Parreñas, R.S. (2001) *Servants of Globalisation: Women, Migration and Domestic Work*. Stanford, CA: Stanford University Press.

Reay, D. (1998) 'Rethinking social class: qualitative perspectives on class and gender', *Sociology*, 32(2): 259–275.

Rumbaut, R.G. and Ima, K. (1988) *The Adaptation of Southeast Asian Refugee Youth: A Comparative Study*. Washington, DC: US Office Refugee Resettlement.

Suksomboon, P. (2007) 'Remittances and "social remittances": their impact on cross-cultural marriage and social transformation', *IIAS Newsletter*, 45: 6.

Thai, H.C. (2014) *Insufficient Funds: The Culture of Money in Low-wage Transnational Families*. Stanford, CA: Stanford University Press.

Zhou, M. (1998) '"Parachute kids" in Southern California: the educational experience of Chinese children in transnational families', *Educational Policy*, 12(6): 682–704.

Zontini, E. (2010) *Transnational Families, Migration and Gender: Moroccan and Filipino Women in Bologna and Barcelona*. New York: Berghahn Books.

Index